5	6	7	8	9
Na な行	Ba ば行	Ma ま行	Ra ら行	Wa わ行
na な	ba ば	ma ま	ra ら	wa わ
ni に	bi び	mi み	ri り	(w)i* い
nu ぬ	bu ぶ	mu む	ru る	(w)u* う
ne ね	be べ	me め	re れ	(w)e* え
no の	bo ぼ	mo も	ro ろ	(w)o* おを**

THE HANDBOOK OF JAPANESE VERBS

A KODANSHA DICTIONARY

THE HANDBOOK OF JAPANESE VERBS

日本語動詞ハンドブック

Taeko Kamiya

KODANSHA INTERNATIONAL
Tokyo • New York • London

Distributed in the United States by Kodansha America, Inc., 575 Lexington Avenue, New York, N.Y. 10022, and in the United Kingdom and continental Europe by Kodansha Europe Ltd., 95 Aldwych, London WC2B 4JF.

Published by Kodansha International Ltd., 17-14 Otowa 1-chome, Bunkyo-ku, Tokyo 112-8652, and Kodansha America, Inc.

First edition, 2001
03 04 05 06 07 08 09 10 10 9 8 7 6 5 4

www.thejapanpage.com

CONTENTS

P R E F A C E

In order to master a foreign language, it is crucial for students to acquire a solid knowledge of its verbs and their usage. Japanese is no exception.

Japanese verbs are often said to be difficult and complicated and hard to learn. That is not true. In fact, they are simple and less complicated to learn than those of many other languages. Unlike some European languages, you do not have to memorize different forms to indicate the number or person or gender of the subject of the sentence. The verb *kaku*, for instance, could mean I/we write, you (sing./pl.) write, he/she/it writes or they write. Moreover, Japanese verbs are highly regular in the way they make their forms. Once you grasp certain rules for making such forms as the negative, conjunctive, conditional forms, etc., you will be able to apply these rules to almost any verbs.

The purpose of this book is to describe in detail not only how Japanese verbs conjugate, but how you should use the verb forms in connection with sentence structures.

The book is divided into two parts. Part I deals with the conjugations of the three types of verbs—regular I, regular II and irregular verbs, as well as copulas (be-verbs) and auxiliaries. A conjugation practice follows the description of a verb or a group of verbs. Part II deals with the usage of various verb forms. Each usage is illustrated with example sentences, and exercises are provided every few lessons to allow you to test your understanding.

I do hope that this book will prove to be helpful—you will discover how simple and easy conjugating and using Japanese verbs can be.

I N T R O D U C T I O N

This section deals with some of the important features of Japanese verbs that are different from English verbs. You are advised to read this section carefully before you move on to the detailed explanation of verb conjugations.

TENSES OF VERBS

Japanese verbs have two tenses: the present and the past. The same verb form is used to express both present and future tenses.

Jimu wa hon o **yomimasu**.
ジムは本を**読みます**。
Jim reads/will read a book.

The same past form is used for the past, present perfect and past perfect tenses.

Jimu wa hon o **yomimashita**.
ジムは本を**読みました**。
Jim read/has read/had read a book.

LEVELS OF SPEECH

Japanese verbs express plain and polite styles of speech. The plain style is used among friends, family and others with whom one is familiar. This style is also used in writing in newspapers, magazines and books. The polite style is used among adults who are not close friends.

PLAIN:

Kare wa Kyōto e **iku**.
かれは京都へ行く。

Kare wa Kyōto e **itta**.
かれは京都へ行った。

POLITE:

Kare wa Kyōto e **ikimasu**.
かれは京都へ行きます。
He goes/will go to Kyoto.

Kare wa Kyōto e **ikimashita**.
かれは京都へ行きました。
He went to Kyoto.

In addition to these styles, there are the honorific and humble styles. The honorific style is used to elevate the listener who is older or higher in social status than the speaker. The humble style is used to lower oneself or one's family member to elevate the listener indirectly.

HONORIFIC:

Hara-sensei ga **o-hanashi ni narimasu**.
原先生が**お話しになります**。
Prof. Hara will speak about it.

HUMBLE:

Chichi ga **o-hanashi itashimasu**.
父が**お話しいたします**。
My father will speak about it.

VERB GROUPINGS

Japanese verbs may be divided into three groups: regular I, regular II and irregular. These can be recognized as follows:

1. Regular I verbs

The dictionary form of a regular I verb has a consonant plus *u* ending.

-ku	く	kaku	書く	write
-gu	ぐ	oyogu	泳ぐ	swim
-su	す	hanasu	話す	speak
-tsu	つ	matsu	待つ	wait
-nu	ぬ	shinu	死ぬ	die
-bu	ぶ	tobu	飛ぶ	fly
-mu	む	yomu	読む	read
-ru	る	toru	取る	take
-(w)u*	う	ka(w)u	買う	buy

*In modern Japanese, *w* disappears before all vowels except *a*.

2. Regular II verbs

The dictionary from of a regular II verb has a vowel (*e* or *i*) plus *ru* ending.

-eru	taberu	食べる	eat
-iru	miru	見る	see, look, watch

EXCEPTIONS: Note that some verbs ending with *-eru/-iru* are regular I verbs, such as the following:

kaeru	帰る	return	hashiru	走る	run
hairu	入る	enter	kiru	切る	cut
iru	要る	need	shiru	知る	know

3. Irregular verbs

There are only two irregular verbs. Their dictionary forms are as follows:

kuru	来る	come
suru	する	do

The verb *suru* is combined with nouns to make a noun into a verb. It may also be attached to foreign loan words.

benkyō 勉強 (study)	benkyō **suru** 勉強**する**	study
yushutsu 輸出 (export)	yushutsu **suru** 輸出**する**	export
doraibu ドライブ (drive)	doraibu **suru** ドライブ**する**	drive
dansu ダンス (dance)	dansu **suru** ダンス**する**	dance

COPULAS (BE-VERBS)

The Japanese copulas *da* (plain style) and *desu* (polite style) are equivalent to the English am, is, or are. They are used as follows:

1. The A is B construction

   Yamada-san wa bengoshi da/desu.

   山田さんは弁護士だ・です。

   Mr. Yamada is a lawyer.

2. As a substitute for other verbs (when the meaning is clear from the context)

   Watashi wa omuretsu da/desu.

   私はオムレツだ・です。

   I'll have an omelet.

AUXILIARIES

Auxiliaries are adjuncts that are attached to main verbs to give them additional meanings. They are used to make various verb forms such as polite, negative, passive, causative, potential, etc. Some verbs such as *iru* (exist) or *morau* (receive) may be used as auxiliaries in conjunction with other verbs.

1. **Chichi wa rokuji ni okimasu.**   (polite)

   父は六時に起きます。

   My father gets up at six o'clock.

2. **Biru wa sakana o tabenai.**   (negative)

   ビルは魚を食べない。

   Bill does not eat fish.

13

3. Sara wa sensei ni home**rareta**.　　　(passive)
サラは先生にほめ**られた**。

Sarah was praised by her teacher.

4. Sensi wa gakusei ni kanji o kaka**seru**.　(causative)
先生は学生に漢字を書か**せる**。

The teacher makes students write kanji.

5. Hiragana wa sugu oboe**rareru**.　　　(potential)
ひらがなはすぐ覚え**られる**。

I can learn hiragana easily.

6. Rainen Kanada e iki**tai**.　　　　　(desire)
来年カナダへ行き**たい**。

I want to go to Canada next year.

7. Ono-san wa Furansugo ga wakaru **sō da**. (hearsay)
小野さんはフランス語が分かる**そうだ**。

I hear that Miss Ono understands French.

8. Yamada-san wa ima hon o yonde **iru**.　(progressive)
山田さんは今本を読んで**いる**。

Mr. Yamada is reading a book now.

TRANSITIVE AND INTRANSITIVE

A transitive verb is a verb that requires a direct object to complete its meaning. It usually expresses an action done by the subject to the object. An intransitive verb, on the other hand, does not require a direct object. It expresses an action or state related only to the subject of the sentence.

TRANSITIVE:

Watashi wa o-cha o **nomu**.

私はお茶を**飲む**。

I drink tea.

INTRANSITIVE:

Watashi wa toshokan made **aruku**.

私は図書館まで**歩く**。

I walk to the library.

NOTE: Some English transitive verbs are intransitive in Japanese.

Tomu wa Nihongo ga **wakaru**.

トムは日本語が**分かる**。

Tom understands Japanese. (To Tom, Japanese is understandable.)

Koko kara umi ga **mieru**.

ここから海が**見える**。

We can see the ocean from here. (From here the ocean is visible.)

PART **I** CONJUGATION

1 Regular I Verbs

VERBS AND THE FIVE BASES

As we have seen earlier, the dictionary form of a regular I verb has a
consonant plus *u* ending. Therefore, all regular I verbs end with -ku
く, -gu ぐ, -su す, -tsu つ, -nu ぬ, -bu ぶ, -mu む, -ru る, -(w)u う,
or exceptionally, as noted previously, -eru/iru える/いる. Their
conjugations are simple and highly systematic. They can be learned
easily by using the Japanese syllabary chart. All the regular I verbs
conjugate on the five bases (1st/A, 2nd/I, 3rd/U, 4th/E, 5th/O) of the
nine rows (Ka, Ga, Sa, etc.) of the following chart.

	1	2	3	4	5	6	7	8	9
BASE	Ka か行	Ga が行	Sa さ行	Ta た行	Na な行	Ba ば行	Ma ま行	Ra ら行	Wa わ行
1st A	ka か	ga が	sa さ	ta た	na な	ba ば	ma ま	ra ら	wa わ
2nd I	ki き	gi ぎ	shi し	chi ち	ni に	bi び	mi み	ri り	(w)i* い
3rd U	ku く	gu ぐ	su す	tsu つ	nu ぬ	bu ぶ	mu む	ru る	(w)u* う
4th E	ke け	ge げ	se せ	te て	ne ね	be べ	me め	re れ	(w)e* え
5th O	ko こ	go ご	so そ	to と	no の	bo ぼ	mo も	ro ろ	(w)o* おを**

*In modern Japanese, *w* disappears before all vowels except *a*.
**を is used as a particle to mark the object of a sentence.

FUNCTIONS OF BASES

Each base functions to create various verb forms (which will be discussed in detail in Part II) and is named according to its main function as shown in parentheses.

1. The first base (negative base) is used in creating the plain negative form of a verb by adding *nai*. E.g. *Tegami o kakanai.* 手紙を書かない。(I don't write letters.)

2. The second base (conjunctive base) functions as the conjunction "and." E.g. *Shi o kaki, shi o yomu.* 詩を書き、詩を読む。(I write poems and read them.) It is also used in creating the polite style of speech by adding *masu*. E.g. *Shi o kakimasu* 詩を書きます。(I write poems.)

3. The third base (dictionary base) is the dictionary form which is used as the plain style of speech. E.g. *Shi o kaku.* 詩を書く。(I write poems.)

4. The fourth base (conditional/imperative base) is used in creating the conditional form by adding *ba*. E.g. *Tegami o kakeba,* 手紙を書けば、 (If I write a letter,). This base is also the imperative form of a verb which is used as a command in very abrupt male speech. E.g. *Tegami o kake.* 手紙を書け。(Write a letter!)

5. The fifth base (volitional base) is used in creating the volitional form by making the final vowel *o* a long sound *ō*. E.g. *Tegami o kakō.* 手紙を書こう。(I will write a letter.)

CONJUGATION

1. Ka Row: **kaku** 書く write

BASE & FORM	Ka か行	CONJUGATION	
1st Negative	ka か	ka**ka**(nai) 書か（ない）	(I) don't write
2nd Conjunctive	ki き	ka**ki**(masu) 書き（ます）	(I) write
3rd Dictionary	ku く	ka**ku** 書く	(I) write
4th Conditional	ke け	ka**ke**(ba) 書け（ば）	if (I) write
Imperative	ke け	ka**ke** 書け	write
5th Volitional	ko こ	ka**ko**(o) 書こ（う）	(I) will write

*The final o becomes a long sound: ko → koo or kō. Here oo (instead of ō) is used to clarify the conjugation.

Practice 1: Conjugate the following verbs.

1. saku 咲く bloom   2. iku 行く go   3. aruku 歩く walk
4. hataraku 働く work   5. tsuku 着く arrive

2. Ga Row: **oyogu** 泳ぐ swim

BASE & FORM	Ga が行	CONJUGATION	
1st Negative	ga が	oyo**ga**(nai) 泳が（ない）	(I) don't swim
2nd Conjunctive	gi ぎ	oyo**gi**(masu) 泳ぎ（ます）	(I) swim
3rd Dictionary	gu ぐ	oyo**gu** 泳ぐ	(I) swim
4th Conditional	ge げ	oyo**ge**(ba) 泳げ（ば）	if (I) swim
Imperative	ge げ	oyo**ge** 泳げ	swim
5th Volitional	go ご	oyo**go** (o)* 泳ご（う）	(I) will swim

*The final o becomes a long sound: go → goo or gō. Here oo (instead of ō) is used to clarify the conjugation.

Practice 2: Conjugate the following verbs.

1. isogu 急ぐ hurry   2. sawagu 騒ぐ make a noise
3. nugu 脱ぐ take off (clothing)

3. Sa Row: **hanasu** 話す speak

BASE & FORM	Sa さ行	CONJUGATION	
1st Negative	sa さ	hanasa(nai) 話さ（ない）	(I) don't speak
2nd Conjunctive	shi し	hanashi(masu) 話し（ます）	(I) speak
3rd Dictionary	su す	hanasu 話す	(I) speak
4th Conditional	se せ	hanase(ba) 話せ（ば）	if (I) speak
Imperative	se せ	hanase 話せ	speak
5th Volitional	so そ	hanaso(o)* 話そ（う）	(I) will speak

*The final o becomes a long sound: so → soo or sō. Here oo (instead of ō) is used to clarify the conjugation.

Practice 3: Conjugate the following verbs.

1. kaesu 返す return   2. naosu 直す correct   3. sagasu 探す look for
4. okosu 起こす wake someone up   5. kasu 貸す lend

4. Ta Row: **matsu** 待つ wait

BASE & FORM	Ta た行	CONJUGATION	
1st Negative	ta た	mata(nai) 待た（ない）	(I) don't wait
2nd Conjunctive	chi ち	machi(masu) 待ち（ます）	(I) wait
3rd Dictionary	tsu つ	matsu 待つ	(I) wait
4th Conditional	te て	mate(ba) 待て（ば）	if (I) write
Imperative	te て	mate 待て	wait
5th Volitional	to と	mato (o)* 待と（う）	(I) will wait

*The final o becomes a long sound: to → too or tō. Here oo (instead of ō) is used to clarify the conjugation.

Practice 4: Conjugate the following verbs.

1. motsu 持つ hold   2. tatsu 立つ stand   3. tatsu 建つ be built
4. utsu 打つ hit   5. katsu 勝つ win

5. Na Row: **shinu** 死ぬ die

BASE & FORM	Na な行	CONJUGATION	
1st Negative	na な	shi**na**(nai) 死な（ない）	(I) don't die
2nd Conjunctive	ni に	shi**ni**(masu) 死に（ます）	(I) die
3rd Dictionary	nu ぬ	shi**nu** 死ぬ	(I) die
4th Conditional	ne ね	shi**ne**(ba) 死ね（ば）	if (I) die
Imperative	ne ね	shi**ne** 死ね	die
5th Volitional	no の	shi**no**(o)* 死の（う）	(I) will die

*The final o becomes a long sound: no → noo or nō. Here oo (instead of ō) is used to clarify the conjugation.

NOTE: In modern Japanese, *shinu* is the only commonly used verb conjugated in the Na row.

6. Ba Row: **tobu** 飛ぶ fly

BASE & FORM	Ba ば行	CONJUGATION	
1st Negative	ba ば	to**ba**(nai) 飛ば（ない）	(I) don't fly
2nd Conjunctive	bi び	to**bi**(masu) 飛び（ます）	(I) fly
3rd Dictionary	bu ぶ	to**bu** 飛ぶ	(I) fly
4th Conditional	be べ	to**be**(ba) 飛べ（ば）	if (I) fly
Imperative	be べ	to**be** 飛べ	fly
5th Volitional	bo ぼ	to**bo**(o)* 飛ぼ（う）	(I) will fly

*The final o becomes a long sound: bo → boo or bō. Here oo (instead of ō) is used to clarify the conjugation.

Practice 5: Conjugate the following verbs.

1. asobu 遊ぶ play   2. hakobu 運ぶ carry   3. erabu 選ぶ choose
4. manabu 学ぶ study   5. yobu 呼ぶ call

7. Ma Row: **yomu** 読**む** read

BASE & FORM	Ma ま行	CONJUGATION	
1st Negative	ma ま	**yoma**(nai) 読ま （ない）	(I) don't read
2nd Conjunctive	mi み	**yomi**(masu) 読み （ます）	(I) read
3rd Dictionary	mu む	**yomu** 読む	(I) read
4th Conditional	me め	**ome**(ba) 読め （ば）	if (I) read
Imperative	me め	**yome** 読め	read
5th Volitional	mo も	**yomo**(o)* 読も （う）	(I) will read

*The final o becomes a long sound: mo → moo or mō. Here oo (instead of ō) is used to clarify the conjugation.

Practice 6: Conjugate the following verbs.

1. nomu 飲む drink　　2. sumu 住む reside　　3. tanomu 頼む ask
4. yasumu 休む rest, take a day off　　5. tanoshimu 楽しむ enjoy

8. Ra Row: **toru** 取**る** take

BASE & FORM	Ra ら行	CONJUGATION	
1st Negative	ra ら	**tora**(nai) 取ら （ない）	(I) don't take
2nd Conjunctive	ri り	**tori**(masu) 取り （ます）	(I) take
3rd Dictionary	ru る	**toru** 取る	(I) take
4th Conditional	re れ	**tore**(ba) 取れ （ば）	if (I) take
Imperative	re れ	**tore** 取れ	take
5th Volitional	ro ろ	**toro**(o)* 取ろ （う）	(I) will take

*The final o becomes a long sound: ro → roo or rō. Here oo (instead of ō) is used to clarify the conjugation.

Exceptions: Some verbs on the Ra row conjugate in slightly different ways from other regular I verbs as shown on p. 22.

Practice 7: Conjugate the following verbs.

1. hairu 入る enter　　2. hashiru 走る run　　3. kaeru 帰る return
4. noru 乗る get on (a bus)　　5. tsukuru 作る make

(1) aru ある there is/are; have

BASE & FORM	Ra ら行	CONJUGATION	
1st Negative	ra ら	nai* ない	there is/are not; don't have

*Not *aranai*.

(2) gozaru ござる there is/are; have

2nd Conjunctive	ri り	gozai*(masu) ござい（ます）	there is/are not; don't have

*R is dropped before -*masu*. Only the conjunctive form is used in modern Japanese.

(3) irassharu (honorific) いらっしゃる be/go/come

2nd Conjunctive	ri り	irasshai*(masu) いらっしゃい（ます）	(he) is/goes/comes
4th Imperative	re れ	irasshai* いらっしゃい	be/go/come

*R is dropped before -*masu* and in the imperative form. Other honorific verbs conjugated in the same way are: *nasaru* なさる (do), *ossharu* おっしゃる (say), and *kudasaru* くださる (give).

9. Wa Row: kau 買う buy

BASE & FORM	Wa わ行	CONJUGATION	
1st Negative	wa わ	kawa(nai) 買わ（ない）	(I) don't buy
2nd Conjunctive	i い	kai(masu) 買い（ます）	(I) buy
3rd Dictionary	u う	kau 買う	(I) buy
4th Conditional	e え	kae(ba) 買え（ば）	if (I) buy
Imperative	e え	kae 買え	buy
5th Volitional	o お	kao(o)* 買お（う）	(I)will buy

*The final o becomes a long sound: o → oo or ō. Here oo (instead of ō) is used to clarify the conjugation.

Practice 8: Conjugate the following verbs.

1. au 会う meet
2. iu 言う say
3. narau 習う learn
4. utau 歌う sing
5. tsukau 使う use

TE, TA, TARA, TARI FORMS

In addition to the forms we have seen so far, Japanese verbs have various other forms such as *te, ta, tara,* and *tari* forms. The *te* form functions as a conjunction among other usages. E.g. *Hon o karite yomu.* 本を借りて読む。 (I borrow books and read them.) The *ta* form is the past tense in the plain style. E.g. *Hon o karita.* 本を借りた。 (I borrowed a book.) The *tara* form is conditional. E.g. *Hon o karitara,* 本を借りたら、 (If/when I borrow a book,). The *tari* form followed by *suru* indicates alternative or an indefinite number of actions or events. E.g. *Hon o karitari suru.* 本を借りたりする。 (I do things like borrowing books and ~; or, I sometimes borrow books and sometimes ~.)

FORMATION

The *te* form is made in the following four ways. For the other three forms, simply replace *te* by *ta, tara,* or *tari*. If the final consonant is voiced, the *t* sound of *te, ta, tara,* and *tari* is changed to a *d* sound, *de, da, dara* and *dari*.

1. Verbs in the **Ka** row and **Gu** row

Change the *-ku* ending to *-ite/-ita/-itara/-itari* and the *-gu* ending to *-ide/-ida/-idara/-idari*.

(1) ka**ku** 書く write

FORM	CONJUGATION	
Te	ka**ite** 書いて	(I) write and ~
Ta (Past)	ka**ita** 書いた	(I) wrote
Tara (Conditional)	ka**itara** 書いたら	if/when (I) write
Tari	ka**itari** (suru) 書いたり（する）	(I do things like) writing and ~

(2) EXCEPTION: **iku** 行く go

FORM	CONJUGATION	
Te	**itte** 行って	(I) go and ~
Ta (Past)	**itta** 行った	(I) went
Tara (Conditional)	**ittara** 行ったら	if/when (I) go
Tari	**ittari** (suru) 行ったり（する）	(I) sometimes go and sometimes ~

(3) oyo**gu** 泳ぐ swim

FORM	CONJUGATION	
Te	oyo**ide** 泳いで	(I) swim and ~
Ta (Past)	oyo**ida** 泳いだ	(I) swam
Tara (Conditional)	oyo**idara** 泳いだら	if/when (I) swim
Tari	oyo**idari** (suru) 泳いだり（する）	(I do things like) swimming and ~

Practice 9: Conjugate the following verbs (**te**, **ta**, **tara**, **tari** forms).

1. ugoku 動く move.
2. naku 鳴く chirp.
3. hiku 弾く play (musical instrument).
4. isogu 急ぐ hurry.
5. nugu 脱ぐ take off (clothing).

2. Verbs in the **Sa** row

Change the *-su* ending to *-shite/-shita/-shitara/-shitari*.

hana**su** 話**す** speak

FORM	CONJUGATION	
Te	hana**shite** 話して	(I) speak and ~
Ta (Past)	hana**shita** 話した	(I) spoke
Tara (Conditional)	hana**shitara** 話したら	if/when (I) speak
Tari	hana**shitari** (suru) 話したり（する）	(I) sometimes speak and sometimes ~

Practice 10: Conjugate the following verbs.

1. otosu 落とす drop.　　2. herasu 減らす decrease.　　3. utsusu 移す move.
4. sugosu 過ごす spend (time).　　5. watasu 渡す hand over.

3. Verbs in the Na row, Ba row and Ma row

Change *-nu, -bu, -mu* endings to *-nde/-nda/-ndara/-ndari*.

(1) shi**nu** 死**ぬ** die

FORM	CONJUGATION	
Te	shi**nde** 死んで	(it) dies and ~
Ta (Past)	shi**nda** 死んだ	(it) died
Tara (Conditional)	shi**ndara** 死んだら	if/when (it) dies
Tari	shi**ndari** (suru) 死んだり（する）	(it) sometimes dies and sometimes ~

(2) **tobu** 飛ぶ fly

FORM	CONJUGATION	
Te	**tonde** 飛んで	(it) flies and ~
Ta (Past)	**tonda** 飛んだ	(it) flew
Tara (Conditional)	**tondara** 飛んだら	if/when (it) flies
Tari	**tondari** (suru) 飛んだり（する）	(it) sometimes flies and sometimes ~

(3) **yomu** 読む read

FORM	CONJUGATION	
Te	**yonde** 読んで	(I) read and ~
Ta (Past)	**yonda** 読んだ	(I) read
Tara (Conditional)	**yondara** 読んだら	if/when (I) read
Tari	**yondari** (suru) 読んだり（する）	(I do things like) reading and ~

Practice 11: Conjugate the following verbs (**te**, **ta**, **tara**, **tari** forms).

1. narabu 並ぶ line up   2. korobu 転ぶ fall down   3. sumu 済む finish
4. susumu 進む advance   5. tsutsumu 包む wrap

4. Verbs in the **Ta** row, Ra row and Wa row

Change -*tsu*, -*ru*, -(*w*)*u* endings to -*tte*/- *tta*/-*ttara*/-*ttari*.

(1) **matu** 待つ wait

FORM	CONJUGATION	
Te	**matte** 待って	(I) wait and ~
Ta (Past)	**matta** 待った	(I) waited
Tara (Conditional)	**mattara** 待ったら	if/when (I) wait
Tari	**mattari** (suru) 待ったり （する）	(I) sometimes wait and sometimes ~

(2) **toru** 取る take

FORM	CONJUGATION	
Te	**totte** 取って	(I) take and ~
Ta (Past)	**totta** 取った	(I) took
Tara (Conditional)	**tottara** 取ったら	if/when (I) take
Tari	**tottari** (suru) 取ったり （する）	sometimes take and sometimes ~

(3) **kau** 買う buy

FORM	CONJUGATION	
Te	**katte** 買って	(I) buy and ~
Ta (Past)	**katta** 買った	(I) bought
Tara (Conditional)	**kattara** 買ったら	if/when (I) buy
Tari	**kattari** (suru) 買ったり（する）	(I do things like) buying and ~

Practice 12: Conjugate the following verbs (**te**, **ta**, **tara**, **tari** forms).

1. medatsu 目立つ stick out   2. okuru 送る send   3. uru 売る sell
4. omou 思う think   5. harau 払う pay

② Regular II Verbs

VERB STEM

The dictionary form of a regular II verb has a vowel (*e* or *i*) plus -*ru* ending. E.g. *taberu* 食べる (eat); *miru* 見る (see, look, watch). The conjugations of regular II verbs is simple and easy to remember. Unlike regular I verbs, they do not conjugate on the five bases of the Japanese syllabary chart. The regular II verbs with -*iru* ending conjugate only on the second/I base and those with -*eru* ending conjugate only on the fourth/E base of the syllabary chart. However, you need not know which row a verb belongs to or which bases it conjugates on. All you have to do is to drop the -*ru* ending and add an appropriate ending to the stem.

CONJUGATION

1. Verbs with -*iru* ending

(1) mi**ru** 見る see, look, watch

FORM	CONJUGATION	
Negative	mi(nai) 見 (ない)	(I) don't see
Conjunctive	mi(masu) 見 (ます)	(I) see
Dictionary	mi**ru** 見る	(I) see
Conditional	mi**re**(ba) 見れ (ば)	if/when (I) see
Imperative	mi**ro**/mi**yo** 見ろ・見よ	look
Volitional	mi**yō** 見よう	(I) will see

Te	**mite** 見て	(I) see and ~
Ta (Past)	**mita** 見た	(I) saw
Tara (Conditional)	**mitara** 見たら	if/when (I) see
Tari	**mitari** (suru) 見たり（する）	(I) sometimes see and sometimes ~

2. Verbs with -*eru* ending

(2) **taberu** 食べる eat

FORM	CONJUGATION	
Negative	**tabe**(nai) 食べ（ない）	(I) don't eat
Conjunctive	**tabe**(masu) 食べ（ます）	(I) eat
Dictionary	**taberu** 食べる	(I) eat
Conditional	**tabere**(ba) 食べれ（ば）	if (I) eat
Imperative	**tabero/tabeyo** 食べろ・食べよ	eat
Volitional	**tabeyō** 食べよう	(I) will eat
Te	**tabete** 食べて	(I) eat and ~
Ta (Past)	**tabeta** 食べた	(I) ate
Tara (Conditional)	**tabetara** 食べたら	if/when (I) eat
Tari	**tabetari** (suru) 食べたり（する）	(I) sometimes eat and sometimes ~

Practice 13: Give the negative, conjunctive, conditional (-*ba*), volitional and *te* forms of the following verbs.

1. kiru 着る wear   2. okiru 起きる get up   3. kotaeru 答える answer
4. miseru 見せる show   5. akeru 開ける open

3. Verbs converted from regular I verbs:

When regular I verbs take the potential form, they become regular II verbs with an *-eru* ending. This form, expressing competence or ability, is made by adding *-ru* to the stem of the conditional form (4th base) of regular I verbs, e.g. *kake(ba)* → *kakeru* 書ける (can write). All potential verbs are regular II verbs.

(1) **yomeru** 読める can read

FORM	CONJUGATION	
Negative	yome(nai) 読め（ない）	(I) can't read
Conjunctive	yome(masu) 読め（ます）	(I) can read
Dictionary	yome**ru** 読める	(I) can read
Te	yome**te** 読めて	(I) can read and ~
Ta (Past)	yome**ta** 読めた	(I) could read
Tara (Conditional)	yome**tara** 読めたら	if/when (I) can read
Tari	yome**tari** (suru) 読めたり（する）	(I) sometimes can read and sometimes ~

Practice 14: Give the potential dictionary, negative, conjunctive and *te* forms of the following verbs.

1. oyogu 泳ぐ swim
2. utau 歌う sing
3. hanasu 話す speak
4. nomu 飲む drink
5. motsu 持つ hold

③ Irregular Verbs

There are only two irregular verbs: *kuru* 来る (come) and *suru* する (do). The *suru*-verb which is a combination of a noun and *suru*, e.g. *denwa suru* 電話する (make a phone call), conjugates in the same way as *suru*.

CONJUGATION

kuru 来る come

FORM	CONJUGATION	
Negative	ko(nai) 来 （ない）	(I) don't come
Conjunctive	ki(masu) 来 （ます）	(I) come
Dictionary	kuru 来る	(I) come
Conditional	kure(ba) 来れ （ば）	if (I) come
Imperative	koi 来い	come
Volitional	koyō 来よう	(I) will come
Te	kite 来て	(I) come and ~
Ta (Past)	kita 来た	(I) came
Tara (Conditional)	kitara 来たら	if/when (I) come
Tari	kitari (suru) 来たり （する）	(I) sometimes come and sometimes ~

suru する do

FORM	CONJUGATION	
Negative	shi(nai) し（ない）	(I) don't do
Conjunctive	shi(masu) し（ます）	(I) do
Dictionary	suru する	(I) do
Conditional	sure(ba) すれ（ば）	if (I) do
Imperative	seyo/shiro せよ・しろ	do
Volitional	shiyō しよう	(I) will do
Te	shite して	(I) do and ~
Ta (Past)	shita した	(I) did
Tara (Conditional)	shitara したら	if/when (I) do
Tari	shitari (suru) したり（する）	(I) sometimes do and sometimes ~

Practice 15: Give the negative, conjunctive, conditional (-*ba*), volitional and *ta* forms of the following verbs.

1. kuru 来る come   2. suru する do   3. shigoto suru 仕事する work
4. shitsumon suru 質問する ask a question

4 Copulas (Be-Verbs)

The Japanese copulas, *da* (plain style) and *desu* (polite style), are equivalent to the English am, is, or are.

CONJUGATION

da だ

FORM	CONJUGATION	
Negative	(gakusei) de (wa) nai (学生) で (は) ない	(he) is not (a student)
Dictionary	(gakusei) da (学生) だ	(he) is (a student)
Conditional	(gakusei) nara (学生) なら	if (he) is a student
Presumptive	(gakusei) darō (学生) だろう	(he) is probably (a student)
Te	(gakusei) de (学生) で	(he) is (a student) and ~
Ta (Past)	(gakusei) datta (学生) だった	(he) was (a student)
Tara (Conditional)	(gakusei) dattara (学生) だったら	if (he) is (a student)
Tari	(gakusei) dattari (suru) (学生) だったり (する)	(he) sometimes is (a student) and sometimes ~

desu です

FORM	CONJUGATION	
Negative	(sensei) de (wa) arimasen (先生) で（は）ありません	(he) is not (a teacher)
Dictionary	(sensei) desu (先生) です	(he) is (a teacher)
Conditional	----------	----------
Presumptive	(sensei) deshō (先生) でしょう	(he) is probably (a teacher)
Te	(sensei) deshite (先生) でして	(he) is (a teacher) and ~
Ta (Past)	(sensei) deshita (先生) でした	(he) was (a teacher)
Tara (Conditional)	(sensei) deshitara (先生) でしたら	if (he) is (a teacher)
Tari	(sensei) deshitari (suru) (先生) でしたり（する）	(he) sometimes is (a teacher) and sometimes ~

	AFFIRMATIVE	NEGATIVE
Present	da/desu だ・です	de (wa) nai/de (wa) arimasen で（は）ない・で（は）ありません
Past	datta/deshita だった・でした	de (wa) nakatta/de (wa) arimasen deshita で（は）なかった・で（は）ありませんでした
Presumptive	darō/deshō だろう・でしょう	de (wa) nai daroo/de (wa) nai deshoo で（は）ないだろう・で（は）ないでしょう

Practice 16: Change the underlined parts into the negative.

1. Amerikajin <u>desu</u>. アメリカ人<u>です</u>。 (He) is an American.
2. Hoteru <u>deshō</u>. ホテル<u>でしょう</u>。 (It) is probably a hotel.
3. Isha <u>deshita</u>. 医者<u>でした</u>。 (He) was a doctor.
4. Hara-san <u>darō</u>. 原さん<u>だろう</u>。 (He) is probably Mr. Hara.
5. Resutoran <u>datta</u>. レストラン<u>だった</u>。 (It) was a restaurant.
6. Bengoshi <u>da</u>. 弁護士<u>だ</u>。 (He) is a lawyer.

⑤ Auxiliaries

Auxiliaries are adjuncts that are attached to main verbs to give them additional meanings. The following show some common auxiliaries and their conjugations.

Masu ます

Masu is attached to the conjunctive form of all verbs to make the tone of speech polite.

FORM	CONJUGATION	
Negative	(iki)masen/masen deshita (行き) ません・ませんでした	(I) don't/didn't go
Dictionary	(iki)masu (行き) ます	(I) go
Conditional	(iki)masureba* (行き) ますれば	if (I) go
Imperative	(irasshai) mase/mashi** (いらっしゃい) ませ・まし	please go/come
Volitional	(iki)mashō (行き) ましょう	(I) will go
Te	(iki)mashite*** (行き) まして	(I) go and ~
Ta (Past)	(iki)mashita (行き) ました	(I) went
Tara (Conditional)	(iki)mashitara*** (行き) ましたら	if/when (I) go

*Seldom used in modern Japanese
**Attached only to the imperative form of honorific verbs such as *nasaru* なさる (do) and *ossharu* おっしゃる (say)
***Very polite level of speech

Practice 17: Give the *masu* form and the negative, past, and past-negative forms of the following verbs.

1. aku 開く open   2. tetsudau 手伝う help   3. kangaeru 考える think
4. tsuzukeru 続ける continue   5. kenbutsu suru 見物する go sightseeing

Nai ない

Nai is attached to the negative form of all verbs to indicate negation.

FORM	CONJUGATION	
Negative	(kawa)naku wa nai (買わ) なく は ない	it isn't that (I) don't buy
Conjunctive	(kawa)naku (買わ) なく	(I) don't buy and ~
Dictionary	(kawa)nai (買わ) ない	(I) don't buy
Conditional	(kawa)nakereba (買わ) なければ	if (I) don't buy
Te	(kawa)nakute (買わ) なくて	(I) don't buy and ~
Ta (Past)	(kawa)nakatta (買わ) なかった	(I) didn't buy
Tara (Conditional)	(kawa)nakattara (買わ) なかったら	if/when (I) don't buy

Practice 18: Negate the following verbs by adding *nai* and *nakatta* (past).

1. naku 泣く cry   2. yameru 辞める resign   3. kimeru 決める decide
4. kuru 来る come   5. fukushū suru 復習する review (lessons)

Tai たい

Tai is attached to the conjunctive form of all verbs to express a first person (I, we) desire to do something.

FORM	CONJUGATION	
Negative	(narai)takunai (習い) たくない	(I) don't want to learn
Conjunctive	(narai)taku (習い) たく	(I) want to learn and ~
Dictionary	(narai)tai (習い) たい	(I) want to learn
Conditional	(narai)takereba (習い) たければ	if (I) want to learn

Te	(narai)takute (習い) たくて	(I) want to learn and ~
Ta (Past)	(narai)takatta (習い) たかった	(I) wanted to learn
Tara (Conditional)	(narai)takattara (習い) たかったら	if (I) want to learn

Practice 19: Add *tai* and *takatta* (past) to the following verbs to express first person desire.

1. kotowaru 断る refuse   2. iwau 祝う celebrate   3. nokosu 残す leave
4. sodateru 育てる bring up   5. kitai suru 期待する expect

Tagaru たがる

Tagaru is attached to the conjunctive form of all verbs to express a third person desire to do something. With *tagaru*, all verbs become regular verbs, conjugated in the Ra row. There are no conditional, imperative or volitional forms. The *tara* form is used for conditional.

BASE & FORM	Ra ら行	CONJUGATION	
1st Negative	ra ら	(asobi)tagara (nai) (遊び) たがら （ない）	(he) doesn't want to play
2nd Conjunctive	ri り	(asobi)tagari (masu) (遊び) たがり （ます）	(he) wants to play
3rd Dictionary	ru る	(asobi)tagaru (遊び) たがる	(he) wants to play
Te		(asobi)tagatte (遊び) たがって	(he) wants to play and ~
Ta (Past)		(asobi)tagatta (遊び) たがった	(he) wanted to play
Tara (Conditional)		(asobi)tagattara (遊び) たがったら	if (he) wants to play

Practice 20: Add *tagaru* to the following verbs to express third person desire.

1. oyogu 泳ぐ swim   2. shiru 知る know   3. miru 見る see, look, watch
4. kariru 借りる borrow   5. ryokō suru 旅行する travel

Hoshii ほしい

Hoshii is attached to the *te* form of all verbs to express a desire to have someone do something.

FORM	CONJUGATION	
Negative	(mite) hoshikunai (見て) ほしくない	(I) don't want (him) to see
Conjunctive	(mite) hoshiku (見て) ほしく	(I) want (him) to see and ~
Dictionary	(mite) hoshii (見て) ほしい	(I) want (him) to see
Conditional	(mite) hoshikereba (見て) ほしければ	if (I) want (him) to see
Te	(mite) hoshikute (見て) ほしくて	(I) want (him) to see and ~
Ta (Past)	(mite) hoshikatta (見て) ほしかった	(I) wanted (him) to see
Tara (Conditional)	(mite) hoshikattara (見て) ほしかったら	if (I) want (him) to see

Practice 21: Add *hoshii* and *hoshikatta* (past) to the following verbs.

1. makasu 負かす defeat
2. ganbaru 頑張る hold on
3. atsumeru 集める collect
4. akirameru あきらめる give up
5. shusseki suru 出席する attend

Rashii らしい

Rashii is attached to the dictionary form and the *ta* form of all verbs to express conjecture based on some reliable infromation.

FORM	CONJUGATION	
Conjunctive	(kaeru/kaetta) rashiku (帰る・帰った) らしく	it seems (he) will return/ has returned and ~
Dictionary	(kaeru/kaetta) rashii (帰る・帰った) らしい	it seems (he) will return/ has returned
Te	(kaeru/kaetta) rashikute (帰る・帰った) らしくて	it seems (he) will return/ has returned and ~

NOTE: Use the negative form of a verb for negative conjecture. E.g. *kaeranai/kaeranakatta rashii* 帰らない・帰らなかったらしい (it seems (he) won't return/hasn't returned).

Practice 22: Change the ending of the following verbs and add *rashii*.
1. maniaimasu 間に合います be in time
2. dekakemashita 出かけました left   3. okuremasu 遅れます be late
4. sanka shimashita 参加しました participated

Sō da そうだ

a. *Sō da* is attached to the dictionary and *ta* forms of all verbs to report hearsay.

FORM	CONJUGATION	
Dictionary	(kuru/kita) sō da (来る・来た) そうだ	I hear that (he) will come/ has come

b. *Sō da* is attached to the conjunctive form of all verbs to express conjecture based on what the speaker sees or feels.

FORM	CONJUGATION	
Dictionary	(taore) sō da (倒れ) そうだ	it looks like (it) will fall down
Conditional	(taore) sō nara (倒れ) そうなら	if it looks like (it) will fall down
Ta (Past)	(taore) sō datta (倒れ) そうだった	it looked like (it) would fall down

Practice 23: Change the endings of the following verbs and add *sō da* to express (a) hearsay and (b) conjecture.

a. 1. kimasu 来ます come   2. akimasu 開きます open
   3. kaimashita 買いました bought
   4. susumemashita 勧めました recommended

b. 1. warau 笑う laugh   2. furu 降る rain   3. yameru 辞める resign
   4. naku 泣く cry   5. hatten suru 発展する develop

Seru/saseru せる・させる

Seru is attached to the negative form of regular I verbs and *saseru* to the stem of regular II verbs to make the causative form: "to make/let someone do something." For irregular verbs, see c (below). With *seru/saseru*, all verbs become regular II.

a. Regular I verbs

aruku 歩く walk   aruka + seru → aruka**seru** 歩か**せる**

FORM	CONJUGATION	
Negative	aruka**se** (nai) 歩かせ（ない）	(I) don't make/let (him) walk
Conjunctive	aruka**se** (masu) 歩かせ（ます）	(I) make/let (him) walk
Dictionary	aruka**seru** 歩かせる	(I) make/let (him) walk
Conditional	aruka**sere**(ba) 歩かせれ（ば）	if (I) make/let (him) walk
Imperative	aruka**sero**/aruka**seyo** 歩かせろ・歩かせよ	make/let (him) walk
Volitional	aruka**seyō** 歩かせよう	(I) will make/let (him) walk
Te	aruka**sete** 歩かせて	(I) make/let (him) walk and ~
Ta (Past)	aruka**seta** 歩かせた	(I) made/let (him) walk

Practice 24: Make the causative *masu* and *ta* forms of the following verbs.

1. kaku 書く write   2. hakobu 運ぶ carry   3. suwaru 座る sit down
4. hirou 拾う pick up 5. shimesu 示す indicate

b. Regular II verbs

taberu 食べる eat　tabe + saseru → (tabe**saseru** 食べさせる)

FORM	CONJUGATION	
Negative	tabe**sase** (nai) 食べさせ（ない）	(I) don't make/let (him) eat
Conjunctive	tabe**sase** (masu) 食べさせ（ます）	(I) make/let (him) eat
Dictionary	tabe**saseru** 食べさせる	(I) make/let (him) eat
Conditional	tabe**sasere**(ba) 食べさせれ（ば）	if (I) make/let (him) eat
Imperative	tabe**sasero**/tabe**saseyo** 食べさせろ・食べさせよ	make/let (him) eat
Volitional	tabe**saseyō** 食べさせよう	(I) will make/let (him) eat
Te	tabe**sasete** 食べさせて	(I) make/let (him) eat and ~
Ta (Past)	tabe**saseta** 食べさせた	(I) made/let (him) eat

Practice 25: Make the causative *masu* and *ta* forms of the following verbs.

1. atsumeru 集める collect　2. kiru 着る wear　3. shimeru 閉める close
4. tomeru 止める stop　　　5. oriru 降りる get off

c. Irregular verbs

kuru 来る come → kosaseru 来させる

FORM	CONJUGATION	
Negative	kosase(nai) 来させ（ない）	(I) don't make/let (him) come
Conjunctive	kosase(masu) 来させ（ます）	(I) make/let (him) come
Dictionary	kosaseru 来させる	(I) make/let (him) come
Conditional	kosasere(ba) 来させれ（ば）	if (I) make/let (him) come

Imperative	kosasero/kosaseyo 来させろ・来させよ	make/let (him) come
Volitional	kosaseyō 来させよう	(I) will make/let (him) come
Te	kosasete 来させて	(I) make/let (him) come and ~
Ta (Past)	kosaseta 来させた	(I) made/let (him) come

suru する do → saseru させる

FORM	CONJUGATION	
Negative	sasa(nai) させ（ない）	(I) don't make/let (him) do
Conjunctive	sase(masu) させ（ます）	(I) make/let (him) do
Dictionary	saseru させる	(I) make/let (him) do
Conditional	sasere(ba) させれ（ば）	if (I) make/let (him) do
Imperative	sasero/saseyo させろ・させよ	make/let (him) do
Volitional	saseyō させよう	(I) will make/let (him) do
Te	sasete させて	(I) make/let (him) do and ~
Ta (Past)	saseta させた	(I) made/let (him) do

Practice 26: Make the causative *masu* and *ta* forms of the following verbs.
1. kuru 来る come　　2. suru する do　3. setsumei suru 説明する explain

There is a shortened form for causative verbs which is formed by changing the final -*seru* せる to -*su* す. In this form, all verbs become regular I verbs and conjugate on the Sa row.

aruka**seru** 歩かせる → aruka**su** 歩か**す**
tabesa**seru** 食べさせる → tabesa**su** 食べさ**す**

kosa**seru** 来させる → kosa**su** 来さす
sa**seru** させる → sa**su** さす

This shortened causative form tends to express more direct causation. For example, *kodomo o arukasu* means "help a child walk by giving him a hand," while *kodomo o arukaseru* means "make/let a child walk."

Reru/rareru れる・られる

Reru is attached to the negative form of regular I verbs, and *rareru* is attached to the stem of regular II verbs to make the passive form. For the irregular verbs, see c (below). With *reru/rareru*, all verbs become regular II verbs.

a. Regular I verbs

yomu 読む read   yoma + reru → yoma**reru** 読ま**れる**

FORM	CONJUGATION	
Negative	yoma**re**(nai) 読ま**れ**（ない）	(it) isn't read
Conjunctive	yoma**re**(masu) 読ま**れ**（ます）	(it) is read
Dictionary	yoma**reru** 読ま**れる**	(it) is read
Te	yoma**rete** 読ま**れて**	(it) is read and ~
Ta (Past)	yoma**reta** 読ま**れた**	(it) was read

b. Regular II verbs

homeru ほめる praise home + rareru → home**rareru** ほめ**られる**

FORM	CONJUGATION	
Negative	home**rare**(nai) ほめられ（ない）	(I) am not praised
Conjunctive	home**rare**(masu) ほめられ（ます）	(I) am praised
Dictionary	home**rareru** ほめられる	(I) am praised
Te	home**rarete** ほめられて	(I) am praised and ~
Ta (Past)	home**rareta** ほめられた	(I) was praised

c. Irregular verbs

kuru 来る come → korareru 来られる

FORM	CONJUGATION	
Negative	korare(nai) 来られ（ない）	(he) doesn't come (and I am happy)
Conjunctive	korare(masu) 来られ（ます）	(he) comes (and I am unhappy)
Dictionary	korareru 来られる	(he) comes (and I am unhappy)
Te	korarete 来られて	(he) comes and (I am unhappy)
Ta (Past)	korareta 来られた	(he) came (and I was unhappy)

NOTE: Japanese intransitive verbs may be used in the passive form, in which the speaker is suffering from someone else's action.

suru する do → sareru される

FORM	CONJUGATION	
Negative	sare(nai) され（ない）	(it) is not done
Conjunctive	sare(masu) され（ます）	(it) is done
Dictionary	sareru される	(it) is done
Te	sarete されて	(it) is done and ~
Ta (Past)	sareta された	(it) was done

This passive form is also used for potential and honorific expressions as follows.

Tomu wa kanji ga yomareru. (potential)
トムは漢字が読まれる。

Tom can read kanji.

NOTE: The potential equivalent for the verb *suru* is *dekiru,* not *sareru.* E.g. *tenisu ga dekiru* テニスができる (can play tennis).

Yamada-sensei ga hon o yomareta.　　(honorific)
山田先生が本を読まれた。

Prof. Yamada read the book.

Practice 27: Make the passive *masu* and *ta* forms of the following verbs

1. sasou 誘う invite　　2. shikaru 叱る scold　　3. shinu 死ぬ die
4. tasukeru 助ける save　　5. chūkoku suru 忠告する advise

Rareru られる with causative verbs

Rareru is attached to the stem of the causative verb to make the causative-passive form. These verbs are regular II verbs.

kakaseru 書かせる make/let someone write
kakase + rareru → kakase**rareru** 書かせ**られる**

FORM	CONJUGATION	
Negative	kakase**rare** (nai) 書かせられ（ない）	(I) am not made to write
Conjunctive	kakase**rare** (masu) 書かせられ（ます）	(I) am made to write
Dictionary	kakase**rareru** 書かせられる	(I) am made to write
Te	kakase**rarete** 書かせられて	(I) am made to write and ~
Ta (Past)	kakase**rareta** 書かせられた	(I) was made to write

The causative-passive form is also made by attaching *reru* to the negative form of shortened causative verbs (regular I verbs only: e.g. *arukasu* 歩かす).

arukasu 歩かす make/let someone walk
arukasa + reru → arukasa**reru** 歩かさ**れる**

FORM	CONJUGATION	
Negative	arukasa**re**(nai) 歩かされ（ない）	(I) am not made to walk
Conjunctive	arukasa**re**(masu) 歩かされ（ます）	(I) am made to walk
Dictionary	arukasa**reru** 歩かされる	(I) am made to walk
Te	arukasa**rete** 歩かされて	(I) am made to walk and ~
Ta (Past)	arukasa**reta** 歩かされた	(I) was made to walk

Practice 28: Make the causative-passive forms (dictionary) of the following verbs.

1. matsu 待つ wait　　　2. nomu 飲む drink　　　3. odoru 踊る dance
4. suteru 捨てる throw away　　5. kuru 来る come
6. hōkoku suru 報告する report

In Part I, we have seen how Japanese verbs are grouped, how they conjugate and make numerous forms, and how they are combined with various auxiliaries to give them additional meanings. Part II deals with how each of these verb forms is used in connection with sentence structures. Let's begin with the conjunctive form which occurs in the most used expressions and then proceed to the dictionary form, to the negative form and so forth. In each form, expressions are numbered and arranged from easy to difficult.

 1 Conjunctive Form

Conjunctive form (Vconj)

Regular I Verb (2nd base)	Regular II Verb (Verb stem)	Irregular Verb
kaki 書き (write) oyogi 泳ぎ (swim)	mi 見 (see, look) tabe 食べ (eat)	ki 来 (come) shi し (do)

SENTENCE PATTERNS

1.1 | **Vconj + masu ます** | "do/will do," "there is/will be"

Vconj *masu* expresses actions or states which regularly take place/exist or will take place/exist. The auxiliary *masu* makes the tone of speech polite.

EXAMPLES:

1. Tomu wa mainichi toshokan e **iki**masu.
トムは毎日図書館へ**行き**ます。

   Tom goes to the library every day.

2. Ashita Tanaka-san wa **ki**masen.
明日田中さんは**来**ません。

   Miss Tanaka won't come tomorrow.

3. Chichi wa sakki made koko ni **i**mashita.
父はさっきまでここに**い**ました。

   My father was here a while ago.

4. Sumisu-san wa kinō gorufu o **shi**masen deshita.
スミスさんは昨日ゴルフを**し**ませんでした。

   Mr. Smith did not play golf yesterday.

1.2 | Vconj + **mashō** ましょう | "I will," "Let's ~"

Vconj *mashō* expresses the first person's volition, invitation or suggestion.

EXAMPLES:

1. Watashi ga **tetsudai**mashō.
私が**手伝い**ましょう。

   I will help you.

2. Kono dēta wa watashi-tachi ga **shirabe**mashō.
このデータは私達が**調べ**ましょう。

   We will check this data.

3. Ano heya de **benkyō shi**mashō.
あの部屋で勉強しましょう。

Let's study in that room.

1.3 | Vconj + **mashō ka/masen ka** ましょうか・ませんか

"Shall I ~ ?" "Wouldn't you ~ ?"

Vconj *mashō ka/masen ka* expresses a first person invitation or suggestion in the form of a question. The negative question *masen ka* is more polite than *mashō ka*.

EXAMPLES:

1. O-cha demo **nomi**mashō ka.
   お茶でも**飲み**ましょうか。
   Shall we drink tea or something?

2. Mado o **ake**mashō ka.
   窓を**開け**ましょうか。
   Shall I open the window?

3. Hara-san o pātī ni **shōtai shi**masen ka.
   原さんをパーティーに**招待し**ませんか。
   Wouldn't you (like to) invite Miss Hara to the party?

PRACTICE 1 (1.1–1.3)

Fill in the blanks with the appropriate forms of the verbs provided at the end of the sentences.

1. Haha wa maiasa rokuji ni _____. (okiru)
   母は毎朝六時に _____。（起きる）

My mother gets up at six o'clock every moring.

2. Hikōki wa gogo yoji ni _____. (tsuku)
   飛行機は午後四時に_____。（着く）
   The airplane will arrive at 4 p.m.

3. Yamada-san wa kinō _____ ga, Kimura-san wa
   _____ . (kuru)
   山田さんは昨日_____が、木村さんは_____。（来る）
   Mr. Yamada came yesterday, but Mr. Kimura didn't.

4. Ima kara bideo o _____. (miru)
   今からビデオを_____。（見る）
   Let's watch the video now.

5. Kono tegami wa watashi ga Eigo ni_____ ka.
   (yakusu)
   この手紙は私が英語に_____か。（訳す）
   Shall I translate this letter into English?

6. Kida-san o watashi-tachi no gurūpu ni _____ ka.
   (shōkai suru)
   木田さんを私達のグループに_____か。（紹介する）
   Wouldn't you (like to) introduce Miss Kida to our group?

1.4 | Vconj + **nasai** なさい | "Do ~"

Vconj *nasai* expresses a plain imperative, used, for example, by teachers or parents to their students or children.

EXAMPLES:

1. Soto de **asobi**nasai.

   外で**遊び**なさい。

   Play outside.

2. Nihongo de **kotae**nasai.

   日本語で**答え**なさい。

   Answer in Japanese.

3. Kanji o nando mo **renshū shi**nasai.

   漢字を何度も**練習し**なさい。

   Practice kanji many times.

1.5 | o + Vconj + **kudasai** お .... ください |

"Would you please do ~"

O Vconj *kudasai* expresses a polite imperative to superiors or customers.

EXAMPLES:

1. Sanji made ni o-**kaeri** kudasai.

   三時までにお**帰り**ください。

   Would you please return by three o'clock.

2. Dōzo o-**kake** kudasai.

   どうぞお**かけ**ください。

   Would you please sit down.

NOTE: Some verbs also use special polite alternative words, e.g. *miru* 見る (look) → *Goran kudasai.* ご覧ください。 (Would you please look.); *iku/kuru* 行く・来る (go/come) → *Oide kudasai.* おいでください。 (Would you please go/come.) For *suru*-verbs, the following polite imperative form is used: e.g. *setsumei suru* 説明する (explain) → *Go-setsumei kudasai.* ご説明ください。 (Would you please explain.) Normally, the polite prefix *o* is attached to Japanese verbs and *go* to *suru*-verbs of Chinese origin.

1.6 | **o** + Vconj + **shimasu/itashimasu** お .... します・いたします

"I'll do ~," "I'd like to do ~"

O Vconj *shimasu/itashimasu* expresses the speaker's volition in the humble style. The verb *itasu* is the humble equivalent of *suru*.

EXAMPLES:

1. Robī de o-**machi** shimasu/itashimasu.
   ロビーでお**待ち**します・いたします。

   I'll wait for you in the lobby.

2. Shinamono wa ashita o-**todoke** shimasu/itashimasu.
   品物は明日お**届け**します・いたします。

   We'll deliver the article tomorrow.

NOTE: Some verbs use special humble words, e.g. *iku/kuru* 行く・来る (go/come) → *mairimasu.* 参ります。(I'll go/come.); *taberu/nomu* 食べる・飲む (eat/drink) → *itadakimasu.* いただきます。(I'll eat/drink.) For *suru*-verbs, the following humble form is used: e.g. *renraku suru* 連絡する (contact) → *Go-renraku itashimasu.* ご連絡いたします。(I'll contact you.)

PRACTICE 2 (1.4–1.6)

A. Make the plain and polite imperatives of the following verbs.

1. narabu 並ぶ line up.   2. harau 払う pay.   3. toru 取る take.
4. arau 洗う wash.   5. miseru 見せる show.

B. Complete the following sentences in the humble style with the verbs provided.

1. Kono nimotsu wa ashita made _____ . (azukaru)
   この荷物は明日まで _____。（預かる）

   I'll keep this baggage for you until tomorrow.

2. Sono go-shōtai wa _____. (kotowaru)

   そのご招待は _____ 。（断る）

   I declined the invitation.

3. Kono shorui wa sugu _____. (shiraberu)

   この書類はすぐ _____ 。（調べる）

   I'll check this document right away.

1.7 | **Vconj, Vconj + masu ます** | "do ~ and do ~ "

By linking two or more verbs, Vconj, Vconj *masu* expresses actions in succession.

EXAMPLES:

1. Maiasa kōhī o **nomi**, hachiji ni ie o demasu.

   毎朝コーヒーを飲み、八時に家を出ます。

   Every morning I drink coffee and leave my house at eight o'clock.

2. Rokuji ni **oki**, ha o **migaki**, shawā o **abi**mashita.

   六時に起き、歯を磨き、シャワーを浴びました。

   I got up at six o'clock, brushed my teeth and took a shower.

3. Kuruma ga **koshō shi**, kaigi ni **okure**mashita.

   車が故障し、会議に遅れました。

   My car broke down and I was late for the meeting.

1.8 | Vconj | used as a noun

Vconj of regular I and regular II verbs is used as a noun by itself.
Desu may be added to adjectives to make the speech polite.

EXAMPLES

1. Doi-sensei no **hanashi** wa itsumo omoshiroi (desu).
   土井先生の**話**はいつも面白い（です）。

   Prof. Doi's talk is always interesting.

2. Kono shōhin wa **mōke** ga ōi (desu).
   この商品は**もうけ**が多い（です）。

   These goods bring in a large profit.

1.9 | Vconj + **ni** に + motion verb |

"go/come/return/enter/leave to do something"

Vconj *ni* may be used only with motion verbs such as *iku* 行く (go),
kuru 来る (come), *kaeru* 帰る (return), *hairu* 入る (enter), *deru* 出る
(leave) to express purpose when a person moves from one place to
another.

EXAMPLES

1. Kusuri o **kai** ni mise ni hairimashita.
   薬を**買い**に店に入りました。

   I entered a store to buy medicine.

2. Hayashi-san wa kodomo o **mukae** ni eki e ikimasu.
   林さんは子供を**迎え**に駅へ行きます。

   Mrs. Hayashi is going to the station to pick up her child.

3. Jimu wa Nihongo o **benkyō shi** ni Nihon e kimashita.

ジムは日本語を勉強しに日本へ来ました。

Jim came to Japan to study Japanese.

PRACTICE 3 (1.7–1.9)

Fill in the blanks with the appropriate forms of the verbs provided at the end of the sentences.

1. Shinjuku de densha ni _____, Ueno de _____ masu. (noru) (oriru)

   新宿で電車に _____ 、上野で _____ ます。（乗る）（降りる）

   I get on a train at Shinjuku and get off at Ueno.

2. Kono shōsetsu wa _____ kara _____ made omoshiroi desu. (hajimeru) (owaru)

   この小説は _____ から _____ まで面白いです。（始める）（終わる）

   This novel is interesting from beginning to end.

3. Ano saka wa _____ wa raku desu ga, _____ wa tai-hen desu. (kudaru) (noboru)

   あの坂は _____ は楽ですが _____ は大変です。（下る）（上る）

   Coming down that slope is easy, but going up is terrible.

4. Tokidoki gakusei ga shitsumon o _____ ni kimasu. (suru)

   時々学生が質問を _____ に来ます。（する）

   Once in a while students come to ask questions.

5. Shokunin ga terebi o _____ ni kimashita. (naosu)

   職人が テレビを _____ に来ました。(直す)

   A technician came to repair the TV set.

6. Sanji ni gakkō o _____ , toshokan e hon o _____ ni ikimashita. (deru) (kaesu)

   三時に学校を _____ 、図書館へ本を _____ に行きました。(出る)(返す)

   I left school at three o'clock and went to the library to return books.

7. Tōri de Hara-san ni _____ , kissaten ni o-cha o _____ ni hairimashita. (au) (nomu)

   通りで原さんに _____ 、喫茶店にお茶を _____ に入りました。(会う)(飲む)

   I met Miss Hara on the street, and we entered a coffee shop to have tea.

1.10 | Vconj + **nagara** ながら | "while doing ~"

Vconj *nagara* expresses simultaneous actions performed by one subject.

EXAMPLES:

1. Miki-san wa tabako o **sui**nagara shigoto o shimasu.

   三木さんはたばこを**吸い**ながら仕事をします。

   Mr. Miki works while smoking.

2. Akiko-san wa piano **hiki**naraga utaimashita.

   秋子さんはピアノを**弾き**ながら歌いました。

   Akiko sang while playing the piano.

3. **Unten shi**nagara ongaku o kikimasu.
運転しながら音楽を聞きます。

I listen to music while driving.

1.11 | Vconj + **tai/tagaru** たい・たがる | "want to do ~"

Vconj *tai* expresses a first person desire and Vconj *tagaru* expresses a third person desire to do something. *Desu* may be added to the auxiliary *tai* to make the speech polite.

EXAMPLES:

1. Shizuka na tokoro ni **sumi**tai (desu).
静かな所に**住み**たい（です）。

I want to live in a quiet place.

2. Kodomo wa terebi o **mi**tagarimasu.
子供はテレビを**見**たがります。

Children want to watch TV.

3. Otōto wa Amerika no daigaku ni **nyūgaku shi**tagari-mashita.
弟はアメリカの大学に**入学し**たがりました。

My younger brother wanted to enter an American college.

PRACTICE 4 (1.10–1.11)

Fill in the blanks with the appropriate forms of the verbs provided at the end of the sentences.

1. Tēpu o _____ nagara hatsuon o _____ masu. (kiku) (renshū suru)

テープを ＿＿＿＿＿ ながら発音を ＿＿＿＿＿ ます。（聞く）
（練習する）

I practice pronunciation while listening to the tapes.

2. Tomu wa jisho o ＿＿＿＿ nagara tegami o ＿＿＿＿ mashita. (tsukau) (yakusu)

トムは辞書を ＿＿＿＿ ながら手紙を ＿＿＿＿ ました。（使う）
（訳す）

Tom translated the letter while using a dictionary.

3. Musume wa akai doresu o ＿＿＿＿ tagarimasu. (kiru)

娘は赤いドレスを ＿＿＿＿ たがります。（着る）

My daughter wants to wear a red dress.

4. Watashi wa chichi no kaisha de ＿＿＿＿＿ tai desu. (hataraku)

私は父の会社で ＿＿＿＿ たいです。（働く）

I want to work at my father's company.

5. Kodomo wa kōen e ＿＿＿＿＿ ni ＿＿＿＿＿ tagarimasu. (asobu) (iku)

子供は公園へ ＿＿＿＿ に ＿＿＿＿ たがります。（遊ぶ）（行く）

The children want to go to the park to play.

6. Umibe no hoteru de nami o ＿＿＿＿ nagara ＿＿＿＿ tai desu. (miru) (sugosu)

海辺のホテルで波を ＿＿＿＿＿ ながら ＿＿＿＿＿ たいです。
（見る）（過ごす）

I want to spend time at a seaside hotel while watching waves.

1.12 | Vconj + **sō da** そうだ | "look like," "feel like"

Vconj *sō da* expresses the speaker's conjecture based on what he sees or feels. The copula *da* may be replaced by *desu* to make the speech polite.

EXAMPLES:

1. Ame ga **furi** sō da.
   雨が**降り**そうだ。
   It looks like it will rain.

2. Kaze de ki ga **taore** sō da.
   風で木が**倒れ**そうだ。
   It looks like the tree will fall down because of the wind.

3. Ono-san wa chikai uchi ni **intai shi** sō desu.
   小野さんは近いうちに**引退し**そうです。
   It looks like Mr. Ono will retire in the near future.

1.13 | Vconj + **mono/kata** 物・方 | "thing"/"a way of," "how to"

Vconj *mono/kata* creates compound nouns.

EXAMPLES:

1. **nomi**mono 飲み物 (drink), **tabe**mono 食べ物 (food), **ka**imono 買い物 (shopping), **yomi**mono 読み物 (reading material), **wasure**mono 忘れ物 (a thing left behind)

2. **tsukuri**kata 作り方 (how to make), **tsukai**kata 使い方 (usage), **oyogi**kata 泳ぎ方 (a way of swimming), **oshie**kata 教え方 (teaching method), **shi**kata 仕方 (how to do)

1.14 | Vconj + **hajimeru/owaru** 始める・終わる

"begin to"/"finish doing ~"

Vconj *hajimeru/owaru* are compound verbs. The verbs *hajimeru* 始める (begin) and *owaru* 終わる (finish) are used as auxiliaries. Other verbs often used as auxiliaries are *tsuzukeru* 続ける (continue), *wasureru* 忘れる (forget), *naosu* 直す (correct), and *sugiru* すぎる (do/be in excess), as shown in example 3.

EXAMPLES:

1. Yuki ga **furi**hajimemashita.
   雪が**降り**始めました。
   It began to snow.

2. Yatto **tabe**owarimashita.
   やっと**食べ**終わりました。
   I finally finished eating my meal.

3. **yomi**tsuzukeru 読み続ける (continue to read), **harai**wasureru 払い忘れる (forget to pay), **kaki**naosu 書き直す (rewrite), **kyōsō shi**sugiru 競争しすぎる (compete in excess)

PRACTICE 5 (1.12–1.14)

Fill in the blanks with the appropriate forms of the verbs provided at the end of the sentences.

1. Warui tenki ga _____ sō da. (tsuzuku)
   悪い天気が _____ そうだ。（続く）
   It looks like the bad weather will continue.

2. Kono kabin wa _____ mono de wa arimasen. (uru)
   この花びんは _____ 物ではありません。（売る）

   This flower vase is not (an article) for sale.

3. Ashita atari shinamono ga _____ sō desu. (todoku)
   明日あたり品物が _____ そうです。（届く）

   I expect that the article will arrive some time tomorrow.

4. Iroiro na _____ mono ga kono michi o _____ masu.
   (noru) (tōru)
   色々な _____ 物がこの道を _____ ます。（乗る）（通る）

   Various vehicles pass along this road.

5. Basu ga _____ hajimemashita. (ugoku)
   バスが _____ 始めました。（動く）

   The bus began to move.

6. Shukudai o _____ wasuremashita. (dasu)
   宿題を _____ 忘れました。（出す）

   I forgot to submit my homework.

7. Watashi wa ane ni ningyō no _____ kata o _____ mashita. (tsukuru, narau)
   私は姉に人形の _____ 方を _____ ました。（作る）
   （習う）

   I leaned how to make dolls from my older sister.

8. Ame no naka o eki made _____ tsuzukemashita.
   (hashiru)
   雨の中を駅まで _____ 続けました。（走る）

   We continued to run in the rain to the railroad station.

② Dictionary Form

Conjunctive form (Vdic)

Regular I Verb (3rd base)	Regular II Verb (Verb stem + ru)	Irregular Verb
hanasu 話す (speak) matsu 待つ (wait)	kotaeru 答える (answer) kiru 着る (wear)	kuru 来る (come) suru する (do)

SENTENCE PATTERNS

2.1 | **Vdic (cf. 1.1)** | "do/will do," "there is/will be"

Vdic expresses actions or states which regularly take place/exist or will take place/exist. This form is used for the plain style.

EXAMPLES:

1. Asoko ni hon'ya ga **aru**.
   あそこに本屋が**ある**。

   There is a bookstore over there.

2. Watashi wa maiasa rokuji ni **okiru**.
   私は毎朝六時に**起きる**。

   I get up at six o'clock every morning.

3. Tomu wa tokidoki toshokan de **benkyō suru**.
   トムは時々図書館で**勉強する**。

   Sometimes Tom studies at the library.

2.2   Vdic + **tsumori da** つもりだ   "intend to ~"

Vdic *tsumori da* expresses a person's intention. *Tsumori* is a pseudo noun (never used independently) usually followed by a copula, *da/datta* (plain) or *desu/deshita* (polite).

EXAMPLES:

1. Ie o **uru** tsumori da.
   家を売るつもりだ。

   I intend to sell my house.

2. Kare wa gakkō o **yameru** tsumori desu.
   彼は学校を辞めるつもりです。

   He intends to quit school.

3. Gaigi ni **shusseki suru** tsumori datta.
   会議に出席するつもりだった。

   I intended to attend the meeting.

2.3   Vdic + **hazu da** はずだ

    "I expect that ~," "It is expected that ~"

Vdic *hazu da* expresses the speaker's expectation that something will take place/took place. *Hazu* is a pseudo noun usually followed by a copula.

EXAMPLES:

1. Kono kisoku wa **kawaru** hazu da.
   この規則は変わるはずだ。

   It is expected that this regulation will change.

2. Kono machi no jinkō wa **fueru** hazu desu.
   この町の人口は**増える**はずです。

   The population of this town is expected to increase.

3. Ano ken wa Ono-san ga **chōsa suru** hazu deshita.
   あの件は小野さんが**調査する**はずでした。

   As for that matter, we expected that Mr. Ono would investigate it.

2.4 | Vdic + **darō** だろう | "probably"

Vdic *darō* expresses the speaker's conjecture. *Darō*, which is the presumptive form of the copula *da*, is used as an axiliary. *Deshō* may be used for the polite style.

EXAMPLES:

1. Gogo kaze ga **fuku** darō.
   午後風が**吹く**だろう。

   The wind will probably blow in the afternoon.

2. Densha wa juppun hodo **okureru** darō.
   電車は十分ほど**遅れる**だろう。

   The train will probably be about ten minutes late.

3. Kare wa jigyō ni **seikō suru** deshō.
   彼は事業に**成功する**でしょう。

   He will probably succeed in his enterprise.

PRACTICE 6 (2.1–2.4)

Fill in the blanks with the dictionary form of the verbs provided at the end of the sentences.

1. **Eiga wa gogo rokuji ni _____. (hajimarimasu)**
   映画は午後六時に _____ 。（始まります）
   The movie begins at 6 p.m.

2. **Bukka ga dandan _____ deshō. (agarimasu)**
   物価がだんだん _____ でしょう。（上がります）
   Prices will probably go up gradually.

3. **Sono ken wa tsugi no kaigi de _____ tsumori desu. (kimemasu)**
   その件は次の会議で _____ つもりです。（決めます）
   We intend to decide that matter at our next meeting.

4. **Biru ga hon o kari ni _____ hazu desu. (yorimasu)**
   ビルが本を借りに _____ はずです。（寄ります）
   I expect that Bill will stop by to borrow the book.

5. **Jimu wa kaerimasu ga, Tomu wa koko ni _____ deshō. (nokorimasu)**
   ジムは帰りますが、トムはここに _____ でしょう。（残ります）
   Jim is going home, but Tom will probably remain here.

6. **Akachan wa yoku _____. (korobimasu)**
   赤ちゃんはよく _____ 。（転びます）
   Babies often fall down.

7. **Yagate sora wa _____ darō. (haremasu)**
   やがて空は _____ だろう。（晴れます）
   The sky will probably clear up soon.

8. **Ane wa watashi o rokuji ni _____ . (okoshimasu)**
   姉は私を六時に _____ 。（起こします）
   My older sister wakes me up at six o'clock.

2.5 | Vdic + **kamoshirenai かもしれない** | "might"

Vdic *kamoshirenai* expresses the speaker's speculation or guess. *Kamoshiremasen* is the polite style.

EXAMPLES:

1. Kono inu wa **shinu** kamoshirenai.
   この犬は**死ぬ**かもしれない。
   This dog might die.

2. Onna no ko ga **umareru** kamoshiremasen.
   女の子が**生まれる**かもしれません。
   A baby girl might be born (to her).

3. Ane wa rainen **kekkon suru** kamoshiremasen.
   姉は来年**結婚する**かもしれません。
   My older sister might marry next year.

2.6 | Vdic + **ni chigainai にちがいない**

"must be," "There is no doubt that ~"

Vdic *ni chigainai* expresses the speaker's guess with confidence. *Chigaiarimasen* is the polite style.

EXAMPLES:

1. Kodomo-tachi wa **yorokobu** ni chigainai.
   子供達は**喜ぶ**にちがいない。
   There is no doubt that the children will be happy.

2. Nihongo no gakusei ga **fueru** ni chigaiarimasen.
日本語の学生が**増える**にちがいありません。

The (number of) students of Japanese will undoubtedly increase.

3. Gijutsu wa **shinpo suru** ni chigaiarimasen.
技術は**進歩する**にちがいありません。

There is no doubt that technology will make progress.

2.7 | **Vdic + no/koto** の・こと | "~ ing," "to ~," "that ~ "

Both *no* and *koto* are nominalizers which make a verb into a gerund,
or a clause into a noun phrase. *No* indicates concrete actions or
events, while *koto* indicates abstract actions or events. *No* and *koto*
are sometimes interchangeable (Example 3).

EXAMPLES:

1. Watashi wa otoko ga jitensha o **nusumu** no o mimashita.
私は男が自転車を**盗む**のを見ました。

I saw a man stealing a bycicle.

2. **Miru** koto wa **shinjiru** koto desu.
見ることは**信じる**ことです。

Seeing is believing.

3. Hara-san ga Furansu ni **tenkin suru** no/koto o kiki-
mashita.
原さんがフランスに**転勤する**こと・のを聞きました。

I heard that Mr. Hara is going to be transferred to France.

Fill in the blanks with the appropriate forms of the verbs provided at the end of the sentences.

1. Yamada-san ni kono shigoto o _____ kamoshire-masen. (tanomimasu)

   山田さんにこの仕事を _____ かもしれません。（頼みます）

   I might ask Mr. Yamada to do this work.

2. Gakkō no chikaku ni apāto ga _____ kamoshirenai. (mitsukarimasu)

   学校の近くにアパートが _____ かもしれない。（見付かります）

   An apartment might be found near the school.

3. Hitobito wa sono nyūsu ni _____ ni chigaiari-masen. (odorokimasu)

   人々はそのニュースに _____ にちがいありません。（驚きます）

   There is no doubt that people will be surprised at the news.

4. Kono hanashi wa kōsei ni _____ ni chigainai. (tsutawarimasu)

   この話は後世に _____ にちがいない。（伝わります）

   This story must be handed down to posterity.

5. Mori no naka de tori ga _____ no o _____ mashita. (nakimasu) (kiku)

   森の中で鳥が _____ のを _____ ました。（鳴きます）（聞く）

   I heard birds singing in the woods.

6. Abe-san ga _____ koto o _____ masen deshita.
   (nyūin shimasu) (shiru)
   阿部さんが _____ ことを _____ ませんでした。（入院
   します）（知る）

   I didn't know that Mr. Abe will be hospitalized.

7. Watashi wa haha ga _____ no o _____ mashita.
   (sōji shimasu) (tetsudau)
   私は母が _____ のを _____ ました。（掃除します）
   （手伝う）

   I helped my mother clean (the house).

2.8 | **Vdic + koto ga dekiru ことが出来る** | "can," "be able to"

Vdic *koto ga dekiru* expresses potential and ability. This potential
form is used in the *wa-ga* construction: A *wa ~ koto ga dekiru.* A は
～ことが出来る。(A can do ~).

EXAMPLES:

1. Kono shigoto wa Kida-san ni **makasu** koto ga dekiru.
   この仕事は木田さんに**任す**ことが出来る。

   We can leave this job up to Ms. Kida.

2. Kodomo wa sugu kotoba o **oboeru** koto ga dekimasu.
   子供はすぐ言葉を**覚える**ことが出来ます。

   Children can learn words quickly.

3. Kono hon o **chūmon suru** koto ga dekimasu ka.
   この本を**注文する**ことが出来ますか。

   Can I order this book?

2.9 | Vdic + **koto ga aru** ことがある | "There are times when ~"

Vdic *koto ga aru* expresses actions or events that occur sometimes.

EXAMPLES:

1. Yano-san wa enkai de **you** koto ga aru.
   矢野さんは宴会で**酔う**ことがある。

   There are times when Mr. Yano gets drunk at a banquet.

2. Tsuyoi chīmu ga **makeru** koto ga arimasu.
   強いチームが**負ける**ことがあります。

   There are times when a strong team is defeated (by a weak one).

3. Tomodachi to **ryokō suru** koto ga aru.
   友達と**旅行する**ことがある。

   There are times when I travel with my friends.

2.10 | Vdic + **koto ni suru** ことにする | "decide to"

Vdic *koto ni suru* expresses the speaker's decision to do something.

EXAMPLES:

1. Raigetsu Kyōto ni **utsuru** koto ni shimashita.
   来月京都に**移る**ことにしました。

   I decided to move to Kyoto next month.

2. Honbako wa koko ni **naraberu** koto ni suru.
   本箱はここに**並べる**ことにする。

   I will put these bookcases side by side here.

3. Maiasa **sanpo suru** koto ni shimasu.
   毎朝**散歩する**ことにします。

   I'll make it a rule to take a walk every morning.

2.11 | Vdic + **koto ni naru** ことになる

"It will be decided that ~"

Vdic *koto ni naru* expresses a decision made by others, rather than the speaker.

EXAMPLES:

1. Motto sensei o **yatou** koto ni naru darō.
   もっと先生を雇うことになるだろう。

   It will be decided that they will hire more teachers.

2. Sagawa-san wa shiten ni **tsutomeru** koto ni narimasu.
   佐川さんは支店に勤めることになります。

   It will be decided that Mr. Sagawa will work at a branch office.

3. Honda-san ga tōronkai ni **sanka suru** koto ni narimashita.
   本田さんが討論会に参加することになりました。

   It has been decided that Miss Honda will participate in the debate.

PRACTICE 8 (2.8–2.11)

A. Change the following verbs into the potential form.

1. hanashimasu 話します speak   2. yakimasu 焼きます bake
3. kotaemasu 答えます answer   4. tomemasu 止めます stop
5. enzetsu shimasu 演説します make a speech

B. Complete the following sentences with the verbs provided.

1. Konban Chūgoku ryōri o _____. (tsukurimasu)
   今晩中国料理を _____。（作ります）

   I decided to make Chinese food tonight.

2. Shūmatsu ni ane no kodomo o _____.
   (sewa shimasu)
   週末に姉の子供を _____。（世話します）
   There are times when I take care of my older sister's child on
   weekends.

3. Kūkō de kuji ni Toda-san to _____. (aimasu)
   空港で九時に戸田さんと _____。（会います）
   I decided to meet Ms.Toda at the airport at nine o'clock.

4. Kimura-san wa tabun ashita _____. (taiin
   shimasu)
   木村さんは多分明日 _____。（退院します）
   Probably it will turn out that Mr. Kimura will be released from
   the hospital tomorrow.

5. Biru wa nōto o torinagara _____. (nemuri-
   masu)
   ビルはノートを取りながら _____。（眠ります）
   There are times when Bill falls asleep while taking notes.

6. Hara-san no kawari ni watashi ga _____.
   (shutchō shimasu)
   原さんの代わりに私が _____。（出張します）
   It has been decided that I will go on a business trip in place of
   Mr. Hara.

2.12 | Vdic + **tokoro da** ところだ | "be just about to do"

Vdic *tokoro da* expresses an action which is about to take place. In this expression, *tokoro* means "state" or "time."

EXAMPLES:

1. Kuruma wa kado o **magaru** tokoro desu.
   車は角を**曲がる**ところです。
   The car is just about to turn the corner.

2. Akira wa ima **neru** tokoro da.
   明は今**寝る**ところだ。
   Akira is just about to go to bed now.

3. Densha wa **shuppatsu suru** tokoro desu.
   電車は**出発する**ところです。
   The train is just about to depart.

2.13 | Vdic + **hō ga ~ yori** ほうが ～ より | "do ~ than do ~"

Vdic *hō ga ~ yori* expresses a comparison between two actions. *Hō* is a pseudo noun.

EXAMPLES:

1. **Katsu** hō ga **makeru** yori ii.
   勝つほうが**負ける**よりいい。
   Winning is better than losing.

2. Kuruma wa koko ni **tomeru** yori asoko ni **tomeru** hō ga anzen desu.

車はここに**止める**よりあそこに**止める**ほうが安全です。

It is safer to park the car here than (park) over there.

3. Jibun de **ryōri suru** hō ga **gaishoku suru** yori tanoshii desu.

自分で**料理する**ほうが**外食する**より楽しいです。

It is more enjoyable to cook myself than to dine out.

2.14 | Vdic + **kawari ni** 代わりに

"instead of," "to make up for ~"

Vdic *kawari ni* expresses an action which is replaced by another action.

EXAMPLES:

1. Konban **asobu** kawari ni ashita yoku benkyō suru.

今晩**遊ぶ**代わりに明日よく勉強する。

I'll study hard tomorrow to make up for having fun tonight.

2. Kotoba o **oboeru** kawari ni kanji o renshū shimasu.

言葉を**覚える**代わりに漢字を練習します。

Instead of memorizing words, I'll practice kanji.

3. Kaigi ni **shusseki suru** kawari ni repōto o teishutsu shimasu.

会議に**出席する**代わりにレポートを提出します。

Instead of attending the meeting, I'll submit the report.

Fill in the blanks with the appropriate forms of the verbs provided at the end of the sentences.

1. Niwa no ki no eda o _____ tokoro desu. (kirimasu)
   庭の木の枝を _____ ところです。(切ります)

   I am just about to cut the branches of the trees in the garden.

2. Kono ka no atarashii kotoba o _____ tokoro da. (anki shimasu)
   この課の新しい言葉を _____ ところだ。(暗記します)

   I am just about to memorize the new words in this lesson.

3. _____ hō ga _____ yori yasashii desu. (naraimasu) (oshiemasu)
   _____ ほうが _____ より易しいです。(習います)(教えます)

   Learning is easier than teaching.

4. Umi de _____ hō ga yama ni _____ yori suki desu. (oyogimasu) (noborimasu)
   海で _____ ほうが山に _____ より好きです。(泳ぎます)(登ります)

   I like swimming in the ocean better than climbing a mountain.

5. Hito ni _____ kawari ni jibun de _____ koto ni shimasu. (tayorimasu) (yarimasu)
   人に _____ 代わりに自分で _____ ことにします。(頼ります)(やります)

   Instead of depending on others, I will do it myself.

6. Kyō _____ kawari ni ashita _____ tsumori desu. (yasumimasu) (hatarakimasu)

今日 _____ 代わりに明日 _____ つもりです。
（休みます）（働きます）

To make up for taking a day off today, I intend to work tomorrow.

2.15 | Vdic + **mae ni** 前に | "before"

Vdic *mae ni* expresses a temporal relation between one action and another.

EXAMPLES:

1. Kare wa tokidoki beru ga **naru** mae ni kyōshitsu o deru.
彼は時々ベルが**鳴る**前に教室を出る。

Sometimes he leaves the classroom before the bell rings.

2. **Neru** mae ni ha o migakimasu.
寝る前に歯を磨きます。

I brush my teeth before going to bed.

3. **Yoshū suru** mae ni fukushū suru.
予習する前に復習する。

I review (my lessons) before preparing my lessons (for tomorrow).

2.16 | Vdic + **made** まで | "until"

Vdic *made* expresses a temporal limit for an action.

Examples:

1. Apāto ga **aku** made nikagetsu machimashita.
   アパートが**空く**まで二か月待ちました。
   I waited two months until the apartment became vacant.

2. Sora ga **hareru** made hoteru ni imashita.
   空が**晴れる**までホテルにいました。
   I stayed at the hotel until the sky cleared up.

3. Jimu wa **sotsugyō suru** made yoku ganbarimashita.
   ジムは**卒業する**までよく頑張りました。
   Jim held on well until he graduated.

2.17 | Vdic + **made ni** までに | "by the time," "before"

Vdic *made ni* expresses a temporal limit for an action. It may be
replaced by *mae ni*.

EXAMPLES:

1. Hi ga **shizumu** made ni mokutekichi ni tsukitai.
   日が**沈む**までに目的地に着きたい。
   We want to reach our destination before the sun sets.

2. Kare ga ryokō ni **dekakeru** made ni mō ichido aitai desu.
   彼が旅行に**出かける**までにもう一度会いたいです。
   I want to see him once more before he leaves for his trip.

3. Hikōki ga **tōchaku suru** made ni nijikan aru.

飛行機が**到着する**までに二時間ある。

It will be two hours before the airplane arrives.

Fill in the blanks with the appropriate forms of the verbs provided at the end of the sentences.

1. _____ mae ni te o _____ nasai. (tabemasu) (arau)

   _____ 前に手を _____ なさい。（食べます）（洗う）

   Wash your hands before you eat.

2. Pūru ni _____ mae ni _____ masu. (hairimasu) (undō shimasu)

   プールに _____ 前に _____ ます。（入ります）（運動します）

   I exercise before entering the swimming pool.

3. Sasaki-san ga _____ made robī de _____ mashō. (arawaremasu) (matsu)

   佐々木さんが _____ までロビーで _____ ましょう。（現れます）（待つ）

   Let's wait in the lobby until Mr. Sasaki shows up.

4. _____ made _____ nasai. (mitsukarimasu) (sagasu)

   _____ まで _____ なさい。（見付かります）（探す）

   Look for it until it is found.

5. Kare wa sanjussai ni _____ made ni shōsetsu o
_____ kamoshiremasen. (narimasu) (shuppan
shimasu)

彼は三十歳に _____ までに小説を _____ かもしれま
せん。(なります) (出版します)

He might publish a novel by the time he's thirty years old.

6. Pasupōto ga _____ made ni mō ichido umi o
_____ tai. (kiremasu) (wataru)

パスポートが _____ までにもう一度海を _____ た い。
(切れます) (渡る)

Before my passport expires, I want to cross the ocean once more.

2.18 | Vdic + **noni** (1) のに |

"(in order) to," "for the purpose of"

Vdic *noni* (1) expresses the purpose of doing something.

EXAMPLES:

1. Kagu o **hakobu** noni torakku ga iru.
家具を**運ぶ**のにトラックが要る。
We need a truck to transport the furniture.

2. O-kane o **azukeru** noni ano ginkō ga ichiban ii desu.
お金を**預ける**のにあの銀行が一番いいです。
That bank is the best one to deposit money in.

3. **Tsūkin suru** noni chikatetsu o riyō shimasu.
通勤するのに地下鉄を利用します。
I use the subway to commute to the office.

2.19 | Vdic + **noni** (2) のに |

"although," "in spite of the fact that"

Vdic *noni* (2) expresses an action which is followed by a result contrary to expectation.

EXAMPLES:

1. Ichinichi ni nanmairu mo **aruku** noni tsukaremasen.
   一日に何マイルも**歩く**のに疲れません。

   Although I walk many miles a day, I don't get tired.

2. Kanojo wa takusan **taberu** noni futorimasen.
   彼女はたくさん**食べる**のに太りません。

   Although she eats a lot, she doesn't get fat.

3. Tomu wa **doryoku suru** noni seiseki ga agarimasen.
   トムは**努力する**のに成績が上がりません。

   Although Tom makes an effort, his grades do not go up.

2.20 | Vdic + **to** と | "if," "when"

Vdic *to* expresses a condition that brings about an automatic or unexpected result.

EXAMPLES:

1. Beru o **osu** to doa ga akimashita.
   ベルを**押す**とドアが開きました。

   When I pushed the bell, the door opened.

2. O-kane o **kazoeru** to, nisen'en tarimasen deshita.
   お金を**数える**と、二千円足りませんでした。

   When I counted the money, I was 2,000 yen short.

3. Takusan **chūmon suru** to, waribiki ga aru.

たくさん注文すると、割引がある。

If you order a lot, you can get a discount.

Fill in the blanks with the appropriate forms of the verbs provided at the end of the sentences.

1. Sukiyaki o _____ noni gyūniku ya yasai ga _____ masu. (tsukurimasu) (iru)

すき焼きを _____ のに牛肉や野菜が _____ ます。（作ります）（要る）

You need beef and vegetables, among other things, to make sukiyaki.

2. Kaijō ni isu o _____ noni sanjuppun _____ mashita. (narabemasu) (kakaru)

会場にいすを _____ のに三十分 _____ ました。（並べます）（かかる）

It took thirty minutes to line up chairs in the hall.

3. Jimu wa ashita shiken ga _____ noni _____ masen. (arimasu) (benkyō suru)

ジムは明日試験が _____ のに _____ ません。（あります）（勉強する）

Jim doesn't study although he has an examination tomorrow.

4. Samu wa yoku gakkō o _____ noni seiseki ga _____ masen. (yasumimasu) (sagaru)

サムはよく学校を _____ のに成績が _____ ません。（休みます）（下がる）

In spite of the fact that Sam is often absent from school, his grades do not fall.

5. Haru ga _____ to, yama no yuki ga _____ masu.
(kimasu) (tokeru)

春が _____ と、山の雪が _____ ます。（来ます）
（溶ける）

When spring comes, the mountain snow will melt.

6. Mori no naka o _____ to, totsuzen tori no nakigoe
ga _____ mashita. (susumimasu) (kikoeru)

森の中を _____ と、突然鳥の鳴き声が _____ まし
た。（進みます）（聞こえる）

When we proceeded into the woods, the singing of birds was
heard suddenly.

2.21 | **Vdic + (*no*) + nara （の）なら** | "if," "if it is the case that"

Vdic (*no*) *nara* expresses a supposition or condition. Since *nara* is
the conditional form of the copula *da*, it requires a noun. Therefore, *no* is added to nominalize the verb, though this *no* is optional.

EXAMPLES:

1. Ie o **uru** (no) nara, ima ga ii jiki da.
家を**売る**（の）なら、今がいい時期だ。

If you are to sell the house, now is a good time.

2. Konban soto de **taberu** (no) nara, doko ga ii desu ka.
今晩外で**食べる**（の）なら、どこがいいですか。

If we dine out tonight, where is a good place?

3. **Kenbutsu suru** (no) nara, kankō-basu ga ii desu yo.
見物する（の）なら、観光バスがいいですよ。

If you go sightseeing, a tour bus would be good.

2.22 │ Interrogative + (particle) + Vdic + **ka** か │

"(I don't know/can't tell) when, what, etc."

An interrogative (with or without a particle) followed by Vdic *ka* expresses a question embedded in a sentence.

EXAMPLES:

1. Nani ga **okoru** ka wakarimasen.
   何が起こるか分かりません。
   I can't tell what will happen.

2. Dochira ga **makeru** ka wakarimasen.
   どちらが負けるか分かりません。
   Which one of them will lose, I can't tell.

3. Ono-san ga itsu **ryūgaku suru** ka shirimasen.
   小野さんがいつ留学するか知りません。
   I don't know when Miss Ono will study abroad.

2.23 │ Vdic + **ka dō ka** かどうか │

"(I don't know/can't tell) whether or not"

Vdic *ka dō ka* expresses a question embedded in a sentence.

EXAMPLES:

1. Sumisu-san ga Nihongo o **hanasu** ka dō ka shirimasen.
   スミスさんが日本語を話すかどうか知りません。
   I don't know whether Mr. Smith speaks Japanese or not.

2. Pikunikku no hi o **kaeru** ka dō ka shirimasen.
   ピクニックの日を変えるかどうか知りません。
   I don't know whether they will change the date for the picnic or not.

3. Kare ga atarashii kikai o **hatsumei suru** ka dō ka wakari-masen.

彼が新しい機械を**発明する**かどうか分かりません。

I can't tell whether he will invent a new machine or not.

Fill in the blanks with the appropriate forms of the verbs provided at the end of the sentences.

1. Tabako o _____ (no) nara, mado o _____ nasai. (suimasu) (akeru)

たばこを _____ （の）なら、窓を _____ なさい。（吸います）（開ける）

If you smoke, open the window.

2. Niji no densha ni _____ (no) nara, _____ mashō. (norimasu) (isogu)

二時の電車に _____ （の）なら、_____ ましょう。（乗ります）（急ぐ）

If we are to take the two-o'clock train, let's hurry.

3. Doko de sensei no tanjōbi o _____ ka _____ masen. (iwaimasu) (shiru)

どこで先生の誕生日を _____ か _____ ません。（祝います）（知る）

I don't know where we will celebrate our teacher's birthday.

4. Dare ga kaigi ni _____ ka _____ mashō. (demasu) (shiraberu)

だれが会議に _____ か _____ ましょう。（出ます）（調べる）

I'll check who will attend the meeting.

5. **Hikōki ga _____ ka dō ka o- _____ shimasu.**
   (okuremasu) (shiraseru)

   飛行機が _____ かどうかお _____ します。（遅れ
   ます）（知らせる）

   I'll let you know whether the airplane will be delayed or not.

2.24 | **Vdic + yō ni ように** | "so that," "in order that"

Vdic *yō ni* expresses purpose.

EXAMPLES:

1. Netsu ga **sagaru** yō ni asupirin o nominasai.
   熱が**下がる**ようにアスピリンを飲みなさい。

   Take aspirin so that your fever goes down.

2. Kare wa jōshi ga jibun no teian o **mitomeru** yō ni
   nesshin ni hanashimashita.
   彼は上司が自分の提案を**認める**ように熱心に話しました。

   He spoke eagerly so that his superior would approve his proposal.

3. Sensei wa gakusei ga **rikai suru** yō ni yoku setsumei
   shimashita.
   先生は学生が**理解する**ようによく説明しました。

   The teacher explained throughly so that the students would understand.

2.25 | **Vdic + yō ni iu ように言う** | "tell someone to do ~"

Vdic *yō ni iu* expresses an indirect command. The verb *iu* may be
replaced by other verbs such as *tanomu* 頼む (ask) or *susumeru* 勧
める (recommend) to express requests or suggestions.

EXAMPLES:

1. Gakusei ni kabe ni posutā o **haru** yō ni iu.
   学生に壁にポスターを張るように言う。

   I'll tell the students to put posters on the wall.

2. Toda-san ni kaigi no jikan o **tashikameru** yō ni tano-mimasu.
   戸田さんに会議の時間を確かめるように頼みます。

   I'll ask Miss Toda to confirm the meeting time.

3. Buraun-san ni Kyōto de o-tera o **hōmon suru** yō ni susumemashita.
   ブラウンさんに京都でお寺を訪問するように勧めました。

   I recommended to Mr. Brown that he visit temples in Kyoto.

2.26 | Vdic + **yō ni naru** ようになる

"reach the point where ~," "come to ~"

Vdic *yō ni naru* expresses a change that gradually takes place.

EXAMPLES:

1. Akachan wa mō sugu **warau** yō ni naru.
   赤ちゃんはもうすぐ笑うようになる。

   The baby will soon reach the point where he will smile.

2. Kodomo wa jibun de heya o **katazukeru** yō ni narima-shita.
   子供は自分で部屋を片付けるようになりました。

   My child has reached the point where she cleans up her room herself.

3. Sono kōjō wa denki kigu o **seisan suru** yō ni nari-mashita.

その工場は電気器具を**生産する**ようになりました。

The plant has reached the point where it produces electrical appliances.

2.27 | Vdic + **yō ni suru** ようにする |

"make sure that ~" "see to it that ~"

Vdic *yō ni suru* expresses a person's efforts to cause a change in behavior.

EXAMPLES:

1. Shimekiri ni **maniau** yō ni suru.

締め切りに**間に合う**ようにする。

I'll make sure that I'll be in time for the deadline.

2. Rokuji ni mise o **shimeru** yō ni shinasai.

六時に店を**閉める**ようにしなさい。

Make sure that you close up the store at six o'clock.

3. Kanojo wa maitsuki **chokin suru** yō ni shimashita.

彼女は毎月**貯金する**ようにしました。

She made sure that she saved money every month.

PRACTICE 13 (2.24–2.27)

Fill in the blanks with the appropriate forms of the verbs provided at the end of the sentences.

1. Byōki ga _____ yō ni mainichi kusuri o _____ nasai. (naorimasu) (nomu)

病気が_____ ように毎日薬を _____ なさい。（治ります）（飲む）

Take medicine every day so that you will get well.

2. Mizuki-san wa _____ yō ni _____ mashita. (yasemasu) (undō suru)

水木さんは _____ ように _____ ました。(やせます)（運動する）

Ms. Mizuki exercised so that she would lose weight.

3. Kodomo ni kutsu no himo o _____ yō ni iimashita. (musubimasu)

子供にくつのひもを _____ ように言いました。(結びます)

I told my child to tie his shoestrings.

4. Watashi wa Ono-san ni repōto o _____ yō ni tanomimashita. (kakinaoshimasu)

私は小野さんにレポートを _____ ように頼みました。（書き直します）

I asked Mr. Ono to rewrite the report.

5. Sofu wa keisan o _____ yō ni narimashita. (machigaemasu)

祖父は計算を _____ ようになりました。(間違えます)

My grandfather has reached the point where he makes mistakes in calculating.

6. Kono goro samusa o _____ yō ni narimashita. (kanjimasu)

このごろ寒さを _____ ようになりました。(感じます)

Lately we've started to feel the cold.

7. Asa hayaku _____ , yoru hayaku _____ yō ni shimashō. (okiru) (nemasu)

朝早く _____、夜早く _____ ようにしましょう。（起きる）（寝ます）

Let's make sure that we get up early in the morning and go to bed early at night.

8. Pikunikku ni minna o _____ yō ni shimasu. (sasoi-masu)

ピクニックにみんなを _____ ようにします。（誘います）

We'll make sure that we invite everybody to the picnic.

2.28 | **Vdic + kara から** | "because," "since," "so"

Vdic *kara* expresses a cause or a reason personally interpreted by the speaker. The dictionary form (plain style) is normally used in the subordinate clause. The *masu* form may also be used in the subordinate clause in very polite speech (Example 3).

EXAMPLES:

1. Parēdo ga **tōru** kara, mi ni ikimashō.

パレードが**通る**から、見に行きましょう。

The parade will pass by, so let's go to see it.

2. Umi ga **mieru** kara, kono heya o erabimashita.

海が**見える**から、この部屋を選びました。

I chose this room because I can see the ocean (from here).

3. Ryōshin ga **anshin suru**/shimasu kara, maishū denwa shimasu.

両親が**安心する**・しますから、毎週電話します。

Because my parents feel relieved, I call them every week.

2.29 | **Vdic + node ので** | "because," "since," "so"

Vdic *node* expresses a cause or a reason presented more objectively without projecting the speaker's personal opinion. This *node* clause cannot be followed by a main clause involving the speaker's volition, opinion, command or invitation.

EXAMPLES:

1. Ashita bōnasu o **morau** node, ureshii.

明日ボーナスを**もらう**ので、嬉しい。

I'm happy, because I'll receive a bonus tomorrow.

2. Kare wa asa hayaku **okiru** node, hayaku shukkin shimasu.

彼は朝早く**起きる**ので、早く出勤します。

Because he gets up early in the morning, he comes to work early.

3. Yano-san ga **nyūin suru** node, watashi ga enkai ni deru koto ni narimashita.

矢野さんが**入院する**ので、私が宴会に出ることになりました。

Since Mr. Yano will be hospitalized, it's been decided that I will attend the banquet.

2.30 | **Vdic + to iu と言う** | "(He) says that ~"

Vdic *to iu* expresses indirect quotations. The verb *iu* may be replaced by other verbs such as *omou* 思う (think) or *kiku* 聞く (hear) to express what a person thinks or hears.

EXAMPLES:

1. Abe-sensei wa kōgi wa sanji made ni **sumu** to iimashita.

阿部先生は講義は三時までに**済む**と言いました。

Prof. Abe said that the lecture would end by three o'clock.

2. Kare wa itsuka kokyō o **tazuneru** to omou.

   彼はいつか故郷を**訪ねる**と思う。

   I think that he will visit his home town some day.

3. Yamada-san ga atarashii kaisha o **soshiki suru** to kiki-mashita.

   山田さんが新しい会社を**組織する**と聞きました。

   I heard that Mr. Yamada will set up a new company.

Fill in the blanks with the appropriate forms of the verbs provided at the end of the sentences.

1. Densha ga _____ kara, asoko de o-cha demo _____ mashō. (okuremasu) (nomu)

   電車が _____ から、あそこでお茶でも _____ ましょう。(遅れます)(飲む)

   The train will be delayed, so let's have tea or something over there.

2. Kare wa tabemono ni _____ node, _____ ma-sen. (chūi shimasu) (futoru)

   彼は食べ物に _____ ので、_____ ません。(注意します)(太る)

   Because he is careful about food, he doesn't get fat.

3. Mado kara bōru o _____ kara, _____ nasai. (otoshimasu) (hirou)

   窓からボールを _____ から、_____ なさい。(落とします)(拾う)

   I'll drop a ball from the window, so pick it up.

4. Sēru ga _____ kara, mise wa _____ to omoimasu. (arimasu) (komimasu)

セールが _____ から、店は _____ と思います。（あります）（込みます）

I think that the store will be crowded, since there will be a sale.

5. Tomodachi ga _____ node, sukoshi hayaku kaisha o _____ mashita. (kimasu) (deru)

友達が _____ ので、少し早く会社を _____ ました。（来ます）（出る）

I left the office a little early, because my friend was coming.

6. Kare wa nedan ga _____ mae ni kuruma o _____ to iimashita. (agarimasu) (kaimasu)

彼は値段が _____ 前に車を _____ と言いました。（上がります）（買います）

He said that he would buy the car before its price went up.

2.31 | Vdic + rashii らしい (cf. 2.32)

"seem," "look like," "I heard"

Vdic *rashii* expresses the speaker's conjecture based on some reliable information. *Desu* may be added to the auxiliary *rashii* to make the speech polite.

EXAMPLES:

1. Ekimae ni sūpā ga **tatsu** rashii (desu).

駅前にスーパーが**建つ**らしい（です）。

It looks like a supermarket will be built in front of the station.

2. Yukiko-san wa Kanada ryokō o akirameru rashii (desu).
雪子さんはカナダ旅行をあきらめるらしい（です）。

It seems that Yukiko will give up the (idea of) a Canadian trip.

3. Ano kaisha wa tōsan suru rashii (desu).
あの会社は倒産するらしい（です）。

I heard that the company will go bankrupt.

2.32 | Vdic + **sō da** そうだ

"I hear that ~," "I heard that ~," "People say that ~"

Vdic *sō da* expresses hearsay—what the speaker heard or information obtained indirectly.

EXAMPLES:

1. Kare wa ofisu o Yokohama ni **utsusu** sō da.
彼はオフィスを横浜に**移す**そうだ。

I heard that he will move his office to Yokohama.

2. Doa ni keihōki o **tsukeru** sō desu.
ドアに警報機を**付ける**そうです。

I hear that they will put an alarm on the door.

3. Yamada-san wa raishū atari **taiin suru** sō desu.
山田さんは来週あたり**退院する**そうです。

People say that Mr. Yamada will be released from hospital some time next week.

2.33 | Vdic + **kashira/kana** かしら・かな | "I wonder"

Vdic *kashira/kana* expresses uncertainty. *Kashira* is mostly used by women, while *kana* is principally used by men.

EXAMPLES:

1. Byōnin wa **tasukaru** kashira/kana.
   病人は**助かる**かしら・かな。
   I wonder if the patient will be saved.

2. Kare wa kurisumasu purezento ni nani o **kureru** kashira/kana.
   彼はクリスマスプレゼントに何を**くれる**かしら・かな。
   I wonder what he will give me for a Christmas present.

3. Tomu wa shiken ni **gōkaku suru** kashira/kana.
   トムは試験に**合格する**かしら・かな。
   I wonder if Tom will pass the examination.

2.34 | Vdic + **na** な | "Don't ~"

Vdic *na* expresses prohibition and is used by men in very infromal speech.

EXAMPLES:

1. Kare no kotoba o **utagau** na.
   彼の言葉を**疑う**な。
   Don't doubt his words.

2. Sono harigane o **mageru** na.
   その針金を**曲げる**な。
   Don't bend that wire.

3. Anna otoko to **giron suru** na.

あんな男と**議論する**な。

Don't argue with that kind of man.

Fill in the blanks with the appropriate forms of the verbs provided at the end of the sentences.

1. Kaisha wa shain o gopāsento _____ rashii. (herashimasu)

会社は社員を五パーセント _____ らしい。（減らします）

It seems that the company will reduce the number of employees by 5 percent.

2. Yakusoku o _____ na. (wasuremasu)

約束を _____ な。（忘れます）

Don't forget the promise.

3. Hara-san wa fakkusu ga _____ made ofisu ni _____ sō da. (hairimasu) (imasu)

原さんはファックスが _____ までオフィスに _____ そうだ。（入ります）（います）

I hear that Mr. Hara will be in the office until the fax comes in.

4. Masako-san wa shashin o _____ ni _____ kashira. (miseru) (yorimasu)

正子さんは写真を _____ に _____ かしら。（見せる）（寄ります）

I wonder if Masako will stop by to show me the photos.

5. Kare wa yoru _____ nagara daigaku ni _____ sō desu. (hataraku) (kayoimasu)

彼は夜 _____ ながら大学に _____ そうです。(働く)（通います）

I hear that he will attend college while working at night.

2.35 | **Vdic + noun** | to make a relative clause

In the Vdic + noun patten, Vdic is used as a modifier of the following noun, e.g. *iku hito* 行く人 (persons who go); *niji ni deru basu* 二時に出るバス (the bus that leaves at two o'clock). Japanese does not have relative pronouns such as "who," "which," and "that."

EXAMPLES:

1. Kyō watashi ga **au** hito wa chichi no tomodachi da.
今日私が**会う**人は父の友達だ。

The person whom I'll meet today is my father's friend.

2. Ogawa-sensei no kawari ni **oshieru** sensei wa Noda-sensei desu.
小川先生の代わりに**教える**先生は野田先生です。

The teacher who will teach in place of Prof. Ogawa is Prof. Noda.

3. Kore wa shokuhin o **kakō suru** kikai desu.
これは食品を**加工する**機械です。

This is the machine that processes food.

Fill in the blanks with the appropriate forms of the verbs provided at the end of the sentences.

1. Umi ga _____ apāto e _____ tai desu. (mie-masu) (utsuru)

   海が _____ アパートへ _____ たいです。(見えます)(移る)

   I want to move to an apartment from which I can see the ocean.

2. Watashi-tachi wa Abe-san ga yoku _____ bā de kare no shōshin o _____ mashita. (ikimasu) (iwau)

   私達は阿部さんがよく _____ バーで彼の昇進を _____ ました。(行きます)(祝う)

   We celebrated his promotion in the bar which Mr. Abe frequented.

3. Pikunikku ni _____ mono o kono kami ni_____ nasai. (irimasu) (kaku)

   ピクニックに _____ 物をこの紙に _____ なさい。(要ります)(書く)

   Write on this paper the things which you need for the picnic.

4. Kono mise ni wa kodomo ga _____ tagaru hon ga takusan _____ masu. (yomu) (aru)

   この店には子供が _____ たがる本がたくさん _____ ます。(読む)(ある)

   In this store there are many books which children want to read.

5. Ane ga _____ kukkī wa mise de _____ no yori oishii desu. (yakimasu) (kaimasu)

   姉の _____ クッキーは店で _____ のよりおいしいです。(焼きます)(買います)

   The cookies which my older sister bakes are more tasty than those I buy at stores.

2.36 | **Vdic + hodo ほど** | "so ~ that," "to the extent of"

Vdic *hodo* expresses the extent of an action or condition.

EXAMPLES:

1. Kanojo wa byōki ni **naru** hodo yoku hataraku.
   彼女は病気に**なる**ほどよく働く。

   She works hard to the extent of becoming ill.

2. Kono gēmu wa kodomo demo **dekiru** hodo kantan da.
   このゲームは子供でも**出来る**ほど簡単だ。

   This game is so simple that even a child can play it.

3. Kare wa oya ga **shinpai suru** hodo sake o nomimasu.
   彼は親が**心配する**ほど酒を飲みます。

   He drinks to the extent that his parents worry.

2.37 | **Vdic + bakari da ばかりだ** | "be ready to do ~"

Vdic *bakari da* expresses the only action left to do.

EXAMPLES:

1. Mō shinkyo ni **utsuru** bakari da.
   もう新居に**移る**ばかりだ。

   We are ready to move into the new house.

2. Ato wa kagu o **ireru** bakari desu.
   後は家具を**入れる**ばかりです。

   The only thing for us to do is to put in the furniture.

3. Mō **shuppatsu suru** bakari desu.
   もう**出発する**ばかりです。

   I am ready to leave now.

2.38 | Vdic + **bakari de naku ~ (mo)** ばかりでなく〜（も）

"not only ~ but also ~"

Vdic *bakari de naku ~ (mo)* expresses two actions or events in one sentence.

EXAMPLES:

1. Kanojo wa shi **kaku** bakari de naku piano mo hiku.
   彼女は詩を書くばかりでなくピアノも弾く。

   She not only writes poetry but also plays the piano.

2. Aoki-sensei wa Eigo o **oshieru** bakari de naku honyaku mo shimasu.
   青木先生は英語を教えるばかりでなく翻訳もします。

   Prof. Aoki not only teaches English but also does translation.

3. Ano kaisha wa seihin o **yushutsu suru** bakari de naku yunyū mo suru.
   あの会社は製品を輸出するばかりでなく輸入もする。

   That company not only exports but also imports goods.

2.39 | Vdic + **shi** し | "not only ~ but also ~," "and ~"

Vdic *shi* expresses two or more actions or events in one sentence.

EXAMPLES:

1. Oda-san wa e mo **kaku** shi, shashin mo torimasu.
   小田さんは絵も描くし、写真もとります。

   Miss Oda not only does paintings but also takes photographs.

2. Ano hito wa yoku **taberu** shi, yoku **nomu** shi, yoku shaberu.

あの人はよく**食べる**し、よく**飲む**し、よくしゃべる。

He eats a lot, drinks a lot, and chatters a lot.

3. Genryō wa **fusoku suru** shi, seisan wa genshō shimasu.

原料は**不足する**し、生産は減少します。

Raw material becomes insufficient, and production decreases.

Fill in the blanks with the appropriate forms of the verbs provided at the end of the sentences.

1. Kare wa _____ hodo o-kane ga _____ masu. (sutemasu) (aru)

   彼は _____ ほどお金が _____ ます。（捨てます）（ある）

   He has so much money that he can afford to throw it away.

2. Watashi wa hito ni _____ hodo o-kane o _____ masen. (kashimasu) (mōkeru)

   私は人に _____ ほどお金を _____ ません。（貸します）（もうける）

   I don't earn so much money that I can afford to loan it to others.

3. Ato wa tēburu ni sara o _____ bakari desu. (narabe-masu)

   後はテーブルに皿を _____ ばかりです。（並べます）

   The only thing for us to do is set the plates around the table.

4. Hara-san wa yoku _____ bakari de naku, yoku _____ masu. (hatarakimasu) (asobu)

   原さんはよく _____ ばかりでなく、よく _____ ます。（働きます）（遊ぶ）

   Mr. Hara not only works hard but also has a lot of fun.

5. Yano-san wa tenisu mo _____ shi, uma ni mo
   _____ masu. (shimasu) (noru)
   矢野さんはテニスも _____ し、馬にも _____ ます。
   （します）（乗る）

   Ms. Yano not only plays tennis but also rides a horse.

6. Koko wa fuyu ni wa ame mo yoku _____ shi, kaze
   mo tsuyoku _____ masu. (furimasu) (fuku)
   ここは冬には雨もよく _____ し、風も強く _____
   ます。（降ります）（吹く）

   In this place, it rains a lot and the wind blows hard in winter.

③ Negative Form

Negative form (Vneg)

Regular I Verb (1st base)	Regular II Verb (Verb stem)	Irregular Verb
shina 死な (die) toba 飛ば (fly)	mise 見せ (show) oki 起き (get up)	ko 来 (come) shi し (do)

SENTENCE PATTERNS

3.1 | **Vneg + nai ない** | "don't/won't do," "there isn't/won't be"

Vneg *nai* expresses actions or states which regularly don't take
place/exist or won't take place/exist. The auxiliary *nai* is attached
to the verb for negation. This form is used for the plain style. The
copula *desu* may be added to make the expression polite.

EXAMPLES:

1. Kono tori wa **toba**nai (desu).
   この鳥は**飛ば**ない（です）。
   This bird does not fly.

2. Aoki-san wa niku o **tabe**nai (desu).
   青木さんは肉を**食べ**ない（です）。
   Mr. Aoki doesn't eat meat.

3. Yamanaka-san wa tenisu tōnamento ni **sanka shi**nai (desu).
   山中さんはテニストーナメントに**参加し**ない（です）。
   Miss Yamanaka won't participate in the tennis tournament.

3.2 | Vneg + **nai tsumori da** ないつもりだ (cf. 2.2)

"don't intend to ~"

Vneg *nai tsumori da* expresses a person's intention not to do something.

EXAMPLES:

1. Ima wa ie o **kawa**nai tsumori da.
   今は家を**買わ**ないつもりだ。
   I don't intend to buy a house now.

2. Kono kisoku wa **kae**nai tsumori desu.
   この規則は**変え**ないつもりです。
   We don't intend to change this regulation.

3. Watashi wa kare no iken ni **dōi shi**nai tsumori deshita.
   私は彼の意見に**同意し**ないつもりでした。
   I didn't intend to agree with his opinion.

3.3 | Vneg + **nai hazu da** ないはずだ (cf.2.3) |

"I don't expect that ~," "It is not expected that ~"

Vneg *nai hazu da* expresses the speaker's expectation that something won't take place.

EXAMPLES:

1. Kida-san wa kayōbi made ni Amerika kara **kaera**nai hazu da.
   木田さんは火曜日までにアメリカから**帰ら**ないはずだ。
   It is not expected that Mr.Kida will return from America by Tuesday.

2. Asoko ni wa apāto o **tate**nai hazu desu.
   あそこにはアパートを**建て**ないはずです。
   I don't expect that they will build an apartment house over there.

3. Kyō wa **gaishutsu shi**nai hazu datta.
   今日は**外出し**ないはずだった。
   I was not expected to go out today.

3.4 | Vneg + **nai darō** ないだろう (cf. 2.4) | "probably not"

Vneg *nai darō* expresses the speaker's negative conjecture.

EXAMPLES:

1. Tōbun ame wa **yama**nai darō.
   当分雨は**止ま**ないだろう。
   The rain probably won't stop for a while.

2. Waga chīmu wa ashita no shiai ni **yabure**nai darō.
わがチームは明日の試合に**敗れ**ないだろう。

Our team probably won't lose tomorrow's game.

3. Ano mise wa suiyōbi wa **eigyō shi**nai deshō.
あの店は水曜日は**営業し**ないでしょう。

That store probably doesn't do business on Wednesdays.

3.5 | Vneg + **nai kamoshirenai** ないかもしれない (cf. 2.5)

"might not"

Vneg *nai kamoshirenai* expresses the speaker's negative speculation or guess.

EXAMPLES:

1. Ano hito wa Nihongo ga **wakara**nai kamoshirenai.
あの人は日本語が**分から**ないかもしれない。

He might not understand Japanese.

2. Kyō wa Fuji-san ga **mie**nai kamoshiremasen.
今日は富士山が**見え**ないかもしれません。

Mt. Fuji might not be visible today.

3. Kore wa kisoku ni **ihan shi**nai kamoshiremasen.
これは規則に**違反し**ないかもしれません。

This might not violate the regulation.

3.6 | Vneg + **nai ni chigainai** ないにちがいない (cf. 2.6) |

"must not be," "There is no doubt that ~ not ~"

Vneg *nai ni chigainai* expresses the speaker's negative guess with confidence.

EXAMPLES:

1. Ogawa-san wa sake o **noma**nai ni chigainai.
   小川さんは酒を**飲ま**ないにちがいない。
   There is no doubt that Mr. Ogawa does not drink sake.

2. Buraun-san wa mō Nihon ni **i**nai ni chigai arimasen.
   ブラウンさんはもう日本に**い**ないにちがいありません。
   Mr. Brown must not be in Japan any more.

3. Kimura-san wa yoru wa **unten shi**nai ni chigai arimasen.
   木村さんは夜は**運転し**ないにちがいありません。
   There is no doubt that Miss Kimura does not drive at night.

PRACTICE 18 (3.1–3.6)

Change the underlined verbs into the negative form.

1. Michiko-san o pātī ni <u>sasou</u> tsumori desu.
   道子さんをパーティーに<u>誘う</u>つもりです。
   I intend to invite Michiko to the party.

2. Raishū no tenrankai ni wa hito ga ōzei <u>atsumaru</u> darō.
   来週の展覧会には人が大勢<u>集まる</u>だろう。
   Probably many people will come to next week's exhibition.

3. Kare wa gogo ofisu ni <u>iru</u> hazu da.
彼は午後オフィスに<u>いる</u>はずだ。

He is expected to be in the office in the afternoon.

4. Kono kisoku wa <u>nakunaru</u> deshō.
この規則は<u>なくなる</u>でしょう。

This regulation will probably be gone.

5. Shachō wa rainen <u>intai suru</u> kamoshirenai.
社長は来年<u>引退する</u>かもしれない。

The company president might retire next year.

6. Jimu wa Nihon ni nagaku <u>sumu</u> tsumori da.
ジムは日本に長く<u>住む</u>つもりだ。

Jim intends to live long in Japan.

7. Tanaka-san wa kyō <u>kuru</u> ni chigainai.
田中さんは今日<u>来る</u>にちがいない。

There is no doubt that Miss Tanaka will come today.

8. Yamada-sensei no kōgi wa kinyōbi ni <u>aru</u> hazu desu.
山田先生の講義は金曜日に<u>ある</u>はずです。

It is expected that Prof. Yamada's lecture will be on Friday.

3.7 | Vneg + **nai no/koto** ないの・こと (cf. 2.7)

"not ~ ing," "not to ~," "that ~ not ~ "

Both *no* and *koto* are nominalizers which make a negative verb into a negative gerund, or a negative clause into a negative noun phrase.

EXAMPLES:

1. Yakusoku o **yabura**nai koto wa taisetsu desu.
   約束を**破ら**ないことは大切です。

   Not breaking promises is important.

2. Yasai o **tabe**nai no wa karada ni warui.
   野菜を**食べ**ないのは体に悪い。

   It is bad for the health not to eat vegetables.

3. Hara-san ga Orinpikku ni kuni o **daihyō shi**nai no/ koto
   o shirimasen deshita.
   原さんがオリンピックに国を**代表し**ないの・ことを知り
   ませんでした。

   I didn't know that Mr. Hara would not represent the country in
   the Olympics.

3.8 | Vneg + **nai de/zu ni** ないで・ずに |

"don't do ~ and," "without doing"

Vneg *nai de/zu ni* expresses non-performance of an action. The
auxiliaries *nai* and *zu* are used for negation. The *zu ni* form for
suru-verbs is *sezu ni* (not *shizu ni*).

EXAMPLES:

1. Samu wa gakkō e **ika**nai de/**ika**zu ni uchi ni imashita.
   サムは学校へ**行か**ないで・**行か**ずにうちにいました。

   Sam did not go to school and stayed home.

2. Gakusei wa tokidoki kyōshitsu no mado o **shime**naide/
   shimezu ni kaerimasu.
   学生は時々教室の窓を**閉め**ないで・**閉め**ずに帰ります。

Sometimes students go home without closing the windows of the classroom.

3. Yūbe wa **benkyō shi**nai de/**benkyō se**zu ni nemashita.
   ゆうべは勉強しないで・勉強せずに寝ました。

   Last night I didn't study and went to bed.

3.9　Vneg + **nai de kudasai** ないでください　"Please don't ~"

Vneg *nai de kudasai* expresses a negative request.

EXAMPLES:

1. Rōka no dentō o **kesa**nai de kudasai.
   廊下の電灯を消さないでください。

   Please don't turn off the lights in the corridor.

2. Sono doa o **ake**nai de kudasai.
   そのドアを開けないでください。

   Please don't open that door.

3. Gogo rokuji igo wa shinamono o **haitatsu shi**nai de kudasai.
   午後六時以後は品物を配達しないでください。

   Please don't deliver goods after 6 P.M.

3.10　Vneg + **nai koto ga aru** ないことがある (cf. 2.9)

"There are times when ~ don't ~"

Vneg *nai koto ga aru* indicates that actions or events sometimes do not occur.

1. Kono beru wa **nara**nai koto ga aru.
   このベルは鳴らないことがある。

   There are times when this bell does not ring.

2. Sofu wa asa hayaku **oki**nai koto ga aru.
   祖父は朝早く起きないことがある。

   There are times when my grandfather doesn't get up early in the morning.

3. Koko ni wa chūsha o **kyoka shi**nai koto ga arimasu.
   ここには駐車を許可しないことがあります。

   There are times when they don't permit parking cars here.

3.11 | Vneg + **nai koto ni suru** ないことにする (cf. 2.10)

"decide not to"

Vneg *nai koto ni suru* expresses the speaker's decision not to do something.

EXAMPLES:

1. Ashita kara tabako o **suwa**nai koto ni suru.
   明日からたばこを吸わないことにする。

   I decided not to smoke starting tomorrow.

2. Koko ni hana o **ue**nai koto ni shimashita.
   ここに花を植えないことにしました。

   I decided not to plant flowers here.

3. Shibaraku soto de **shokuji shi**nai koto ni shimasu.
   しばらく外で食事しないことにします。

   I've decided not to dine out for a while.

3.12 | Vneg + **nai koto ni naru** ないことになる (cf. 2.11)

"It will be decided that ~ won't ~"

Vneg *nai koto ni naru* expresses a negative decision made by others, rather than the speaker.

EXAMPLES:

1. Watashi-tachi wa sono ryokan de **tomara**nai koto ni naru darō.

   私達はその旅館で**泊まら**ないことになるだろう。

   It will probably be decided that we won't stay overnight at that Japanese inn.

2. Kida-san wa kaisha o **yame**nai koto ni narimashita.

   木田さんは会社を**辞め**ないことになりました。

   It has been decided that Miss Kida won't quit the company.

3. Akutenkō no tame fune wa **shukkō shi**nai koto ni nari-mashita.

   悪天候のため船は**出航し**ないことになりました。

   It has been decided that the ship won't sail due to the bad weather.

PRACTICE 19 (3.7–3.12)

A. Change the following verbs into the negative gerund form.

1. erabu 選ぶ choose   2. shiraberu 調べる check   3. au 会う meet
4. kuru 来る come   5. oboeru 覚える memorize
6. junbi suru 準備する prepare

B. Make negative requests using the following verbs.

1. iku 行く go   2. suteru 捨てる throw away
3. wasureru 忘れる forget   4. matsu 待つ wait
5. hitei suru 否定する deny   6. machigaeru 間違える make a mistake

C. Complete the following sentences with the verbs provided.

1. Kare wa hachiji made ni shigoto ni _____ .
(kimasu)

   彼は八時までに仕事に _____。（来ます）

   There are times when he does not come to work by eight o'clock.

2. Kono koto wa buchō to _____ . (sōdan shi-masu)

   この事は部長と _____。（相談します）

   As for this matter, I decided not to consult with the department head.

3. Haruko-san wa piano risaitaru o _____ . (okonai-masu)

   春子さんはピアノリサイタルを _____。（行ない ます）

   It has been decided that Haruko won't give a piano recital.

4. Kyōshitsu de wa Eigo de _____. (hanashi-masu)

   教室では英語で _____。（話します）

   Let's decide not to speak in English in the classroom.

5. Watashi wa jūniji made _____. (nemasu)

   私は十二時まで _____。（寝ます）

   There are times when I don't go to bed until twelve o'clock.

6. Kōjō wa seisan o _____. (zōka shimasu)

   工場は生産を _____。（増加します）

   It has been decided that the factory won't increase production.

3.13　Vneg + **nai uchi ni** ないうちに

"before something takes place"

Vneg *nai uchi ni* expresses a temporal limit for a negative action or event. The tense of the sentence is determined by the verb in the main clause.

EXAMPLES:

1. Ame ga **fura**nai uchi ni kaerimashō.
   雨が**降ら**ないうちに帰りましょう。
   Let's go home before it rains.

2. Kodomo ga okinai uchi ni asagohan o tabemashita.
   子供が**起き**ないうちに朝ご飯を食べました。
   I ate breakfast before my child got up.

3. Zairyō ga **fusoku shi**nai uchi ni chūmon shimashita.
   材料が**不足し**ないうちに注文しました。
   We ordered before we were short of the materials.

3.14　Vneg + **nai hō ga ii** ないほうがいい

"be better not to do ~," "had better not do ~"

Vneg *nai hō ga ii* expresses advice not to do something. *Hō* is a pseudo noun. *Desu* may be added to the adjective *ii* to make the speech polite.

EXAMPLES:

1. Kono koto wa dare ni mo **hanasa**nai hō ga ii (desu).
   この事はだれにも**話さ**ないほうがいい (です)。
   As for this matter, it is better not to tell anyone.

2. Pātī de **nomisugi**nai hō ga ii (desu) yo.
パーティーで飲みすぎないほうがいい（です）よ。

You had better not drink too much at the party.

3. Ano kaisha to **keiyaku shi**nai hō ga ii (desu).
あの会社と契約しないほうがいい（です）。

It is better not to contract with that company.

3.15 | **Vneg + nai kawari ni ない代わりに (cf. 2.14)** |

"instead of not doing ~," "make up for not doing ~"

Vneg *nai kawari ni* expresses the thought that a certain action will not be carried out, and that instead another action will take place. Note, as in the first example below, that a verb modifier (in this case, the destination) is often of crucial importance.

EXAMPLES:

1. Kanada e **ika**nai kawari ni Hawai e iku.
カナダへ行かない代わりにハワイへ行く。

Instead of (not) going to Canada, I'll go to Hawaii.

2. Abe-san wa niku o **tabe**nai kawari ni yasai o takusan tabemasu.
阿部さんは肉を食べない代わりに野菜をたくさん食べます。

Miss Abe eats a lot of vegetables to make up for not eating meat.

3. Kyō **shigoto shi**nai kawari ni doyōbi ni shigoto suru.
今日仕事しない代わりに土曜日に仕事する。

I'll work on Saturday to make up for not working today.

Fill in the blanks with the appropriate forms of the verbs provided at the end of the sentences.

1. Tomodachi ga _____ uchi ni heya o _____
   mashita. (kuru) (sōji suru)
   友達が _____ うちに部屋を _____ ました。
   （来る）（掃除する）

   I cleaned the room before my friend came.

2. Sofu wa yo ga _____ uchi ni _____ masu.
   (akeru) (okiru)
   祖父は夜が _____ うちに _____ ます。（明ける）
   （起きる）

   My grandfather gets up before the day breaks.

3. Kono shinamono wa ima nedan o _____ hō ga
   ii desu. (sageru)
   この品物は今値段を _____ ほうがいいです。（下げる）

   It is better not to lower the price of these goods now.

4. Kaigi ga _____ made heya ni _____ hō ga ii
   desu. (owarimasu) (hairu)
   会議が _____ まで部屋に _____ ほうがいい
   です。（終わります）（入る）

   You had better not enter the room until the meeting is over.

5. Kanojo wa _____ kawari ni piano o _____
   mashita. (utau) (hiku)
   彼女は _____ 代わりにピアノを _____ ました。
   （歌う）（弾く）

   She played the piano to make up for not singing.

6. _____ kawari ni sutereo o _____ koto ni shimashita. (ryokō suru) (kaimasu)

_____ 代わりにステレオを _____ ことにしました。(旅行する)(買います)

Instead of (not) going on a trip, I decided to buy a stereo.

3.16 | Vneg + **nai noni** ないのに (cf. 2.19)

"although ~ not," "in spite of the fact that ~ not"

Vneg *nai noni* expresses a negative action which is followed by a result contrary to expectation.

EXAMPLES:

1. Mada goji ni **nara**nai noni, mō hi ga kuremashita.
   まだ五時に**なら**ないのに、もう日が暮れました。
   It's dark already, although it isn't five o'clock yet.

2. Sensei ga **tari**nai noni yatoimasen.
   先生が**足り**ないのに雇いません。
   Although we don't have enough teachers, they won't hire any more.

3. **Chūmon sh**inai noni hon ga todokimashita.
   注文しないのに本が届きました。
   A book arrived in spite of the fact that I did not order it.

3.17 | Vneg + **nai to** ないと (cf. 2.20) | "if ~ not"

Vneg *nai to* expresses a negative condition that brings about an inevitable result.

EXAMPLES:

1. Kusuri o **noma**nai to netsu ga sagaranai.
   薬を飲まないと熱が下がらない。
   If you don't take medicine, your fever won't go down.

2. Dentō o **tsuke**nai to mienai.
   電灯をつけないと見えない。
   If I don't turn on the light, I can't see.

3. Minna ga **kyōryoku shi**nai to kono shigoto wa kansei shimasen.
   みんなが協力しないとこの仕事は完成しません。
   If everyone doesn't cooperate, this job won't be completed.

3.18 | Vneg + **nai** (**no**) **nara** ない（の）なら (cf. 2.21) |

"if ~ not," "if it is not the case ~"

Vneg *nai* (*no*) *nara* expresses a negative supposition or condition.

EXAMPLES:

1. Noda-san ga **ika**nai (no) nara, watashi mo ikanai.
   野田さんが行かない（の）なら、私も行かない。
   If Mr. Noda doesn't go, I won't go either.

2. Terebi o **mi**nai (no) nara, keshi nasai.
   テレビを見ない（の）なら、消しなさい。
   If you're not watching the TV, turn it off.

3. Ima **happyō shi**nai (no) nara, itsu suru tsumori desu ka.
   今発表しない（の）なら、いつするつもりですか。
   If you don't announce it now, when do you intend to do it?

Fill in the blanks with the appropriate forms of the verbs provided at the end of the sentences.

1. Kanojo wa o-kane ga _____ noni, takai mono o _____ masu. (aru) (kau)

   彼女はお金が _____ のに、高いものを _____ ます。（ある）（買う）

   She buys expensive things, although she doesn't have money.

2. _____ noni, hito ga ōzei _____ mashita. (senden suru) (atsumaru)

   _____ のに、人が大勢 _____ ました。（宣伝する）（集まる）

   Although we did not advertise, many people came.

3. Beru ga _____ to, gakusei wa kyōshitsu ni _____ masen. (naru) (hairu)

   ベルが _____ と、学生は教室に _____ ません。（鳴る）（入る）

   Unless the bell rings, students do not enter the classroom.

4. Kachō ga _____ to, nani mo _____ darō. (shusseki suru) (kimaru)

   課長が _____ と、何も _____ だろう。（出席する）（決まる）

   If the section chief does not attend (the meeting), probably nothing will be decided.

5. _____ (no) nara, eki kara _____ mashō. (isogu) (aruku)

_____ （の）なら、駅から _____ ましょう。（急ぐ）
（歩く）

If you're not in a hurry, let's walk from the station.

6. Mō _____ (no) nara, _____ nasai. (tsukau)
(suteru)
もう _____ （の）なら、_____ なさい。（使う）
（捨てる）

If you don't use it any more, throw it away.

3.19 | **Vneg + nai yō ni ないように (cf. 2.24)**

"in order not to," "so that ~ not"

Vneg *nai yō ni* expresses by means of a negative verb a reason or motive for doing something.

EXAMPLES:

1. Kaze o **hika**nai yō ni sētā o kiru.
   かぜを引かないようにセーターを着る。

   I wear a sweater in order not to catch cold.

2. **Nomisugi**nai yō ni ki o tsukemasu.
   飲みすぎないように気をつけます。

   I'll be careful not to drink too much.

3. **Rakudai shi**nai yō ni shikkari benkyō shinasai.
   落第しないようにしっかり勉強しなさい。

   Study hard so that you won't fail the examination.

3.20 | Vneg + **nai yō ni iu** ないように言う (cf. 2.25)

"tell someone not to do ~"

Vneg *nai yō ni iu* expresses an indirect command. The verb *iu* may be replaced by other verbs such as *tanomu* 頼む (ask) or *chūkoku suru* 忠告する (advise) to express requests or suggestions.

EXAMPLES:

1. Kodomo ni rōka o **hashira**nai yō ni iu.
   子供に廊下を**走ら**ないように言う。
   I'll tell the children not to run in the corridor.

2. Watashi wa Ono-san ni mado o **ake**nai yō ni tanomi-mashita.
   私は小野さんに窓を**開け**ないように頼みました。
   I asked Miss Ono not to open the window.

3. Kare wa watashi ni ima kabu ni **tōshi shi**nai yō ni chūkoku shimashita.
   彼は私に今株に**投資し**ないように忠告しました。
   He advised me not to invest in stocks now.

3.21 | Vneg + **nai yō ni naru** ないようになる (cf. 2.26)

"reach the point where ~ not"

Vneg *nai yō ni naru* expresses with a negative verb some change that takes place gradually.

EXAMPLES:

1. Hayashi-san wa tabako o **suwa**nai yō ni narimashita.
   林さんはたばこを**吸わ**ないようになりました。
   Mr. Hayashi has reached the point where he does not smoke.

2. Jimu wa gakkō ni **okure**nai yō ni narimashita.
   ジムは学校に**遅れ**ないようになりました。

   Jim has reached the point where he is not late for school. (Jim is not late for school any more.)

3. Noda-san wa **zangyō shi**nai yō ni narimashita.
   野田さんは**残業し**ないようになりました。

   Miss Noda has reached the point where she doesn't work overtime. (Ms. Noda doesn't work overtime any more.)

3.22 | Vneg + **nai yō ni suru** ないようにする (cf. 2.27)

   "try not to ~," "make sure that ~ not"

Vneg *nai yō ni suru* expresses with a negative verb a person's efforts to cause a change in behavior.

EXAMPLES:

1. Yasai o **nokosa**nai yō ni shinasai.
   野菜を**残さ**ないようにしなさい。

   Make sure that you don't leave vegetables (uneaten).

2. Amari yoru osoku shawā o **abi**nai yō ni suru.
   あまり夜おそくシャワーを**浴び**ないようにする。

   I try not to take a shower late at night.

3. Otōto to **kenka shi**nai yō ni shimasu.
   弟と**けんかし**ないようにします。

   I'll try not to quarrel with my younger brother.

Fill in the blanks with the appropriate forms of the verbs provided at the end of the sentences.

1. Gakkō ni _____ yō ni asa hayaku _____ masu. (okureru) (okiru)

   学校に _____ ように朝早く _____ ます。（遅れる）（起きる）

   I get up early in the morning in order not to be late for school.

2. _____ yō ni yukkuri saka o _____ mashita. (korobu) (kudaru)

   _____ ようにゆっくり坂を _____ ました。（転ぶ）（下る）

   I came down the slope slowly so as not to fall down.

3. Heya de _____ yō ni _____ nasai. (sawagu) (suru)

   部屋で _____ ように _____ なさい。（騒ぐ）（する）

   Don't make noise in the room.

4. Gakusei ni koko ni mono o _____ yō ni iimasu. (oku)

   学生にここに物を _____ ように言います。（置く）

   I'll tell the students not to put things here.

5. Sara wa pātī de Tomu to _____ yō ni narimashita. (odoru)

   サラはパーティーでトムと _____ ようになりました。（踊る）

   Sarah doesn't dance with Tom at a party any more.

6. Shōjo wa ningyō to _____ yō ni narimashita. (asobu)

少女は人形と _____ ようになりました。(遊ぶ)

The girl has reached the point where she does not play with dolls any more.

7. O-kane o _____ yō ni shimasu. (tsukaisugiru)

お金を _____ ようにします。(使いすぎる)

I'll try not to spend too much money.

8. Yoru osoku ano michi o _____ yō ni shimashō. (tōru)

夜おそくあの道を _____ ようにしましょう。(通る)

Let's try not to walk along that road late at night.

3.23 | Vneg + **reru/rareru** (1) れる・られる | "be -ed"

Vneg *reru/rareru* expresses the passive form. *Reru* is attached to regular I verbs and *rareru* to regular II verbs. The irregular verbs *kuru* and *suru* become *korareru* and *sareru*. All passive verbs are regular II verbs.

There are two types of passives in Japanese: direct and indirect. The direct passive is similar to the English passive in which the object of the active sentence becomes the subject of the passive sentence (Example 1). The agent (performer of the action) takes the particle *ni*. The agent may be omitted when it is not important or unknown (Example 2). In the indirect passive, the person who becomes the subject of the passive sentence is the one who is adversely affected by someone else's action or an unpleasant event (Example 3). For this passive, both transitive and intransitive verbs may be used (Examples 3, 4 and 5).

EXAMPLES:

1. Tokidoki Tomu wa Jimu ni **damasa**reru.
   時々トムはジムに**だまさ**れる。
   Sometimes Tom is deceived by Jim.

2. Asoko ni biru ga **tate**raremasu.
   あそこにビルが**建て**られます。
   A building will be built over there.

3. Watashi wa otōto ni pai o **tabe**raremashita.
   私は弟にパイを**食べ**られました。
   I had my pie eaten by my younger brother.

4. Gorufujō de ame ni **fura**remashita.
   ゴルフ場で雨に**降ら**れました。
   We were rained on at the golf course.

5. Watashi wa Akiko-san ni totsuzen uchi e **ko**raremashita.
   私は秋子さんに突然うちへ**来ら**れました。
   Akiko came to my home unexpectedly (and I was unhappy).

3.24 | Vneg + **reru/rareru** (2) れる・られる |

"can do," "be able to"

Vneg *reru/rareru* expresses potential. *Reru* is attached to regular I verbs and *rareru* to regular II verbs. The potential forms for the irregular verbs *kuru* and *suru* are *korareru* and *dekiru* (not *sareru*).

EXAMPLES:

1. Anata wa kyō tenrankai ni **ika**remasu ka.
   あなたは今日展覧会に**行か**れますか。
   Can you go to the exhibition today?

2. Asa goji ni wa **oki**rarenai.
朝五時には**起き**られない。

I can't get up at five o'clock in the morning.

3. Mina-san ashita hachiji made ni **ko**raremasu ka.
皆さん明日八時までに**来**られますか。

Can everyone come by eight o'clock tomorrow?

4. Kono terebi wa **shūri deki**nai.
このテレビは**修理出来**ない。

I can't repair this TV set.

3.25 | Vneg + **reru/rareru** (3) れる・られる | "be -ed"

Vneg *reru/rareru* is used for the honorific style of speech. *Reru* is attached to regular I verbs and *rareru* to regular II verbs. The irregular verbs *kuru* and *suru* become *korareru* and *sareru*.

EXAMPLES:

1. Nakamura-sensei ga Nihon no keizai ni tsuite **hanasa**-remasu.
中村先生が日本の経済について**話さ**れます。

Prof. Nakamura will speak about the Japanese economy.

2. Kin'yōbi ni wa Hara-sensei wa **oshie**rarenai.
金曜日には原先生は**教え**られない。

Prof. Hara does not teach on Fridays.

3. Sono kaigi de Oka-buchō ga nando mo **shitsumon sare**mashita.
その会議で岡部長が何度も**質問され**ました。

Mr. Oka, the department head, asked questions many times at that meeting.

A. Change the following active sentences into passive sentences.

1. Sensei wa kodomo-tachi o shikarimashita. → Kodomo-tachi wa ………
先生は子供達を叱りました。 → 子供達は ………
The teacher scolded the children. → The children were scolded by the teacher.

2. Gakusei wa Ono-sensei o pātī ni shōtai shimashita. → Ono-sensei wa ……
学生は小野先生をパーティーに招待しました。 → 小野先生は ……
The students invited Prof. Ono to the party. → Prof. Ono was invited to the party by the students.

3. Ueitoresu ga watashi no sukāto o yogoshimashita. → Watashi wa ……
ウエイトレスが私のスカートを汚しました。 → 私は ....
A waitress soiled my shirt. → I had my skirt soiled by a waitress.

4. Dorobō ga Kida-san no jitensha o nusumimashita. → Kida-san wa ……
泥棒が木田さんの自転車を盗みました。 → 木田さんは ……
A thief stole Mr. Kida's bicycle. → Mr. Kida had his bicycle stolen by a thief.

5. Yano-san no okusan ga shinimashita. → Yano-san wa ……
矢野さんの奥さんが死にました。 → 矢野さんは ……
Mr. Yano's wife died (and he was unhappy).

6. Maiban kodomo ga nakimasu. → Watashi-tachi wa
......

毎晩子供が泣きます。 → 私達は ......

Every night our child cries (and we are unhappy).

B. Fill in the blanks with the appropriate forms of the verbs given at the end of the sentences.

1. Suzuki-san wa hon'ya ni _____ mashita. (yoru) [honorific]

鈴木さんは本屋に _____ ました。(寄る)

Mr. Suzuki stopped by the bookstore.

2. Ano gaikokujin wa Nihongo no shinbun ga _____ masu. (yomu) [potential]

あの外国人は日本語の新聞が _____ ます。(読む)

That foreigner can read Japanese newspapers.

3. Honda-sensei wa bunpō no hon o _____ mashita. (kaku) [honorific]

本田先生は文法の本を _____ ました。(書く)

Prof. Honda wrote a grammar book.

4. Nigatsu made ni kono shigoto wa _____ masu. (kansei suru) [potential]

二月までにこの仕事は _____ ます。(完成する)

This work can be completed by February.

5. Buchō wa watashi-tachi no iken ni _____ mashita. (sansei suru) [honorific]

部長は私達の意見に _____ ました。(賛成する)

The department head agreed with our opinion.

3.26　Vneg + **seru/saseru** せる・させる

"make/let someone do"

Vneg *seru/saseru* expresses the causative form. *Seru* is attached to regular I verbs and *saseru* to regular II verbs. The irregular verbs *kuru* and *suru* become *kosaseru* and *saseru*. These causative verbs are regular II verbs. The shortened causative form may be obtained by changing the final *seru* to *su*, e.g. *arukaseru → arukasu; tabesaseru → tabesasu; kosaseru → kosasu; saseru → sasu.* The causative verbs of this shortened form are regular I verbs, conjugated on the Sa row. The person who causes someone to do something usually takes the particle *wa* or *ga* and the person who is made or allowed to do something is marked by *o* or *ni*. When the verb is transitive and the direct object maker *o* appears, the person caused to do something must be marked by *ni* (Example 1). When the verb is intransitive, that person takes *ni* if he perfoms an action willingly (Example 2). *O* is used regardless of the person's volition (Example 3).

EXAMPLES:

1. Haha wa imōto ni barē o **narawa**seru/**narawa**su.
   母は妹にバレーを**習わせる・習わす**。
   My mother makes/lets my younger sister learn ballet.

2. Watashi wa kodomo-tachi ni tento de **ne**sasemashita/**nesashi**mashita.
   私は子供達にテントで**寝させました・寝さし**ました。
   I let my children sleep in a tent.

3. Oda-san wa musuko o Amerika ni **ryūgaku sase**mashita/**ryūgaku sashi**mashita.

小田さんは息子をアメリカに**留学させ**ました・**留学さし**ました。

Mr. Oda made/let his son study in America.

3.27 | Vneg + **serareru/saserareru** せられる・させられる

"be made to do"

Vneg *serareru/saserareru* expresses the causative-passive form. *Serareru* is attached to regular I verbs and *saserareru* to regular II verbs. The irregular verbs *kuru* and *suru* become *kosaserareru* and *saserareru*. The shortened causative-passive form is made by attaching *reru* to the negative base of the shortened causative verbs made from regular I verbs; e.g.*matasu* → *matasa* +*reru* → *matasareru* (Example 1). All causative-passive verbs are regular II verbs.

EXAMPLES:

1. Itsumo ginkō de **mata**serareru (**matasa**reru).
   いつも銀行で**待た**せられる (**待たさ**れる)。

   I am always made to wait at the bank.

2. Kachō ni shorui o **shirabe**saseraremashita.
   課長に書類を**調べ**させられました。

   I was made to check the documents by the section chief.

3. Kaigi ni **shusseki sase**raremashita.
   会議に**出席さ**せられました。

   I was made to attend the meeting.

A. Change the following verbs into the causative and causative-passive forms.

1. iku 行く go
2. kangaeru 考える think
3. tetsudau 手伝う help
4. shimeru 閉める close
5. nomu 飲む drink
6. shinpai suru 心配する worry

B. Fill in the blanks with the appropriate forms of verbs given at the end of sentences.

1. Watashi wa kodomo-tachi o kōen de _____ mashita. (asobu)
   私は子供達を公園で _____ ました。（遊ぶ）
   I let the children play in the park.

2. Isha wa Minami-san ni tabako o _____ mashita. (yameru)
   医者は南さんにたばこを _____ ました。（やめる）
   The doctor made Mr. Minami quit smoking.

3. Haha wa imōto ni heya o _____ mashita. (sōji suru)
   母は妹に部屋を _____ ました。（掃除する）
   My mother made my younger sister clean the room.

4. Watashi wa ani ni kutsu o _____ mashita. (migaku)
   私は兄にくつを _____ ました。（磨く）
   I was made to polish the shoes by my older brother.

5. Doi-san wa isha ni _____ mashita. (nyūin suru)
   土井さんは医者に_____ ました。（入院する）
   Mr. Doi was made to enter the hospital by his doctor.

3.28 | Vneg + **nakatta** なかった (cf. 3.1)

"did not do," "there was not"

Vneg *nakatta* is the past tense of Vneg *nai*. The copula *desu* may be added to make the speech polite.

EXAMPLES:

1. Kyonen wa Fuji-san ni **nobora**nakatta (desu).
   去年は富士山に登らなかった (です)。
   I did not climb Mr. Fuji last year.

2. Watashi wa Masako-san ni shashin o **mise**nakatta (desu).
   私は正子さんに写真を見せなかった (です)。
   I did not show the photos to Masako.

3. Waga chīmu wa **yūshō shi**nakatta (desu).
   わがチームは優勝しなかった (です)。
   Our team did not win the championship.

3.29 | Vneg + **nakereba/nakattara** なければ・なかったら

"if ~ not"

Vneg *nakereba/nakattara* expresses a negative condition.

EXAMPLES:

1. **Isoga**nakereba/nakattara, ma ni awanai yo.
   急がなければ・なかったら、間に合わないよ。
   If you don't hurry, you won't be in time.

2. Kiri ga **hare**nakereba/nakattara, hikōki wa tobimasen.
   きりが**晴れ**なければ・なかったら、飛行機は飛びません。

   If the fog doesn't clear up, the airplane won't fly.

3. Shachō ga **kyoka shi**nakereba/nakattara, kono purojekuto wa dekimasen.
   社長が**許可し**なければ・なかったら、このプロジェクト
   は出来ません。

   If the company president doesn't give permission, we cannot do
   this project.

3.30 | Vneg + **nakereba naranai** なければならない |

"have to," "must"

Vneg *nakereba naranai* expresses the idea of obligation or duty.
Nakereba narimasen is the polite style of speech.

EXAMPLES:

1. Nihongo de sakubun o **kaka**nakereba naranai.
   日本語で作文を**書か**なければならない。

   I have to write a composition in Japanese.

2. Kono shinamono wa kayōbi made ni **todoke**nakereba
   narimasen.
   この品物は火曜日までに**届け**なければなりません。

   We must deliver this article by Tuesday.

3. Shiai ga aru kara, mainichi **renshū shi**nakereba naranai.
   試合があるから、毎日**練習し**なければならない。

   Because we'll have a tournament, we have to practice every day.

Fill in the blanks with the appropriate forms of the verbs provided at the end of the sentences.

1. Yano-san ga _____ nakereba, watashi ga kono repōto o _____ nakereba naranai. (kuru) (kaki-naosu)

   矢野さんが _____ なければ、私がこのレポートを _____ なければならない。（来る）（書き直す）

   If Miss Yano doesn't come, I have to rewrite this report.

2. Kusuri o _____ nakatta kara, netsu ga _____ nakatta. (nomu) (sagaru)

   薬を _____ なかったから、熱が _____ なかった。（飲む）（下がる）

   Because I did not take medicine, my fever did not go down.

3. Gakkō ni _____ nai yō ni hachiji no densha ni _____ nakereba narimasen. (okureru) (noru)

   学校に _____ ないように八時の電車に _____ なければなりません。（遅れる）（乗る）

   I have to take the eight-o'clock train, so that I won't be late for school.

4. Jiko o _____ nai yō ni kōtsū kisoku o _____ nakereba naranai. (okosu) (mamoru)

   事故を _____ ないように交通規則を _____ なければならない。（起こす）（守る）

   We must observe the traffic regulations so that we won't cause accidents.

3.31 | Vneg + **nakute** なくて

"do not do ~ and ~," "because ~ do not do ~"

Vneg *nakute* is the negative *te* form of the verb and indicates a cause or reason for an action or event.

EXAMPLES:

1. Hikōki ga teikoku ni **tsuka**nakute enkai ni okuremashita.
   飛行機が定刻に**着か**なくて宴会に遅れました。
   The airplane didn't arrive on schedule and I was late for the banquet.

2. Kanji ga **oboerare**nakute komaru.
   漢字が**覚えられ**なくて困る。
   Because I can't memorize kanji, I'm in trouble.

3. Shukudai o **teishutsu shi**nakute sensei ni shikararemashita.
   宿題を**提出し**なくて先生に叱られました。
   I did not hand in my homework and was scolded by my teacher.

3.32 | Vneg + **nakute mo** なくても

"even if ~ not ~"

Vneg *nakute mo* expresses a negative condition.

EXAMPLES:

1. Ame ga **yama**nakute mo dekakeru tsumori da.
   雨が**止ま**なくても出かけるつもりだ。
   Even if the rain doesn't stop, I intend to go out.

2. Nedan o **sage**nakute mo kono shinamono wa mada yoku ureru.

値段を**下げ**なくてもこの品物はまだよく売れる。

Even though we haven't lowered the price, this article still sells well.

3. Ryōshin ga **sansei shi**nakute mo Furansu e ikitai (desu).

両親が**賛成し**なくてもフランスへ行きたい（です）。

Even if my parents do not approve, I'd like to go to France.

3.33 | Vneg + **nakute mo ii** なくてもいい

"It is all right if ~ not," "don't have to"

Vneg *nakute mo ii* expresses the idea of non-obligation or duty.

EXAMPLES:

1. Kono hagaki ni kitte o **hara**nakute mo ii (desu).

この葉書に切手を**はら**なくてもいい（です）。

You don't have to stick a stamp on this postcard.

2. Shūmatsu wa hayaku **oki**nakute mo ii (desu).

週末は早く**起き**なくてもいい（です）。

I don't have to get up early on weekends.

3. Kono ken wa ima **kettei shi**nakute mo ii (desu).

この件は今**決定し**なくてもいい（です）。

We don't have to decide this matter now.

A. Change the following phrases into the ~ *nakereba naranai* and ~ *nakute mo ii* forms.

1. densha o norikaeru 電車を乗りかえる change trains
2. kutsu o nugu くつを脱ぐ take off shoes
3. shiken o ukeru 試験を受ける take an examination
4. jisho o chūmon suru 辞書を注文する order a dictionary
5. ryōkin o harau 料金を払う pay a fee

B. Fill in the blanks with the appropriate forms of the verbs given at the end of the sentences.

1. Hi ga _____ nakute hana ga _____ masen. (ataru) (saku)
   日が _____ なくて花が _____ ません。（当たる）（咲く）

   Because the sun does not shine, the flowers do not bloom.

2. Anata wa senshū _____ nakatta kara, konshū no doyōbi wa _____ nakute mo ii desu yo. (yasumu) (hataraku)
   あなたは先週 _____ なかったから、今週の土曜日は _____ なくてもいいですよ。（休む）（働く）

   Because you didn't take a day off last week, you don't have to work this Saturday.

3. Ashita ame ga _____ nakute mo tsuri ni _____ nai hō ga ii desu. (furu) (dekakeru)
   明日雨が _____ なくても釣りに _____ ないほうがいいです。（降る）（出かける）

   Even if it doesn't rain tomorrow, it's better not to go out fishing.

4. Tenki ga _____ sō da kara, gogo no shiai wa
   _____ nakute mo ii deshō. (kaifuku suru) (chūshi
   suru)

   天気が _____ そうだから、午後の試合は _____ なく
   てもいいでしょう。（回復する）（中止する）

   It looks like the weather will improve, so we probably don't
   have to call off this afternoon's game.

④ Conditional Form

Conditional form (Vcond)

Regular I Verb (4th base)	Regular II Verb (Verb stem + re)	Irregular Verb
yome 読め (read) tore 取れ (take)	akere 開けれ (open) orire 降りれ (get off)	kure 来れ (come) sure すれ (do)

SENTENCE PATTERNS

4.1 | **Vcond + ba** ば | "if"

Vcond *ba* expresses a condition. The main clause may involve an
inevitable event, or the speaker's volition or hope.

EXAMPLES:

1. Kikai ga **are**ba, Kimura-san o tazunetai (desu).
   機会が**あれ**ば、木村さんを訪ねたい（です）。

   If I have an opportunity, I'd like to visit Miss Kimura.

2. Hachiji ni kochira o **dere**ba, niji made ni achira ni tsuku.
八時にこちらを**出れ**ば、二時までにあちらに着く。

If we leave here at eight o'clock, we will arrive there by two o'clock.

3. Yamada-san ga **kure**ba, issho ni tenisu o suru tsumori da.
山田さんが**来れ**ば、一緒にテニスをするつもりだ。

If Mr. Yamada comes, I intend to play tennis with him.

4.2 | Vcond + **ba ii** ばいい

"you need only," "all you have to do is"

Vcond *ba ii* suggests the only action the listener should take in a certain situation.

EXAMPLES:

1. Wakaranakereba, sensei ni **kike**ba ii (desu).
分からなければ、先生に**聞け**ばいい（です）。

If you don't understand, all you have to do is to ask your teacher.

2. Ashita no tesuto ni wa kono ka no kanji o **oboere**ba ii (desu).
明日のテストにはこの課の漢字を**覚えれ**ばいい（です）。

For tomorrow's test, you need only memorize the kanji in this lesson.

3. Isogu (no) nara, denwa de **chūmon sure**ba ii (desu).
急ぐ（の）なら、電話で**注文すれ**ばいい（です）。

If you want it in a hurry, all you have to do is to order by phone.

4.3 | Vcond + **ba yokatta** ばよかった | "I wish ~ had done ~"

Vcond *ba yokatta* expresses the speaker's regret for something he hasn't done. *Desu* may be added to the adjective *yokatta* (past form of *ii/yoi*) to make the speech polite.

EXAMPLES:

1. Ano hon o **kae**ba yokatta (desu).
   あの本を**買え**ばよかった（です）。
   I wish I had bought that book.

2. Motto yoku **kangaere**ba yokatta (desu).
   もっとよく**考えれ**ばよかった（です）。
   I wish I had given more thought to it.

3. Kono koto wa sensei to **sōdan sure**ba yokatta (desu).
   このことは先生と**相談すれ**ばよかった（です）。
   I wish I had consulted with my teacher about this matter.

4.4 | Vcond + **ba ~ hodo/dake** ば ～ ほど・だけ

"the more ~ the more"

Vcond *ba ~ hodo/dake* expresses a proportional relationship between two actions or states.

EXAMPLES:

1. Minami e **ike**ba iku hodo/dake atatakaku naru.
   南へ**行け**ば行くほど・だけ暖かくなる。
   The further south you go, the warmer it gets.

2. Kono e wa **mire**ba miru hodo/dake utsukushii.
   この絵は**見れ**ば見るほど・だけ美しい。

   The more I look at this picture, the more beautiful it is.

3. Gogaku wa **benkyō sure**ba suru hodo/dake omoshi-
   roku narimasu.
   語学は**勉強すれ**ばするほど・だけ面白くなります。

   The more you study language, the more interesting it becomes.

4.5 | **Vcond + ba koso ばこそ** | "because," "only because"

Vcond *ba koso* expresses emphasis of a reason or cause.

EXAMPLES:

1. O-kane ga **ire**ba koso yoru mo hataraku.
   お金が**要れ**ばこそ夜も働く。

   Only because I need money, I work at night as well.

2. Eigo ga **dekire**ba koso Yano-san wa Amerika no
   daigaku ni hairemasu.
   英語が**出来れ**ばこそ矢野さんはアメリカの大学に入れま
   す。

   Only because she understands English, Miss Yano can enter an
   American college.

3. Piano wa mainichi **renshū sure**ba koso jōzu ni narimasu.
   ピアノは毎日**練習すれ**ばこそ上手になります。

   Only because you practice every day, will you become good at
   the piano.

Fill in the blanks with the appropriate forms of the verbs provided at the end of the sentences.

1. Ano yama ni _____ ba tōku ni umi ga _____ masu. (noboru) (mieru)

   あの山に _____ ば遠くに海が _____ ます。（登る）（見える）

   If you climb that mountain, you can see the ocean in the distance.

2. Kono densha ni _____ ba sanjuppun de shūten ni _____ masu. (noru) (tsuku)

   この電車に _____ ば三十分で終点に _____ ます。（乗る）（着く）

   If you get on this train, you will arrive at the terminal station in thirty minutes.

3. Ishi wa _____ ba migaku hodo _____ masu. (migaku) (hikaru)

   石は _____ ば磨くほど _____ ます。（磨く）（光る）

   The more you polish the stone, the more it shines.

4. Kono pēji no shitsumon ni _____ ba ii. (kotaeru)

   このページの質問に _____ ばいい。（答える）

   All you have to do is answer the questions on this page.

5. Tochū de _____ zu ni Nihongo no benkyō o _____ ba yokatta. (yameru) (tsuzukeru)

   途中で _____ ずに日本語の勉強を _____ ばよかった。（やめる）（続ける）

   I wish I had continued the study of Japanese without giving up in the middle.

6. Nihon ni _____ ba koso Nihongo o hanasu kikai ga takusan _____ masu. (iru) (aru)

日本に _____ ばこそ日本語を話す機会がたくさん _____ ます。（いる）（ある）

Only because you are in Japan, you have a lot of chances to speak Japanese.

5 Imperative Form

Imperative form (Vimp)

Regular I Verb (4th base)	Regular II Verb (Verb stem + ro/yo)	Irregular Verb
kae 買え (buy) ike 行け (go)	tomero/yo 止めろ・よ (stop) kariro/yo 借りろ・よ (borrow)	koi 来い (come) seyo/shiro せよ・しろ (do)

SENTENCE PATTERNS

5.1 | Vimp (cf. 2.34) | "Do ~"

Vimp expresses a direct command and is used by men in very informal speech.

EXAMPLES:

1. Bōshi o **nuge**.
   帽子を脱げ。
   Take off you hat.

2. Hayaku **nigero/nigeyo**.
   早く逃げろ・逃げよ。
   Run away quick!

3. Asaban **undō seyo/undō shiro**.
朝晩**運動せよ・運動しろ**。

Exercise morning and evening.

5.2 | **Vimp + to iu と言う** | "tell someone to do ~"

Vimp *to iu* expresses an indirect command and is used by men. The
passive form *iwareru* 言われる (be told) may be used by men and
women.

EXAMPLES:

1. Ten'in ni sugu mihon o **okure** to iu.
店員にすぐ見本を**送れ**と言う。

I'll tell the clerk to send the sample right away.

2. Itsumo sensei ni Nihongo de **kotaero/kotaeyo** to iware-
masu.
いつも先生に日本語で**答えろ・答えよ**と言われます。

I'm always told by my teacher to answer in Japanese.

3. Buchō ni kaigi o **enki seyo/enki shiro** to iwaremashita.
部長に会議を**延期せよ・延期しろ**と言われました。

I was told by the department head to postpone the meeting.

PRACTICE 28 (5.1–5.2)

Change the underlined verbs into the imperative form.

1. Tsukawanai (no) nara, <u>suteru</u>.
使わない（の）なら、<u>捨てる</u>。

Throw it away, if you don't use it.

2. **Kore o Yamada-san ni <u>watasu</u> to iwaremashita.**
これを山田さんに<u>渡す</u>と言われました。

   I was told to hand this to Miss Yamada.

3. **Kurasu ga owaru made koko de <u>matsu</u>.**
クラスが終わるまでここで<u>待つ</u>。

   Wait here until the class is over.

4. **Kachō no iken o <u>shiji suru</u> to iwaremashita.**
課長の意見を<u>支持する</u>と言われました。

   We were told to support the section chief's opinion.

5. **Soto ga yakamashii kara, doa o <u>shimeru</u>.**
外がやかましいから、ドアを<u>閉める</u>。

   It's noisy outside, so close the door.

 Volitional Form

Volitional form (Vvol)

Regular I Verb (5th base + o)	Regular II Verb (Verb stem + yō)	Irregular Verb
isogō 急ごう (hurry) naosō 直そう (correct)	kimeyō 決めよう (decide) shinjiyō 信じよう (believe)	koyō 来よう (come) shiyō しよう (do)

SENTENCE PATTERNS

6.1 | **Vvol (cf. 1.2)** | "I will," "Let's ~"

Vvol expresses first person volition, invitation or suggestion in the plain style of speech.

EXAMPLES:

1. Gogo toshokan de hon o **yomō**.
   午後図書館で本を**読もう**。
   I'll read a book in the library this afternoon.

2. Kono pai o yottsu ni **wakeyō**.
   このパイを四つに**分けよう**。
   Let's divide this pie in four.

3. Watashi ga o-kyaku-san o kaijō e **annai shiyō**.
   私がお客さんを会場へ**案内しよう**。
   I'll lead the visitors to the assembly hall.

6.2 | **Vvol + ka か (cf. 1.3)** | "Shall I ~"

Vvol *ka* expresses first person invitation or suggestion by asking in the plain style of speech.

EXAMPLES:

1. Honda-san o pikunikku ni **sasoō** ka.
   本田さんをピクニックに**誘おう**か。
   Shall we invite Miss Honda to the picnic?

2. Asoko ni kuruma o **tomeyō** ka.
   あそこに車を**止めよう**か。
   Shall I park the car over there?

3. Watashi ga bazā no uriage o **keisan shiyō** ka.
   私がバザーの売り上げを**計算しよう**か。
   Shall I calculate the proceeds of the bazaar?

6.3 | Vvol + **to omou** と思う | "I think I'll do ~"

Vvol *to omou* expresses the speaker's thoughts about doing something.

EXAMPLES:

1. Rainen atarashii kuruma o **kaō** to omou.
   来年新しい車を**買おう**と思う。
   I think I'll buy a new car next year.

2. Kono shigoto o **yameyō** to omou.
   この仕事を**辞めよう**と思う。
   I think I'll quit this job.

3. Tomodachi o Tanaka-sensei ni **shōkai shiyō** to omoi-masu.
   友達を田中先生に**紹介しよう**と思います。
   I think I'll introduce my friend to Prof. Tanaka.

6.4 | Vvol + **to suru** (1) とする | "try to do ~"

Vvol *to suru* expresses a person's effort to do something (often unsuccessfully).

EXAMPLES:

1. Wakai otoko ga jitensha o **nusumō** to shimashita.
   若い男が自転車を**盗もう**としました。
   A young man tried to steal a bicycle.

2. Ani ni kuruma o **kariyō** to shimashita ga dame deshita.
   兄に車を**借りよう**としましたが駄目でした。
   I tried to borrow the car from my older brother but didn't succeed.

146

3. Akira wa itsumo Masao to **kyōsō shiyō** to shimasu.
明はいつも正男と**競争しよう**とします。

Akira always tries to compete with Masao (without success).

6.5 | **Vvol + to suru (2) とする** | "be about to do ~"

Vvol *to suru* expresses in a conditional clause an action which is about to take place.

EXAMPLES:

1. Densha ni **norō** to suru to, doa ga shimarimashita.
電車に**乗ろう**とすると、ドアが閉まりました。

Just as I was about to get on a train, the doors were closed.

2. Shokuji o **hajimeyō** to suru to, denwa ga narimashita.
食事を**始めよう**とすると、電話が鳴りました。

Just as I was about to start the meal, the telephone rung.

3. **Gaishutsu shiyō** to suru to, itsumo dare ka kuru.
外出しようとすると、いつもだれか来る。

Just as I'm about to go out, someone always comes.

PRACTICE 29 (6.1–6.5)

A. Change the following phrases into the volitional form.

1. kabe of shiroku nuru 壁を白く塗る paint the wall white
2. shiai o chūshi suru 試合を中止する call off the game
3. nimotsu o todokeru 荷物を届ける deliver baggage
4. Fuji-san ni noboru 富士山に登る climb Mt. Fuji

B. Fill in the blanks with the appropriate forms of the verbs given at the end of the sentences.

1. Ofisu o _____ to suru to, fakkusu ga _____ mashita. (deru) (hairu)

   オフィスを _____ とすると、ファックスが _____ ました。（出る）（入る）

   Just as I was about to leave the office, a fax came in.

2. Kyō toshokan e hon o _____ to omoimasu. (kaesu)

   今日図書館へ本を _____ と思います。（返す）

   I think I'll return the books to the library today.

3. Kodomo wa inu o _____ to shimashita. (oyo-gaseru)

   子供は犬を _____ としました。（泳がせる）

   The child tried to make the dog swim.

4. Kore wa watashi ga kachō ni _____ ka. (hōkoku suru)

   これは私が課長に _____ か。（報告する）

   Shall I report this to the section chief?

5. Nedan ga _____ ba sugu _____ . (agaru) (uru)

   値段が _____ ばすぐ _____ 。（上がる）（売る）

   If the price goes up, I'll sell it right away.

7 Te Form

Te form (Vte)

Regular I Verb (cf. pp. 23–28)	Regular II Verb (Verb stem + te)	Irregular Verb
kaite 書いて (write) hanashite 話して (speak) shinde 死んで (die) matte 待って (wait)	shirabete 調べて (check) ite いて (be, stay)	kite 来て (check) shite して (do)

SENTENCE PATTERNS

7.1 | **Vte (1) 〜て (cf. 1.7)** | "and," "do ~ and"

Vte is used as a conjunction to link two or more actions or events.

EXAMPLES:

1. Kami de hikōki o **tsukutte** tobasu.
   紙で飛行機を**作って**飛ばす。

   I make airplanes with paper and fly them.

2. Meguro de densha o **orite** gakkō made arukimasu.
   目黒で電車を**降りて**学校まで歩きます。

   I get off the train at Meguro and walk to school.

3. Ie o **sōji shite** kaimono ni ikimashita.
   家を**掃除して**買い物に行きました。

   I cleaned the house and went shopping.

7.2 | Vte (2) ～て | "do ~, so ~," "because"

Vte expresses the reason for or the cause of the action or event in the main clause.

EXAMPLES:

1. Ame ga **futte** tsuri ni ikemasen deshita.
   雨が**降って**釣りに行けませんでした。
   It rained, so we couldn't go fishing.

2. Kare wa **hatarakisugite** byōki ni narimashita.
   彼は**働きすぎて**病気になりました。
   He became ill, because he worked too hard.

3. Tomodachi ga **kite** issho ni bīru o nomimashita.
   友達が**来て**一緒にビールを飲みました。
   My friend came, so we drank beer together.

7.3 | Vte (3) ～て | "-ing," "-ed"

Vte expresses how an action is performed.

EXAMPLES:

1. Kesa **isoide** uchi o demashita.
   今朝**急いで**うちを出ました。
   I left home in a hurry this morning.

2. Kare wa sofa ni **nete** hon o yomu.
   彼はソファに**寝て**本を読む。
   Lying on the sofa, he reads books.

3. Kankyaku wa **kiritsu shite** hakushu shimashita.
観客は**起立して**拍手しました。

The audience stood up and clapped their hands.

7.4 | Vte + kudasai 〜てください (cf. 3.9) | "Please do ~"

Vte *kudasai* expresses a request.

EXAMPLES:

1. Kono shigoto o **tetsudatte** kudasai.
この仕事を**手伝って**ください。

Please help me with this work.

2. Gakusei ni tenrankai ni iku yō ni **susumete** kudasai.
学生に展覧会に行くように**勧めて**ください。

Please encourage the students to go to the exhibition.

3. Ashita no gozenchū ni kanarazu **renraku shite** kudasai.
明日の午前中に必ず**連絡して**ください。

Please contact me tomorrow morning without fail.

7.5 | Vte + iru (1) 〜ている | "be doing ~"

Vte *iru* expresses an action in progress.

EXAMPLES:

1. Haruko-san wa uta o **utatte** iru.
春子さんは歌を**歌って**いる。

Haruko is singing a song.

2. Sensei ga gakusei ni kanji o **kakasete** imasu.

先生が学生に漢字を**書かせて**います。

A teacher is making students write kanji.

3. Sumisu-sensei wa Nihon bungaku o **kenkyū shite** imasu.

スミス先生は日本文学を**研究して**います。

Prof. Smith is studying Japanese literature.

7.6 | **Vte + iru (2) 〜ている** | "be -ed," "be -ing"

In contrast to Vte *iru* (1), which expresses an ongoing action, Vte *iru* (2) expresses a state of being resulting from a prevous action. Typical Japanese verbs that use this form are *shiru* 知る (learn, realize or know), *motsu* 持つ (possess) and *oboeru* 覚える (remember). In this Vte *iru* form, these verbs indicate states of "knowing," "possessing" or "remembering," usually represented in English by, in the first person, "I know" "I have" and "I remember." Note that the opposite of *shitteiru* is *shiranai* (not *shitte inai*).

EXAMPLES:

1. Ginkō wa sanji made **aite** iru.

銀行は三時まで**開いて**いる。

The bank is open until three o'clock.

2. Toda-san wa akai doresu o **kite** imasu.

戸田さんは赤いドレスを**着て**います。

Ms. Toda is wearing a red dress.

3. Hara-san wa **kekkon shite** iru.

原さんは**結婚して**いる。

Mr. Hara is married.

7.7 | Vte + aru 〜てある (cf. 7.6) | "be -ed"

Like Vte *iru* (2), Vte *aru* expresses a state of being resulting from a previous action. In this form, only transitive verbs are used and the subject of the sentence is always inanimate. In the Vte *aru* form, there is an implication that someone did the action, therefore the resulting state exists. On the other hand, in the Vte *iru* form, there is no such implication but a mere description of fact.

EXAMPLES:

1. Kono taoru wa **tsukatte** arimasu.
   このタオルは**使って**あります。
   This towel has been used.

2. Kyōshitsu no doa ga **shimete** aru.
   教室のドアが**閉めて**ある。
   The door of the classroom is closed.

3. Kono terebi wa **shūri shite** arimasu.
   このテレビは**修理して**あります。
   This TV set has been repaired.

PRACTICE 30 (7.1–7.7)

A. Make the *te* form of the following verbs.

1. kiku 聞く hear   2. narau 習う learn   3 wakaru 分かる understand
4. asobu 遊ぶ play   5. kuru 来る come   6. naosu 直す correct
7. junbi suru 準備する prepare   8. oriru 降りる get off

B. Fill in the blanks with the appropriate forms of the verbs given at the end of the sentences.

1. Mado ga _____ imasu. _____ kudasai. (aku)
   (shimeru)
   窓が _____ います。_____ ください。(開く)(閉める)
   The window is open. Please close it.

2. Wada-san wa _____ repōto o _____ imasu.
   (isogu) (kakinaosu)
   和田さんは _____ レポートを _____ います。(急ぐ)
   (書き直す)
   Miss Hara is rewriting the report in a hurry.

3. Kono heya wa _____ arimasu ka. (sōji suru)
   この部屋は _____ ありますか。(掃除する)
   Has this room been cleaned?

4. Zasshi wa hako ni _____, shinbun wa _____
   kudasai. (ireru) (suteru)
   雑誌は箱に _____、新聞は _____ ください。(入れる)
   (捨てる)
   Please put the magazines in the box and throw the newspapers away.

5. Shinjuku de eiga o _____, kaeri ni hon'ya ni
   _____ mashita. (miru) (yoru)
   新宿で映画を _____、帰りに本屋に _____ ました。
   (見る)(寄る)
   I saw a movie in Shinjuku and on the way back I stopped by a
   bookstore.

6. Yūbe osoku made _____, kesa hayaku _____
   masen deshita. (benkyō suru) (okiru)
   ゆうべ遅くまで _____、今朝早く _____ ませんでし
   た。(勉強する)(起きる)

I studied until late last night, so I could not get up early this morning.

7.8 | Vte + kara 〜てから | "after doing ~," "since doing ~"

Vte *kara* expresses the time relationship (after/since) between actions or events.

EXAMPLES:

1. Kono apāto ni **utsutte** kara sannen ni naru.
   このアパートに**移って**から三年になる。
   It's been three years since I moved into this apartment.

2. Shukudai o **sumasete** kara asobinasai.
   宿題を**済ませて**から遊びなさい。
   Play after you finish your homework.

3. Watashi wa daigaku o **sotsugyō shite** kara ginkō de hataraku tsumori desu.
   私は大学を**卒業して**から銀行で働くつもりです。
   I intend to work in a bank after graduating from college.

7.9 | Vte + **bakari iru** 〜てばかりいる | "be doing nothing but"

Vte *bakari iru* expresses the only action that a person is doing.

EXAMPLES:

1. Tonari no otoko no ko wa ichinichijū hāmonika o **fuite** bakari iru.
   隣の男の子は一日中ハーモニカを**吹いて**ばかりいる。
   The boy next door does nothing but play a harmonica all day long.

2. Yoshiko-san wa shigoto o **kaete** bakari imasu.
良子さんは仕事を**変えて**ばかりいます。

Yoshiko does nothing but change jobs.

3. Mizuki-san wa dōryō to **giron shite** bakari iru.
水木さんは同僚と**議論して**ばかりいる。

Mr. Mizuki does nothing but argue with his colleagues.

7.10 | **Vte + hoshii 〜てほしい** | "want (someone) to do ~"

Vte *hoshii* expresses a desire to have someone (marked by the particle *ni*) do something. This someone is not supposed to be higher in status than the speaker. This pattern is used with the first person in declarative sentences (Example 1) and with the second person in interrogative sentences (Example 2).

EXAMPLES:

1. Watashi wa Minami-san ni kono tegami o **yonde** hoshii.
私は南さんにこの手紙を**読んで**ほしい。

I want Miss Minami to read this letter.

2. Anata wa dare ni Nihongo o **oshiete** hoshii desu ka.
あなたはだれに日本語を**教えて**ほしいですか。

Who do you want to teach you Japanese?

3. Hoteru no yoyaku o **kakunin shite** hoshii desu.
ホテルの予約を**確認して**ほしいです。

I want you to confirm the reservation at the hotel.

Fill in the blanks with the appropriate forms of the verbs provided at the end of the sentences.

1. Kare wa kōto o _____ kara isu ni _____ mashita. (nugu) (suwaru)

   彼はコートを_____ からいすに _____ ました。(脱ぐ)（座る）

   After taking off his coat, he sat down on the chair.

2. Kore o _____ kara mina ni _____ kudasai. (yomu) (mawasu)

   これを_____ から皆に _____ ください。（読む）（回す）

   After you read this, please pass it around to everybody.

3. Toshokan e hon o _____ ni _____ hoshii. (kaesu) (iku)

   図書館へ本を _____ に _____ ほしい。（返す）（行く）

   I want you to go to the library to return the books.

4. Kono inu wa nani mo _____ nai de _____ bakari imasu. (taberu) (neru)

   この犬は何も _____ ないで _____ ばかりいます。（食べる）（寝る）

   This dog does nothing but sleep, without eating anything.

5. Shōjo wa shitsumon ni _____ zu ni _____ bakari imashita. (kotaeru) (naku)

   少女は質問に _____ ずに _____ ばかりいました。（答える）（泣く）

   The girl was doing nothing but weeping without answering questions.

7.11 | **Vte + mo ～ても** | "even if," "although"

Vte *mo* is used as a conjunction to express a condition.

EXAMPLES:

1. Hiroshi wa sankōsho o **katte** mo tsukaimasen.
   宏は参考書を**買って**も使いません。
   Hiroshi doesn't use reference books, even if he buys them.

2. Kono kotoba wa jisho de **shirabete** mo wakarimasen deshita.
   この言葉は辞書で**調べて**も分かりませんでした。
   Although I checked this word in the dictionary, I couldn't understand it.

3. Kare wa **yakusoku shite** mo mamoranai.
   彼は**約束して**も守らない。
   Even if he promises, he doesn't keep it.

7.12 | **Vte + mo ii ～てもいい (cf. 3.33)** | "It is all right if," "may"

Vte *mo* ii expresses permission or concession.

EXAMPLES:

1. Koko de wa tabako o **sutte** mo ii desu.
   ここではたばこを**吸って**もいいです。
   It is all right if you smoke here.

2. Koko ni kuruma o **tomete** mo ii desu ka.
   ここに車を**止めて**もいいですか。
   May I park the car here?

158

3. Kono kisoku wa **haishi shite** mo ii to omou.
   この規則は**廃止して**もいいと思う。

   I think that we can abolish this regulation.

7.13 | Vte + **mo** + Vnakute mo 〜ても〜なくても |

"whether or not"

Vte *mo* Vnakute *mo* expresses a condition with a set of affirmative and negative verb forms. The second verb may be affirmative if it has an opposite meaning to the first verb (Example 3).

EXAMPLES:

1. Ame ga **futte** mo **furanakute** mo iku.
   雨が**降って**も**降らなくて**も行く。

   I'll go whether it rains or not.

2. Kono shigoto wa **tanomarete** mo **tanomarenakute** mo watashi ga yaru.
   この仕事は**頼まれて**も**頼まれなくて**も私がやる。

   I myself will do this work whether asked or not.

3. Honda-san ga kaigi ni **shusseki shite** mo **kesseki shite** mo kamaimasen.
   本田さんが会議に**出席して**も**欠席して**もかまいません。

   It doesn't matter whether Mr. Honda attends the meeting or not.

7.14 | Vte + wa ikenai 〜てはいけない |

"It is not all right if," "must not"

Vte *wa ikenai* expresses prohibition. *Ikemasen* is the polite style. The verb *komaru* 困る (be problematic) may be used in place of *ikenai*.

EXAMPLES:

1. Rōka o **hashitte** wa ikenai.
   廊下を**走って**はいけない。

   You must not run in the corridor.

2. Shukudai o **wasurete** wa komarimasu.
   宿題を**忘れて**は困ります。

   You must not forget your homework.

3. Kare no kotoba o **gokai shite** wa ikemasen.
   彼の言葉を**誤解して**はいけません。

   You must not misunderstand his words.

PRACTICE 32 (7.11–7.14)

A. Change the following phrases into the ~ *te mo ii desu ka* and ~ *te wa ikemasen* forms.

1. enpitsu de kaku 鉛筆で書く write in pencil
2. jugyō ni okureru 授業に遅れる be late for class
3. terebi o kesu テレビを消す turn off the TV
4. shinbun o suteru 新聞を捨てる throw away newspapers
5. kaigi o enki suru 会議を延期する postpone a meeting.

B. Fill in the blanks with the appropriate forms of the verbs given at the end of the sentences.

1. Kono inu wa _____ mo konai. (yobu)
   この犬は _____ も来ない。（呼ぶ）

   This dog doesn't come, even if I call him.

2. Denwa o _____ mo _____ nakute mo ryōkin o
   harawanakereba naranai. (tsukau)
   電話を _____ も _____ なくても料金を払わなければ
   ならない。（使う）

   You have to pay the fee whether you use the telephone or not.

3. Tsuyoi kaze ga _____ mo kono ki wa taorenai deshō.
   (fuku)
   強い風が _____ もこの木は倒れないでしょう。（吹く）

   Even if a strong wind blows, this tree won't fall down.

4. Kono kawa de _____ mo ii desu ka. (oyogu)
   この川で _____ もいいですか。（泳ぐ）

   May I swim in this river?

5. Mō kaigi ga _____ iru kara, ano heya ni _____ wa
   ikemasen. (hajimaru) (hairu)
   もう会議が_____ いるから、あの部屋に _____ は
   いけません。（始まる）（入る）

   Since the meeting has already begun, you must not enter that room.

7.15 | **Vte + ageru ～てあげる** | "do something for someone"

Vte *ageru* expresses a person's doing a favorable action for some-one whose status is about equal to that of the doer (Example 1). Vte *sashiageru* is used for someone whose status is higher than that of the doer (Example 2). Vte *yaru* is used for someone whose status is lower than that of the doer or who is a close friend of the doer. The verbs *ageru* あげる, *sashiageru* さしあげる and *yaru* やる (give) are used as auxiliaries. The indirect object (the receiver of the favorable action marked by the particle *ni*) cannot be the first person.

EXAMPLES:

1. Watashi wa Haruko-san ni konsāto no kippu o **katte agemashita.**

   私は春子さんにコンサートの切符を**買って**あげました。

   I bought a concert ticket for Haruko.

2. Watashi wa sensei ni shashin o **misete** sashiagemashita.

   私は先生に写真を**見せて**さしあげました。

   I showed the photos to my teacher.

3. Watashi wa imōto ni **sentaku shite** yarimashita.

   私は妹に**洗濯して**やりました。

   I washed clothes for my younger sister.

7.16 | Vte + morau ～てもらう

"have someone do something"

Vte *morau* indicates that a person receives a favorable action from someone whose status is about equal to or lower than that of the receiver. Vte *itadaku* is used when the favorable action comes from someone whose status is higher than that of the receiver (Example 2). The verbs *morau* もらう and *itadaku* いただく (receive) are used as auxiliaries. The indirect object (the doer of the favorable action marked by the particle *ni*) cannot be the first person.

EXAMPLES:

1. Toda-san wa tokidoki Ogawa-san ni kuruma o **aratte** morau.

   戸田さんは時々小川さんに車を**洗って**もらう。

   Miss Toda sometimes has Mr. Ogawa wash the car for her.

2. Watashi-tachi wa Takagi-sensei ni kanji o **oshiete** itadakimasu.

   私達は高木先生に漢字を**教えて**いただきます。

   We have Prof. Takagi teach us kanji. (Prof. Takagi teaches us kanji.)

3. Watashi wa tomodachi ni machi o **annai shite** moraimashita.

   私は友達に町を**案内して**もらいました。

   I had my friend show me the town.

7.17 | Vte + kureru ～てくれる

"do something (for me or someone)"

Vte *kureru* indicates that someone is doing a favorable action for the speaker (the first person) or someone who is close to the speaker. Vte *kudasaru* is used when the status of the doer of the favorable action is higher than that of the receiver (Example 3). The verbs *kureru* くれる and *kudasaru* くださる (give) are used as auxiliaries.

EXAMPLES:

1. Tokidoki ane ga (watashi ni) kukkī o **yaite** kureru.

   時々姉が（私に）クッキーを**焼いて**くれる。

   Once in a while my older sister bakes cookies for me.

2. Dare ga (anata ni) sono nyūsu o **shirasete** kuremashita ka.
   だれが（あなたに）そのニュースを**知らせて**くれましたか。
   Who informed you of that news?

3. Hara-sensei ga (watashi-tachi ni) jisho no tsukaikata
   o **setsumei shite** kudasaimashita.
   原先生が（私達に）辞書の使い方を**説明して**くださいま
   した。
   Prof. Hara explained to us how to use the dictionary.

Complete the following sentences with the verbs provided.

1. Watashi wa tomodachi no nimotsu o _____ . (hakobu)
   私は友達の荷物を _____ 。（運ぶ）
   I carried my friend's baggage (for him).

2. Tomu wa sensei ni Nihongo no tegami o _____ .
   (yakusu)
   トムは先生に日本語の手紙を _____ 。（訳す）
   Tom had his teacher translate the letter written in Japanese for him.

3. Kimura-san wa otōto ni kuruma o _____ . (kasu)
   木村さんは弟に車を _____ 。（貸す）
   Mr. Kimura lent his car to my younger brother.

4. Watashi wa Masako-san ni hitoban heya ni _____
   tsumori desu. (tomeru)
   私は正子さんに一晩部屋に _____ つもりです。（泊める）
   I intend to have Masako put me up in her room overnight.

5. Watashi wa imōto no shigoto o _____. (tetsudau)

私は妹の仕事を _____。（手伝う）

I helped my younger sister with her work.

6. Tanaka-sensei ga sakubun o _____. (naosu)

田中先生が作文を _____。（直す）

Prof. Tanaka corrected my composition (for me).

7. Watashi wa sensei ni denwachō de denwa bangō o _____. (shiraberu)

私は先生に電話帳で電話番号を _____。（調べる）

I checked the phone number in the phone book for my teacher.

7.18 | Vte + iru toki (ni) 〜ている時（に） | "when ~ doing ~"

Vte *iru toki (ni)* expresses the time when an action or event is/was taking place. *Toki* 時 (time) is used as a pseudo noun and functions as a conjunction. The tense of the sentence is determined by the verb in the main clause.

EXAMPLES:

1. Watashi ga Yamada-san to **hanashite** iru toki (ni), kozutsumi ga todokimashita.

私が山田さんと**話して**いる時（に）、小包が届きました。

While I was talking with Mrs. Yamada, a package arrived.

2. Asagohan o **tabete** iru toki (ni), denwa ga narimashita.

朝ご飯を**食べて**いる時（に）、電話が鳴りました。

While I was eating breakfast, the telephone rung.

3. Kare wa itsumo watashi ga **benkyō shite** iru toki (ni) kuru.

彼はいつも私が**勉強して**いる時（に）、来る。

He always comes when I am studying.

7.19 | **Vte + iru aida (ni) ～ている間（に）** | "while ~ doing ~"

Vte *iru aida (ni)* expresses the time during which an action or event is/was taking place. *Aida* without *ni* indicates that the two actions or events in the main clause and subordinate clause (the *aida*-clause) cover the same span of time (Examples 1, 2). *Aida* with *ni* indicates that an action or event in the main clause occurs within the time span of an action or event in the *aida*-clause (Example 3).

EXAMPLES:

1. Samu wa sensei ga **hanashite** iru aida hon o yonde imashita.

サムは先生が**話して**いる間本を読んでいました。

Sam was reading a book while the teacher was talking.

2. Kodomo ga ehon **mite** iru aida watashi wa kēki o yaite imashita.

子供が絵本を**見て**いる間私はケーキを焼いていました。

I was baking a cake while my child was looking at a picture book.

3. Kida-san ga **shutchō shite** iru aida ni o-tōsan ga naku-narimashita.

木田さんが**出張して**いる間にお父さんが亡くなりました。

While Mr. Kida was on a business trip, his father passed away.

7.20 **Vte iru uchi ni ～ているうちに** (cf. 7.19)

"while ~ doing ~"

Vte *iru uchi ni* expresses the time during which an action or event is/was taking place. This pattern may be replaced by Vte *iru aida ni*.

EXAMPLES:

1. Kare o **matte** iru uchi ni kanji o oboemashita.
   彼を**待って**いるうちに漢字を覚えました。
   I memorized kanji while waiting for him.

2. Kodomo ga **nete** iru uchi ni hon o yomu.
   子供が**寝て**いるうちに本を読む。
   I read books while my child is sleeping.

3. **Sanpo shite** iru uchi ni ame ga furihajimemashita.
   散歩しているうちに雨が降り始めました。
   It started to rain while I was taking a stroll.

7.21 **Vte iru/aru + noun** (cf. 2.35)   to make a relative clause

In the Vte *iru/aru* + noun pattern, Vte *iru/aru* is used as a modifier of the following noun, e.g. *asonde iru kodomo* 遊んでいる子供 (a child who is playing); *hako ni irete aru hon* 箱に入れてある本 (the books put in the box).

EXAMPLES:

1. Asoko ni **tatte** iru hito wa dare desu ka.
   あそこに**立って**いる人はだれですか。
   Who is the person standing over there?

2. Ano megane o **kakete** iru otoko no hito ga watashi-tachi no sensei desu.

あの眼鏡を**かけ**ている男の人が私達の先生です。

That man who is wearing glasses is our teacher.

3. **Shūri shite** aru terebi wa asoko ni oite aru.

修理してあるテレビはあそこにおいてある。

The TV sets which have been repaired have been put over there.

Fill in the blanks with the appropriate forms of the verbs provided at the end of the sentences.

1. Kōgi o _____ uchi ni nemuku narmashita. (kiku)

講義を _____ うちに眠くなりました。(聞く)

I became sleepy while listening to the lecture.

2. Ano chairo no zubon o _____ hito ga buchō desu. (haku)

あの茶色のズボンを _____ 人が部長です。(はく)

The person who is wearing brown trousers is the department head.

3. Sono jiko wa _____ toki ni okorimashita. (jikken suru)

その事故は _____ 時に起こりました。(実験する)

The accident occurred when we were doing an experiment.

4. Asoko ni _____ kuruma wa dare no desu ka. (tomeru)

あそこに _____ 車はだれのですか。(止める)

Whose car is it that's been parked over there?

168

5. Watashi ga piano _____ aida haha wa jitto kiite imashita. (hiku)

私がピアノを _____ 間母はじっと聞いていました。（弾く）

While I was playing the piano, my mother was listening intently.

6. Tomodachi ga Amerika ni _____ aida ni asobi ni ikitai. (ryūgaku suru)

友達がアメリカに _____ 間に遊びに行きたい。（留学する）

I want to go to visit my friend while she is studying in America.

7. Ame ga _____ uchi ni dekakemashō. (yamu)

雨が _____ うちに出かけましょう。（やむ）

Let's go out while the rain is stopped.

8. _____ shītsu wa dore desu ka. (arau)

_____ シーツはどれですか。（洗う）

Which sheets are the ones that have been washed?

7.22 | **Vte + miru 〜てみる** | "do ~ and see," "try to do ~"

Vte *miru* expresses a person's attempt at doing something to see what it is like. The verb *miru* みる (see) is used as an auxiliary.

EXAMPLES:

1. Akira wa hajimete bīru o **nonde** mimashita.

明は始めてビールを**飲んで**みました。

Akira drunk beer for the first time (to see what it is like).

2. Rainen ano yama o kuruma de **koete** mimasu.
   来年あの山を車で**超えて**みます。

   I'll try to cross that mountain by car next year.

3. Kono keikaku o **jikkō shite** miru tsumori da.
   この計画を**実行して**みるつもりだ。

   I intend to try to put this plan into practice.

7.23 | **Vte + iku 〜ていく** |　　"go on ~ ing," "become," "grow"

Vte *iku* expresses an action which goes away from the location of
the speaker or moves into the future. The verb *iku* いく (go) is used
as an auxiliary.

EXAMPLES:

1. Tori ga **tonde** iku.
   鳥が**飛んで**いく。

   Birds are flying away.

2. Dorobō ga achira e **nigete** ikimashita.
   泥棒があちらへ**逃げて**いきました。

   The thief escaped in that direction.

3. Kono machi wa **henka shite** iku deshō.
   この町は**変化して**いくでしょう。

   This town probably will go on changing.

7.24 | Vte + kuru ～てくる | "come about," "begin to," "grow"

Vte *kuru* expresses an action which comes toward the location of the speaker or up to a current point of time. The verb *kuru* くる (come) is used as an auxiliary.

EXAMPLES:

1. Kyū ni tsuyoi kaze ga **fuite** kimashita.
   急に強い風が**吹いて**きました。
   Suddenly a strong wind began to blow.

2. Ōkii hako ga kaigan ni **nagarete** kimashita.
   大きい箱が海岸に**流れて**きました。
   A big box drifted to the seashore.

3. Niwa no wakagi ga **seichō shite** kimashita.
   庭の若木が**成長して**きました。
   The young trees in the garden have grown.

7.25 | Vte + oku ～ておく | "do something in advance"

Vte *oku* expresses an action which is performed in advance for future convenience. The verb *oku* おく (put) is used as an auxiliary.

EXAMPLES:

1. Tomodachi ga kuru kara, o-kashi o **katte** oku.
   友達が来るから、お菓子を**買って**おく。
   Because my friends are coming, I'll buy some sweets.

2. Kaigi ga hajimaru mae ni mō ichido shorui o **shirabete** okimashita.

会議が始まる前にもう一度書類を**調べて**おきました。

Before the meeting began, I had checked the document once more.

3. Kore wa nedan ga agaranai uchi ni, sugu **chūmon shite** okimashō.

これは値段が上がらないうちに、すぐ**注文して**おきましょう。

Let's order this right away, before the price goes up.

7.26 | **Vte + shimau 〜てしまう** | "have done," "finish doing 〜"

Vte *shimau* expresses with emphasis the completion of an action and, in some cases, may imply a sense of regret for an action being totally completed (Example 2). The verb *shimau* しまう (finish or put away) is used as an auxiliary.

EXAMPLES:

1. Sono koto wa mō sensei ni **hanashite** shimaimashita.

そのことはもう先生に**話して**しまいました。

I have already spoken to my teacher about that matter.

2. Jimu wa sengetsu gakkō o **yamete** shimaimashita.

ジムは先月学校を**辞めて**しまいました。

Jim quit school last month (to my regret).

3. Raigetsujū ni kono purojekuto o **kansei shite** shimaō to omou.

来月中にこのプロジェクトを**完成して**しまおうと思う。

I think that I will finish up this project within the next month.

A. Complete the following sentences with the verbs provided.

1. Ashita shiken ga aru kara, konban _____ .
   (fukushū suru)
   明日試験があるから、今晩 _____。（復習する）
   Since I have an examination tomorrow, I'll review the lessons tonight.

2. Kare wa itsumo pātī de _____. (nomisugiru)
   彼はいつもパーティーで _____。（飲みすぎる）
   He always drinks too much at a party (to my regret).

3. Sora ga dandan _____. (hareru)
   空がだんだん _____。（晴れる）
   The sky has gradually cleared up.

4. Atarashii kamera o _____. (tsukau)
   新しいカメラを _____。（使う）
   I used the new camera (to see how it would work).

5. Kono ki wa kore kara _____. (sodatsu)
   この木はこれから _____。（育つ）
   This tree will grow from now on.

6. Watashi wa hitoban de sono shōsetsu o _____ .
   (yomu)
   私は一晩でその小説を _____。（読む）
   I finished reading that novel in one night.

7. Sensei ga kuru mae ni kokuban o _____. (kesu)
   先生が来る前に黒板を _____。（消す）
   I erased the blackboard before the teacher came (for his convenience).

B. Fill in the blanks with the appropriate forms of the verbs given at the end of the sentences.

1. Shukudai o _____, sensei ni _____ shimai-mashita. (wasureru) (shikaru)

   宿題を _____、先生に _____ しまいました。(忘れる)(叱る)

   I forgot my homework and was scolded by my teacher.

2. Kodomo ga soto de _____ iru uchi ni heya o _____ okimasu. (asobu) (katazukeru)

   子供が外で _____ いるうちに部屋を _____ おきます。(遊ぶ)(片付ける)

   I will clean up the room while my children are playing outside.

3. Oya ga _____ mo kono shigoto o _____ miru tsumori desu. (hantai suru) (yaru)

   親が _____ もこの仕事を _____ みるつもりです。(反対する)(やる)

   Even if my parents object, I intend to do this work (and see what will happen).

4. Kare wa yoku _____ iru kara, dandan seiseki ga _____ iku darō. (ganbaru) (agaru)

   彼はよく _____ いるから、だんだん成績が _____ いくだろう。(頑張る)(上がる)

   Because he is doing his best, his grades will gradually go up.

5. Kanojo wa takusan _____ nai noni _____ kimashita. (taberu) (futoru)

   彼女はたくさん _____ ないのに _____ きました。(食べる)(太る)

   Although she doesn't eat a lot, she has become heavier.

(8) Ta Form

Ta form (Vta)

Regular I Verb (cf. pp.23–28)	Regular II Verb (Verb stem + ta)	Irregular Verb
oyoida 泳いだ (swim) hanashita 話した (speak) tonda 飛んだ (fly) totta 取った (take)	oboeta 覚えた (memorize) sugita 過ぎた (pass by)	kita 来た (come) shita した (do)

SENTENCE PATTERNS

8.1 ｜ **Vta 〜た (cf. 2.1)** ｜ "did," "there was"

Vta is the past tense of Vdic and expresses actions or states which have taken place/took place or existed. This form is used for the plain style.

EXAMPLES:

1. Kare wa sono shashin o mite ōkii koe de **waratta**.
   彼はその写真を見て大きい声で笑った。
   Looking at the picture, he laughed loudly.

2. Sensei wa gakusei o mittsu no gurūpu ni **waketa**.
   先生は学生を三つのグループに分けた。
   The teacher divided the students into three groups.

3. Machi no jinkō ga nibai ni **zōka shita**.
   町の人口が二倍に増加した。
   The population of the city increased by two times.

175

8.2 | Vta + **tsumori da** 〜たつもりだ (cf. 2.2)

"be convinced that ~"

Vta *tsumori da* expresses the speaker's conviction about having done something.

EXAMPLES:

1. Sono shorui wa senjitsu Noda-san ni **watashita** tsumori da.

   その書類は先日野田さんに**渡した**つもりだ。

   I'm convinced that I handed the documents to Mr. Noda the other day.

2. Watashi wa Hara-san to no yakusoku no jikan o **kaeta** tsumori datta.

   私は原さんとの約束の時間を**変えた**つもりだった。

   I was convinced that I had changed the appointment time with Miss Hara.

3. Sono ken wa kono mae no kaigi de **hōkoku shita** tsumori desu.

   その件はこの前の会議で**報告した**つもりです。

   I'm convinced that I reported on that matter in the last meeting.

8.3 | Vta + **hazu da** 〜たはずだ (cf. 2.3)

"I expect that ~," "It is expected that ~"

Vta *hazu da* expresses the speaker's feeling or certainty that something took place.

EXAMPLES:

1. Fukeiki de uriage ga **hetta** hazu desu.
不景気で売り上げが**減った**はずです。

It is felt that sales decreased due to the recession.

2. Kare wa sono ban uchi ni **ita** hazu da.
彼はその晩うちに**いた**はずだ。

I expect (I'm quite sure) that he was at home on that night.

3. Tamura-san wa kyonen **intai shita** hazu desu.
田村さんは去年**引退した**はずです。

I am quite sure that Mr. Tamura retired last year.

8.4 | **Vta + darō 〜ただろう (cf. 2.4)** | "probably did"

Vta *darō* expresses the speaker's conjecture about past actions or events.

EXAMPLES:

1. Kimura-san no ryokō no yotei wa mō **kimatta** darō.
木村さんの旅行の予定はもう**決まった**だろう。

Miss Kimura's travel plans have probably been decided by now.

2. Kyonen no jishin de ano tatemono wa **kowareta** deshō.
去年の地震であの建物は**壊れた**でしょう。

That building was probably destroyed by last year's earthquake.

3. Honkon kara no hikōki wa ichijikan mae ni **tōchaku shita** darō.
香港からの飛行機は一時間前に**到着した**だろう。

The plane from Hong Kong probably arrived one hour ago.

A. Make the *ta* form of the following verbs.

1. shinu 死ぬ die   2. suwaru 座る sit down   3. tokeru 溶ける melt
4. tetsudau 手伝う help 5. taosu 倒す knock down
6. saku 咲く bloom   7. sakeru 避ける avoid
8. bōshi suru 防止する prevent

B. Fill in the blanks with the appropriate forms of the verbs given at the end of the sentences.

1. Yoji ni shigoto o _____ te, hayame ni ofisu o
   _____ ta. (owaru) (deru)
   四時に仕事を _____ て、早めにオフィスを _____
   た。（終わる）（出る）
   I finished my work at four o'clock and left the office early.

2. Tegami o _____ ni yūbinkyoku e _____ ta.
   (dasu) (iku)
   手紙を _____ に郵便便局へ _____ た。（出す）（行く）
   I went to the post office to mail letters.

3. Shinamono wa senjitsu _____ hazu desu ga,
   mada _____ masen ka. (okuru) (todoku)
   品物は先日 _____ はずですが、まだ _____ ません
   か。（送る）（届く）
   We are sure that we sent out the article the other day; hasn't it arrived yet?

4. Suzuki-san wa _____ kara ikkagetsu de _____
   ta. (taiin suru) (nakunaru)
   鈴木さんは _____ から一か月で _____ た。（退院
   する）（亡くなる）
   Mrs. Suzuki passed away one month after she left the hospital.

5. Kare wa furui konpyutā o _____ te atarashii no o
_____ darō. (uru) (kau)

彼は古いコンピューターを _____ て新しいのを
_____ だろう。（売る）（買う）

He probably sold his old computer and bought a new one.

6. Sono shōtai o _____ tsumori da ga, mata shōtaijō
ga _____ ta. (kotowaru) (kuru)

その招待を _____ つもりだが、また招待状が
_____ た。（断る）（来る）

I'm sure that I declined the invitation but a letter of invitation
came again.

8.5 | Vta + kamoshirenai 〜たかもしれない (cf. 2.5)

"might have ~"

Vta *kamoshirenai* expresses the speaker's speculation or guess about
past actions or events.

EXAMPLES:

1. Buraun-san wa Ginza de michi ni **mayotta** kamoshirenai.

ブラウンさんは銀座で道に**迷った**かもしれない。

Mr. Brown might have lost his way in Ginza.

2. Tanaka-san wa kyō no yakusoku o **wasureta** kamoshiremasen.

田中さんは今日の約束を**忘れた**かもしれません。

Miss Tanaka might have forgotten today's appointment.

3. Kaisha ga hiyō o **futan shita** kamoshirenai.
会社が費用を**負担した**かもしれない。

The company might have born the expense.

8.6 | Vta + **ni chigainai** 〜たにちがいない (cf. 2.6)

"must have ~," "There is no doubt that ~"

Vta *ni chigainai* expresses with confidence the speaker's guess about past actions or events.

EXAMPLES:

1. Dare ka kono heya de tabako o **sutta** ni chigainai.
だれかこの部屋でたばこを**吸った**にちがいない。

Someone must have been smoking in this room.

2. Nete iru aida ni denki ga **kieta** ni chigai arimasen.
寝ている間に電気が**消えた**にちがいありません。

The electricity must have gone off while I was sleeping.

3. Ano kaisha wa **tōsan shita** ni chigai arimasen.
あの会社は**倒産した**にちがいありません。

There is no doubt that the company went bankrupt.

8.7 | Vta + **no/koto** 〜たの・こと (cf. 2.7) | "that ~ "

Both *no* and *koto* are nominalizers. Vta *no/koto* expresses a noun phrase.

EXAMPLES:

1. Saifu o **otoshita** no/koto ni kizukimasen deshita.
   財布を**落とした**の・ことに気づきませんでした。

   I was not aware that I had lost my wallet.

2. Waga chīmu ga kesshōsen de **maketa** no/koto wa jitsu ni zannen da.
   我がチームが決勝戦で**負けた**の・ことは実に残念だ。

   It is truly regrettable that our team lost in the final game.

3. Keisatsu ga hannin o **taiho shita** no/koto o shitte imasu ka.
   警察が犯人を**逮捕した**の・ことを知っていますか。

   Are you aware that the police arrested the criminal?

PRACTICE 37 (8.5–8.7)

Fill in the blanks with the appropriate forms of the verbs provided at the end of the sentences.

1. Ofisu no doa ga _____ iru. Kare wa mō _____ komo shirenai. (shimaru) (kaeru)
   オフィスのドアが_____いる。彼はもう_____かもしれない。（閉まる）（帰る）

   The door of the office is closed. He might have gone home already.

2. Masako wa shigoto ga _____ kara sūpā ni _____ ni chigainai. (owaru) (yoru)
   正子は仕事が_____からスーパーに_____にちがいない。（終わる）（寄る）

   Masako must have stopped by a supermarket after her work was done.

3. Biru wa seiseki ga _____ te, sensei ni _____ ni chigainai. (sagaru) (chūi suru)

ビルは成績が _____ て、先生に _____ にちがいない。（下がる）（注意する）

There is no doubt that Bill was cautioned by his teacher, because his grades fell.

4. Watashi wa Hayashi-san ga ginkō de _____ nagara hitori de kodomo o _____ no o shiranakatta. (hataraku) (sodateru)

私は林さんが銀行で _____ ながら一人で子供を _____ のを知らなかった。（働く）（育てる）

I didn't know that Mrs. Hayashi raised her child by herself while working at a bank.

8.8 | Vta + koto ga aru ～たことがある (cf. 2.9)

"have done ~," "have had experience doing ~"

Vta *koto ga aru* expresses a person's experience.

EXAMPLES:

1. Watashi wa nando mo Chūgoku e **itta** koto ga aru.
   私は何度も中国へ**行った**ことがある。
   I have been to China many times.

2. Harisu-san wa Tōkyō no daigaku de Eigo o **oshieta** koto ga arimasu.
   ハリスさんは東京の大学で英語を**教えた**ことがあります。
   Ms Harris has taught English at a university in Tokyo.

3. Kare wa yasei dōbutsu no seitai o **kansatsu shita** koto ga aru.

彼は野生動物の生態を観察したことがある。

He has had the experience of observing the life of wild animals.

8.9 | Vta + **tokoro da** 〜たところだ (cf. 2.12)

"have just done ~ "

Vta *tokoro da* expresses an action which has just been completed.

EXAMPLES:

1. Ima repōto o **kakiowatta** tokoro da.
   今レポートを書き終わったところだ。
   I have just finished writing the report.

2. Haha wa kaimono ni **dekaketa** tokoro desu.
   母は買い物に出かけたところです。
   My mother has just left for shopping.

3. Yamamoto-san ikka wa Hokkaidō ni **iten shita** tokoro desu.
   山本さん一家は北海道に移転したところです。
   The Yamamoto family has just moved to Hokkaido.

8.10 | Vta + **hō ga ii** 〜たほうがいい (cf. 3.14)

"had better do ~ " "should"

Vta *hō ga ii* expresses advice to do something.

EXAMPLES:

1. Kuraku naranai uchi ni **kaetta** hō ga ii.
   暗くならないうちに帰ったほうがいい。
   You had better go home before it gets dark.

2. Kono shigoto wa ashita made ni **sumaseta** hō ga ii desu ka.
この仕事は明日までに**済ませた**ほうがいいですか。

Should I finish this work by tomorrow?

3. Kimura-san wa shibaraku **kinshu shita** hō ga ii desu.
木村さんはしばらく**禁酒した**ほうがいいです。

Mr. Kimura had better quit drinking for a while.

8.11 | Vta + **noni** 〜たのに (cf. 2.19)

"although," "in spite of the fact that"

Vta *noni* expresses a past action or event which is followed by a result contrary to expectation.

EXAMPLES:

1. **Ayamatta** noni kare wa mada okotte iru.
謝ったのに彼はまだ怒っている。

Although I apologized to him, he is still angry.

2. Yakusoku no jikan ga **sugita** noni Oda-san wa mada konai.
約束の時間が**過ぎた**のに小田さんはまだ来ない。

Although it is past the appointment time, Mr. Oda hasn't come yet.

3. Kare wa daigaku ni **nyūgaku shita** noni ichinen de yamete shimaimashita.
彼は大学に**入学した**のに一年で辞めてしまいました。

In spite of the fact that he got into college, he quit in one year (to my regret).

Fill in the blanks with the appropriate forms of the verbs provided at the end of the sentences.

1. Tēpu o _____ nagara kotoba o _____ hō ga ii desu yo. (kiku) (oboeru)
   テープを _____ ながら言葉を_____ ほうがいいですよ。(聞く)(覚える)

   You had better memorize words while listening to the tapes.

2. Kodomo wa hirugohan o _____ ni _____ tokoro desu. (taberu) (kaeru)
   子供は昼ご飯を _____ に _____ ところです。(食べる)(帰る)

   My child has just come home to eat lunch.

3. _____ noni niji no densha ni _____ nakatta. (isogu) (maniau)
   _____ のに二時の電車に _____ なかった。(急ぐ)(間に合う)

   Although I hurried, I wasn't in time for the two o'clock train.

4. Sono hito ni _____ koto ga aru ga isshoni _____ koto wa nai. (au) (shokuji suru)
   その人に _____ ことがあるが一緒に _____ ことはない。(会う)(食事する)

   I have met that person but haven't had a meal with him.

5. Ono-san ga _____ koto o mina ni _____ hō ga ii desu. (nyūin suru) (shiraseru)
   小野さんが _____ ことを皆に _____ ほうがいいです。(入院する)(知らせる)

   We had better inform everybody that Mr. Ono has been hospitalized.

8.12 | Vta + (no) + nara 〜た（の）なら (cf. 2.21) |

"if," "if it is the case that"

Vta *(no) nara* expresses a supposition or condition about past actions or events.

EXAMPLES:

1. Heya ga **aita** (no) nara sugu utsuritai.
   部屋が**空いた**（の）ならすぐ移りたい。
   If the room has been vacated, I'd like to move in right away.

2. Benkyō ni **akita** (no) nara sukoshi yasuminasai.
   勉強に**飽きた**（の）なら少し休みなさい。
   If you get tired of studying, take a short break.

3. Ikeda-san ga **kōshō shita** (no) nara banji umaku iku deshō.
   池田さんが**交渉した**（の）なら万事うまく行くでしょう。
   If Mr. Ikeda has conducted the negotiations, everything should go well.

8.13 | Interrogative + (particle) + Vta + ka 〜たか (cf. 2.22) |

"(I don't know/can't tell) when, what, etc."

An interrogative (with or without a particle) followed by Vta *ka* expresses a question about past actions or events embedded in a sentence.

EXAMPLES:

1. Kinō no shiai de dochira ga **katta** ka shiranai.
   昨日の試合でどちらが**勝った**か知らない。
   I don't know which one won yesterday's game.

2. Yūbe Wada-san to nanji ni **wakareta** ka oboete imasen.
ゆうべ和田さんと何時に**別れた**か覚えていません。

I don't remember what time I parted from Mr. Wada last night.

3. Hara-san ga itsu **tenkin shita** ka wakaranai.
原さんがいつ**転勤した**か分からない。

I can't say when Mr. Hara was transferred.

8.14 | **Vta + ka + dō ka** ～たかどうか (cf. 2.23)

"(I don't know/can't tell) whether or not"

Vta *ka dō ka* expresses a question about past actions or events embedded in a sentence.

EXAMPLES:

1. Mō sakura no hana ga **chitta** ka dō ka shirimasen.
もう桜の花が**散った**かどうか知りません。

I don't know whether the cherry blossoms have fallen or not.

2. Kanojo ga kare o **akirameta** ka dō ka shiranai.
彼女が彼を**あきらめた**かどうか知らない。

I don't know whether she gave him up or not.

3. Matsui-san ga atarashii jigyō ni **seikō shita** ka dō ka wakarimasen.
松井さんが新しい事業に**成功した**かどうか分かりません。

I can't tell whether Mr. Matsui has succeeded in his new enterprise.

8.15 Vta + **kara** 〜たから (cf. 2.28) "because," "since," "so"

Vta *kara* expresses a cause or reason for past actions or events personally interpreted by the speaker.

EXAMPLES:

1. Kēki o **tsukutta** kara tabete kudasai.
   ケーキを**作った**から食べてください。
   I made a cake, so please eat it.

2. Ii resutoran o **eranda** kara chūshokukai wa tanoshikatta.
   いいレストランを**選んだ**から昼食会は楽しかった。
   Because we chose a good restaurant, our luncheon (party) was enjoyable.

3. Kare wa tōshi ni **shippai shita** kara gakkari shite imasu.
   彼は投資に**失敗した**からがっかりしています。
   Since he failed in the investment, he is disheartened.

8.16 Vta + **node** 〜たので (cf. 2.29) "because," "since," "so"

Vta *node* expresses a cause or reason for past actions or events presented more objectively, without projecting the speaker's personal opinion.

EXAMPLES:

1. Kuruma no jiko ga **atta** node ano michi wa tōrenai.
   車の事故が**あった**のであの道は通れない。
   Because there was a car accident, you can't go along that road.

2. Kanojo wa **hatarakisugita** node byōki ni narimashita.

   彼女は**働きすぎた**ので病気になりました。

   She worked too hard, so she got sick.

3. Yūbe **teiden shita** node benkyō dekinakatta.

   ゆうべ**停電した**ので勉強出来なかった。

   I couldn't study last night, because we had a power failure.

PRACTICE 39 (8.12–8.16)

Fill in the blanks with the appropriate forms of the verbs provided at the end of the sentences.

1. Kida-san ga _____ no nara watashi wa _____ mo
   ii desu ka. (kuru) (kaeru)

   木田さんが _____ のなら私は _____ もいいですか。
   （来る）（帰る）

   If Mr.Kida has come, may I go home?

2. Kono taoru o _____ kara _____ oite kudasai.
   (tsukau) (arau)

   このタオルを _____ から _____ おいてください。
   （使う）（洗う）

   I used these towels, so please wash them (for the future use).

3. Pasupōto ga _____ node atarashii no o _____
   nakereba narimasen. (kireru) (shinsei suru)

   パスポートが _____ ので新しいのを _____ なければ
   なりません。（切れる）（申請する）

   Since my passport expired, I must apply for a new one.

4. Terebi o _____ nakatta kara doko de jishin ga
_____ ka shiranai. (tsukeru) (okoru)
テレビを _____ なかったからどこで地震が _____ か
知らない。（つける）（起こる）
I didn't turn on the TV, so I don't know where the earthquake occurred.

5. Kyō gakkō o _____ node sono kōgi ga _____ ka
dō ka wakaranai. (yasumu) (aru)
今日学校を _____ のでその講義が _____ かどうか分
からない。（休む）（ある）
Since I was absent from school today, I can't tell whether the lecture was held or not.

8.17 | Vta + rashii 〜たらしい (cf. 2.31)

"seem," "look like," "I heard"

Vta *rashii* expresses the speaker's conjecture about past actions or events based on reliable information.

EXAMPLES:

1. Kinō no arashi de gyosen ga **shizunda** rashii desu.
昨日の嵐で漁船が**沈んだ**らしいです。
I heard that a fishing boat sank due to yesterday's storm.

2. Tomu wa sensei ni **shikarareta** rashii.
トムは先生に**叱られた**らしい。
It seems that Tom was scolded by his teacher.

3. Miki-san wa demo (kōshin) ni **sanka shita** rashii desu.

三木さんはデモ（行進）に**参加した**らしいです。

It looks like Mr. Miki participated in the demonstration (parade).

8.18 | **Vta + sō da 〜たそうだ (cf. 2.32)**

"I hear that ~," "I heard that ~," "People say that ~ "

Vta *sō da* expresses hearsay about past actions or events.

EXAMPLES:

1. Kyūshū de kinō yuki ga **futta** sō da.
   九州で昨日雪が**降った**そうだ。

   I hear that it snowed in Kyushu yesterday.

2. Akiko-san ni onna no akachan ga **umareta** sō desu.
   秋子さんに女の赤ちゃんが**生まれた**そうです。

   I heard that a baby girl was born to Akiko.

3. Hawai de mata kazan ga **bakuhatsu shita** sō da.
   ハワイでまた火山が**爆発した**そうだ。

   People say that a volcano erupted again in Hawaii.

8.19 | **Vta + kashira/kana 〜たかしら・かな (cf. 2.33)**

"I wonder"

Vta *kashira/kana* expresses uncertainty about past actions or events.

EXAMPLES:

1. Ano ko wa neru mae ni ha o **migaita** kashira/kana.
   あの子は寝る前に歯を**磨いた**かしら・かな。

   I wonder if the child brushed his teeth before going to bed.

2. Kare wa seifu kara hojokin ga **moraeta** kashira/kana.
彼は政府から補助金が**貰えた**かしら・かな。

I wonder if he could get a grant from the government.

3. Kanojo wa daigaku no nyūgaku shiken ni **gōkaku shita** kashira/kana.
彼女は大学の入学試験に**合格した**かしら・かな。

I wonder if she passed the entrance examination for the university.

8.20 | **Vta + mama 〜たまま** | "leave as is," "unchanged"

Vta *mama* indicates that the already existing state the subject is in remains unchanged.

EXAMPLES:

1. Kare wa bōshi o **kabutta** mama heya ni haitta.
彼は帽子を**かぶった**まま部屋に入った。

He entered the room with his hat on.

2. Atsui kara mado o **aketa** mama neta.
暑いから窓を**開けた**まま寝た。

Because it was warm, I slept leaving the windows open.

3. Gakusei wa **kiritsu shita** mama sensei no hanashi o kikimashita.
学生は**起立した**まま先生の話を聞きました。

Students listened to the teacher's speech while standing.

8.21 | Vta + ato de ～たあとで (cf. 7.8) | "after doing ~"

Vta *ato de* indicates that an action or event takes place after another action or event has taken place.

EXAMPLES:

1. Honda-san wa Kanada kara **modotta** ato de byōki ni narimashita.
   本田さんはカナダから戻ったあとで病気になりました。
   Miss Honda became ill after she came back from Canada.

2. Kono futatsu o yoku **kurabeta** ato de kochira ni kimeta.
   この二つをよく比べたあとでこちらに決めた。
   After comparing these two thoroughly, I decided on this one.

3. Kare wa kyō no ka o **fukushū shita** ato de ashita no ka o yoshū shimasu.
   彼は今日の課を復習したあとで明日の課を予習します。
   He prepares tomorrow's lessons after reviewing today's lessons.

PRACTICE 40 (8.17–8.21)

Fill in the blanks with the appropriate forms of the verbs provided at the end of the sentences.

1. Neruson-san ga _____ ato de kono kozutsumi ga _____ ta. (kikoku suru) (todoku)
   ネルソンさんが _____ あとでこの小包が _____ た。
   （帰国する）（届く）
   After Mr. Nelson returned to his country, this package arrived.

2. Kutsu o _____ mama kono heya ni _____ wa
   ikemasen. (haku) (hairu)
   くつを _____ ままこの部屋に _____ はいけません。
   （はく）（入る）

   You must not enter this room with your shoes on.

3. Kare wa hikōki ga _____ te, kūkō de nijikan mo
   _____ so desu. (okureru) (matsu)
   彼は飛行機が _____ て、空港で二時間も _____ そう
   です。（遅れる）（待つ）

   The plane was delayed, so he had to wait as long as two hours at
   the airport.

4. Yukiko-san wa kinō saka de _____ te, _____
   rashii desu. (suberu) (korobu)
   雪子さんは昨日坂で _____ て、_____ らしいです。
   （滑る）（転ぶ）

   I heard that Yukiko slipped and fell on the slope yesterday.

5. Yakusoku no jikan ga _____ noni kare wa mada
   konai. Hi o _____ kana. (sugiru) (machigaeru)
   約束の時間が _____ のに彼はまだ来ない。日を
   _____ かな。（過ぎる）（間違える）

   Although it is past the appointment time, he hasn't come yet. I
   wonder if he got the wrong date.

8.22 | **Vta + toki (ni)** 〜た時（に）**(cf. 7.18)** | "when ~ did ~"

Vta *toki (ni)* indicates when an action or event took place.

EXAMPLES:

1. Shōnen wa saifu o **hirotta** toki (ni) sugu keisatsu ni todokemashita.

少年は財布を**拾った**時（に）すぐ警察に届けました。

When the boy picked up the wallet, he took it to the police immediately.

2. Watashi-tachi ga Doitsu ni **ita** toki (ni) chōnan ga umareta.

私達がドイツに**いた**時（に）長男が生まれた。

While we were in Germany, our eldest son was born.

3. Basu ga densha ni **shōtotsu shita** toki (ni) ōku no hito ga shibō shimashita.

バスが電車に**衝突した**時（に）多くの人が死亡しました。

When a bus collided with a train, many people died.

8.23 | **Vta + noun (cf. 2.35, 7.21)** | to make a relative clause

In the Vta + noun pattern, Vta is used as a modifier of the following noun, e.g. *kinō kita hito* 昨日来た人 (a person who came yesterday); *watashi ga yonda hon* 私が読んだ本 (the book which I read).

EXAMPLES:

1. Chichi ga **tsutta** sakana o tabeta.

父が**釣った**魚を食べた。

We ate the fish that our father caught.

2. Kinō **oboeta** kanji o wasurete shimatta.

昨日**覚えた**漢字を忘れてしまった。

I forgot (to my regret) the kanji that I memorized yesterday.

3. Kono kikai o **hatsumei shita** hito ga kaijō ni kite imasu.

この機械を**発明した**人が会場に来ています。

The person who invented this machine is in the assembly hall.

8.24 | **Vta + bakari de naku ~ (mo)** 〜たばかりでなく〜（も）(cf. 2.38)

"not only ~ but also ~ "

Vta *bakari de naku ~ (mo)* expresses two past actions or events in one sentence.

EXAMPLES:

1. Kare wa kusa o **katta** bakari de naku umi e kodomo o tsureteitta.*

彼は草を**刈った**ばかりでなく海へ子供を連れて行った。

He not only mowed the grass but also took his children to the ocean.

Tsureteiku is a compound verb made up of *tsureru* 連れる (take) and *iku* 行く (go). This is used for animate things. For inanimate things, *motteiku* 持って行く is used. These verbs conjugate like the verb *iku*.

2. Arukisugite, ashi ga **tsukareta** bakari de naku nodo mo kawaita.

歩きすぎて、足が**疲れた**ばかりでなく喉も乾いた。

I walked too much, so not only did my feet get tired, but I got thirsty.

3. Jon wa Nihon no daigaku o **sotsugyō shita** bakari de naku Nihon no kaisha ni shūshoku shimashita.

ジョンは日本の大学を**卒業した**ばかりでなく日本の会社に就職しました。

John not only graduated from a Japanese university but also found a job at a Japanese company.

8.25 | Vta + **shi** 〜たし (cf. 2.39)

"not only ~ but also ~ " "and ~"

Vta *shi* expresses two or more past actions or events in one sentence.

EXAMPLES:

1. Natsu ni wa yama ni mo **nobotta** shi, umi de mo oyoi-da.

   夏には山にも**登った**し、海でも泳いだ。

   I not only climbed a mountain but also swam in the ocean during the summer.

2. Taifū de ie mo **tsubureta** shi, hashi mo nagaremashita.

   台風で家も**潰れた**し、橋も流れました。

   Not only were houses destroyed by the tyhoon but also bridges were washed away.

3. Kyō wa sōji mo **shita** shi, sentaku mo **shita** shi, kai-mono mo shita.

   今日は掃除も**した**し、洗濯も**した**し、買い物もした。

   Today I cleaned house, washed clothes, and did some shopping.

PRACTICE 41 (8.22–8.25)

Fill in the blanks with the appropriate forms of the verbs provided at the end of the sentences.

1. Toda-san ni watashi ga Pari de _____ shashin o _____ agemashita. (toru) (miseru)

   戸田さんに私がパリで _____ 写真を _____ あげました。（とる）（見せる）

   I showed Miss Toda the photos that I took in Paris.

2. Kinō no pātī de mukashi no tomodachi ni _____ bakari de naku hoka no hito ni mo _____ ta. (au) (shōkai suru)

昔日のパーティーで昔の友達に _____ ばかりでなく外の人にも _____ た。（会う）（紹介する）

At yesterday's party, I not only met old friends but also was introduced to others.

3. Watashi mo Nobuko-san ga _____ tsuā ni _____ tai. (mōshikomu) (sanka suru)

私も信子さんが _____ ツアーに _____ たい。（申し込む）（参加する）

I also want to join the tour that Nobuko has signed up for.

4. Kore wa umibe no hoteru ni _____ toki ni _____ kai desu. (tomaru) (atsumeru)

これは海辺のホテルに _____ 時に _____ 貝です。（泊まる）（集める）

These are the shells that I collected when I stayed at the seaside hotel.

5. Gaikoku de _____ toki, shinsetsu na hito ga _____ kureta. (komaru) (tasukeru)

外国で _____ 時、親切な人が _____ くれた。（困る）（助ける）

When I was in trouble in a foreign country, a kind person helped me.

9 Tara Form

Tara form (Vtara)

Regular I Verb (cf. pp.23–28)	Regular II Verb (Verb stem + tara)	Irregular Verb
ugoitara 動いたら (move) otoshitara 落としたら (drop) yondara 読んだら (read) kattara 買ったら (buy)	netara 寝たら (sleep) dekitara 出来たら (can)	kitara 来たら (come) shitara したら (do)

SENTENCE PATTERNS

9.1 | **Vtara (1) ～たら (cf. 3.29)** | "if"

Vtara expresses a condition.

EXAMPLES:

1. Jikan ga **attara** asobi ni kite kudasai.
   時間が**あったら**遊びに来てください。
   If there's time, please come to visit me.

2. Mō sukoshi **yasetara** kono sukāto ga hakeru.
   もう少し**痩せたら**このスカートがはける。
   If I lose a little more weight, I can wear this skirt.

3. Dare ka hana o **mottekitara**,* kono kabin ni ikete kudasai.
   だれか花を**持って来たら**、この花びんに生けてください。
   If someone brings some flowers, please arrange them in this vase.

*Mottekuru is a compound verb made up of motsu 持つ (carry or hold) and kuru 来る (come). This is used for inanimate things. For animate things, tsuretekuru 連れて来る is used. These verbs conjugate like the irregular verb kuru.

9.2 | Vtara (2) ～たら | "when," "after"

Vtara indicates that the action or event in the subordinate clause (the *tara*-clause) takes place before the action or event in the main clause.

EXAMPLES:

1. Eki ni **tsuitara** densha ga deta tokoro deshita.
   駅に**着いたら**電車が出たところでした。
   When I arrived at the station, (I found that) the train had just left.

2. Rokuji o **sugitara** uchi e kaeranakereba naranai.
   六時を**過ぎたら**うちへ帰らなければならない。
   When it's six o'clock, I must go home.

3. Kono shigoto o **kansei** shitara, Hawai e iku tsumori desu.
   この仕事を**完成**したら、ハワイへ行くつもりです。
   I intend to go to Hawaii after completing this work.

9.3 | Vtara (3) ～たら | "Why not ~," "How about ~"

Vtara expresses a suggestion or proposal in casual conversation.

EXAMPLES:

1. Kono kēki o futatsu ni **kittara**.
   このケーキを二つに**切ったら**。
   How about cutting this cake in two?

2. Mō iranai (no) nara **sutetara**.
   もう要らない（の）なら**捨てたら**。
   If you don't need it any more, why not throw it away?

3. **Sono shoku ni ōboshitara.**

その職に**応募したら**。

Why not apply for that job?

A. Make the *tara* form of the following verbs.

1. hakaru 計る measure　　2. hiku 引く pull　　3. kayou 通う commute
4. hareru 腫れる swell　　　5. fukumu 含む contain
6. nareru 慣れる get used to　7. oreru 折れる break
8. shidō suru 指導する lead

B. Fill in the blanks with the appropriate form of the verbs given at the end of the sentences.

1. Wada-san ni _____ tara kono fūtō o _____ kuda-sai. (au) (watasu)

   和田さんに _____ たらこの封筒を _____ ください。
   （会う）（渡す）

   When you see Mr. Wada, please hand this envelope to him.

2. Anata ga _____ ningyō o Buraun-san ni_____ tara. (tsukuru) (ageru)

   あなたが _____ 人形をブラウンさんに _____ たら。
   （作る）（上げる）

   Why not give Mrs. Brown the doll you made?

3. Penki ga _____ tara heya ni isu o _____ kudasai. (kawaku) (hakobu)

   ペンキが _____ たら部屋にいすを _____ ください。
   （乾く）（運ぶ）

   When the paint gets dry, please carry the chairs into the room.

4. Takarakuji o _____ tara o-kane o nani ni _____
tai desu ka. (ateru) (tsukau)

宝くじを _____ たらお金を何に _____ たいですか。
（当てる）（使う）

If you win the lottery, what do you want to spend the money for?

⑩ Tari Form

Tari form (Vtari)

Regular I Verb (cf. pp. 23–28)	Regular II Verb (Verb stem + tari)	Irregular Verb
naitari 鳴いたり (chirp) hanashitari 話したり (speak) tsutsundari 包んだり (wrap) uttari 売ったり (sell)	detari 出たり (leave) nitari 煮たり (boil)	kitari 来たり (come) shitari したり (do)

SENTENCE PATTERNS

10.1 Vtari + Vtari suru ～たり～たりする

"do things like ~ and ~," "sometimes do ~ and sometimes do ~ "

Vtari ~ Vtari *suru* expresses an alternative or an indefinite number of actions or events in no particular sequence. A single action or event may be listed as a representative of others (Example 3).

EXAMPLES:

1. Pātī de **nondari tabetari odottari** shita.

パーティーで**飲んだり食べたり踊ったり**した。

We did things like drinking, eating and dancing at the party.

2. Watashi-tachi wa sensei ni **homeraretari shikararetari**
shimasu.
私達は先生に**誉められたり叱られたり**します。

Sometimes we are praised and sometimes scolded by our teachers.

3. Natsu ni wa **tozan shitari** suru.
夏には**登山したり**する。

In summer I do things like mountain climbing.

10.2 | **Vtari + Vnakattari suru** 〜たり〜なかったりする

"sometimes do ~ and sometimes don't ~ "

Vtari ~ Vnakattari *suru* expresses a pair of opposite actions or events.

EXAMPLES:

1. Watashi wa asa kōhī o **nondari nomanakattari** suru.
私は朝コーヒーを**飲んだり飲まなかったり**する。

Sometimes I drink coffee in the morning and sometimes I don't.

2. Tenki ni yotte Fuji-san ga **mietari mienakattari** shimasu.
天気によって富士山が**見えたり見えなかったり**します。

Sometimes Mt. Fuji can be seen and sometimes it can't be seen,
depending on the weather.

3. Kinyōbi ni wa Kimura-san wa **kitari konakattari** shimasu.
金曜日には木村さんは**来たり来なかったり**します。

On Fridays, Mr. Kimura sometimes comes and sometimes he
doesn't.

Fill in the blanks with the appropriate forms of the verbs provided at the end of the sentences.

1. Kesa kara ame ga _____ tari _____ dari shite imasu. (furu) (yamu)

   今朝から雨が _____ たり _____ だりしています。（降る）（やむ）

   It has been raining off and on since this morning.

2. Kōen de bōru o _____ tari jitensha ni_____ tari shite asonda. (nageru) (noru)

   公園でボールを _____ たり自転車に _____ たりして遊んだ。（投げる）（乗る）

   We played in the park, doing things like throwing a ball and riding bicycles.

3. Kare wa tabako o _____ tari _____ nakattari shimasu. (suu)

   彼はたばこを _____ たり _____ なかったりします。（吸う）

   Sometimes he smokes, and sometimes he doesn't.

4. Sensei wa gakusei ni hon o _____ tari kanji o _____ tari suru. (yomu) (kaku)

   先生は学生に本を _____ たり漢字を _____ たりする。（読む）（書く）

   The teacher does things like making students read books and write kanji.

A P P E N D I X E S

ANSWERS TO PRACTICES (PART I, CONJUGATION)

Practice 1

1. sakanai, sakimasu, saku, sakeba, sake, sakō
   咲かない、咲きます、咲く、咲けば、咲け、咲こう
2. ikanai, ikimasu, iku, ikeba, ike, ikō
   行かない、行きます、行く、行けば、行け、行こう
3. arukanai, arukimasu, aruku, arukeba, aruke, arukō
   歩かない、歩きます、歩く、歩けば、歩け、歩こう
4. hatarakanai, hatarakimasu, hataraku, hatarakeba, hatarake, hatarakō
   働かない、働きます、働く、働けば、働け、働こう
5. tsukanai, tsukimasu, tsuku, tsukeba, tsuke, tsukō
   着かない、着きます、着く、着けば、着け、着こう

Practice 2

1. isoganai, isogimasu, isogu, isogeba, isoge, isogō
   急がない、急ぎます、急ぐ、急げば、急げ、急ごう
2. sawaganai, sawagimasu, sawagu, sawageba, sawage, sawagō
   騒がない、騒ぎます、騒ぐ、騒げば、騒げ、騒ごう
3. nuganai, nugimasu, nugu, nugeba, nuge, nugō
   脱がない、脱ぎます、脱ぐ、脱げば、脱げ、脱ごう

Practice 3

1. kaesanai, kaeshimasu, kaesu, kaeseba, kaese, kaesō
   返さない、返します、返す、返せば、返せ、返そう
2. naosanai, naoshimasu, naosu, naoseba, naose, naosō
   直さない、直します、直す、直せば、直せ、直そう
3. sagasanai, sagashimasu, sagasu, sagaseba, sagase, sagasō

探さない、探します、探す、探せば、探せ、探そう

4. okosanai, okoshimasu, okosu, okoseba, okose, okosō
起こさない、起こします、起こす、起こせば、起こせ、起こそう

5. kasanai, kashimasu, kasu, kaseba, kase, kasō
貸さない、貸します、貸す、貸せば、貸せ、貸そう

Practice 4

1. motanai, mochimasu, motsu, moteba, mote, motō
持たない、持ちます、持つ、持てば、持て、持とう

2. tatanai, tachimasu, tatsu, tateba, tate, tatō
立たない、立ちます、立つ、立てば、立て、立とう

3. tatanai, tachimasu, tastu, tatebe, (no imperative, no volitional)
建たない、建ちます、建つ、建てば、

4. utanai, uchimasu, utsu, uteba, ute, utō
打たない、打ちます、打つ、打てば、打て、打とう

5. katanai, kachimasu, katsu, kateba, kate, katō
勝たない、勝ちます、勝つ、勝てば、勝て、勝とう

Practice 5

1. asobanai, asobimasu, asobu, asobeba, asobe, asobō
遊ばない、遊びます、遊ぶ、遊べば、遊べ、遊ぼう

2. hakabanai, hakobimasu, hakobu, hakobeba, hakobe, hakobō
運ばない、運びます、運ぶ、運べば、運べ、運ぼう

3. erabanai, erabimasu, erabu, erabeba, erabe, erabō
選ばない、選びます、選ぶ、選べば、選べ、選ぼう

4. manabanai, manabimasu, manabu, manabeba, manabe, manabō
学ばない、学びます、学ぶ、学べば、学べ、学ぼう

5. yobanai, yobimasu, yobu, yobeba, yobe, yobō
呼ばない、呼びます、呼ぶ、呼べば、呼べ、呼ぼう

Practice 6

1. nomanai, nomimasu, nomu, nomeba, nome, nomō
飲まない、飲みます、飲む、飲めば、飲め、飲もう

2. sumanai, sumimasu, sumu, sumeba, sume, sumō
住まない、住みます、住む、住めば、住め、住もう

3. tanomanai, tanomimasu, tanomu, tanomeba, tanome, tanomō
頼まない、頼みます、頼む、頼めば、頼め、頼もう

4. yasumanai, yasumimasu, yasumu, yasumeba, yasume, yasumō
休まない、休みます、休む、休めば、休め、休もう

5. tanoshimanai, tanoshimimasu, tanoshimu, tanoshimeba, tanoshime, tanoshimō
楽しまない、楽しみます、楽しむ、楽しめば、楽しめ、楽しもう

Practice 7

1. hairanai, hairimasu, hairu, haireba, haire, hairō
   入らない、入ります、入る、入れば、入れ、入ろう
2. hashiranai, hashirimasu, hashiru, hashireba, hashire, hashirō
   走らない、走ります、走る、走れば、走れ、走ろう
3. kaeranai, kaerimasu, kaeru, kaereba, kaere, kaerō
   帰らない、帰ります、帰る、帰れば、帰れ、帰ろう
4. noranai, norimasu, noru, noreba, nore, norō
   乗らない、乗ります、乗る、乗れば、乗れ、乗ろう
5. tsukuranai, tsukurimasu, tsukuru, tsukureba, tsukure, tsukurō
   作らない、作ります、作る、作れば、作れ、作ろう

Practice 8

1. awanai, aimasu, au, aeba, ae, aō
   会わない、会います、会う、会えば、会え、会おう
2. iwanai, iimasu, iu, ieba, ie, iō
   言わない、言います、言う、言えば、言え、言おう
3. narawanai, naraimasu, narau, naraeba, narae, naraō
   習わない、習います、習う、習えば、習え、習おう
4. utawanai, utaimasu, utau, utaeba, utae, utaō
   歌わない、歌います、歌う、歌えば、歌え、歌おう
5. tsukawanai, tsukaimasu, tsukau, tsukaeba, tsukae, tsukaō
   使わない、使います、使う、使えば、使え、使おう

Practice 9

1. ugoite, ugoita, ugoitara, ugoitari
   動いて、動いた、動いたら、動いたり
2. naite, naita, naitara, naitari
   鳴いて、鳴いた、鳴いたら、鳴いたり
3. hiite, hiita, hiitara, hiitari
   弾いて、弾いた、弾いたら、弾いたり
4. isoide, isoida, isoidara, isoidari
   急いで、急いだ、急いだら、急いだり
5. nuide, nuida, nuidara, nuidari
   脱いで、脱いだ、脱いだら、脱いだり

Practice 10

1. otoshite, otoshita, otoshitara, otoshitari
   落として、落とした、落としたら、落としたり
2. herashite, herashita, herashitara, herashitari
   減らして、減らした、減らしたら、減らしたり

3. utsushite, utsushita, utsushitara, utsushitari
移して、移した、移したら、移したり

4. sugoshite, sugoshita, sugoshitara, sugoshitari
過ごして、過ごした、過ごしたら、過ごしたり

5. watashite, watashita, watashitara, watashitari
渡して、渡した、渡したら、渡したり

Practice 11

1. narande, naranda, narandara, narandari
並んで、並んだ、並んだら、並んだり

2. koronde, koronda, korondara, korondari
転んで、転んだ、転んだら、転んだり

3. sunde, sunda, sundara, sundari
済んで、済んだ、済んだら、済んだり

4. susunde, susunda, susundara, susundari
進んで、進んだ、進んだら、進んだり

5. tsutsunde, tsutsunda, tsutsundara, tsutsundari
包んで、包んだ、包んだら、包んだり

Practice 12

1. medatte, medatta, medattara, medattari
目立って、目立った、目立ったら、目立ったり

2. okutte, okutta, okuttara, okuttari
送って、送った、送ったら、送ったり

3. utte, utta, uttara, uttari
売って、売った、売ったら、売ったり

4. omotte, omotta, omottara, omottari
思って、思った、思ったら、思ったり

5. haratte, haratta, harattara, harattari
払って、払った、払ったら、払ったり

Practice 13

1. kinai, kimasu, kireba, kiyō, kite
着ない、着ます、着れば、着よう、着て

2. okinai, okimasu, okireba, okiyō, okite
起きない、起きます、起きれば、起きよう、起きて

3. kotaenai, kotaemasu, kotaereba, kotaeyō, kotaete
答えない、答えます、答えれば、答えよう、答えて

4. misenai, misemasu, misereba, miseyō, misete
見せない、見せます、見せれば、見せよう、見せて

5. akenai, akemasu, akereba, akeyō, akete
開けない、開けます、開ければ、開けよう、開けて

Practice 14

1. oyogeru, oyogenai, oyogemasu, oyogete
   泳げる、泳げない、泳げます、泳げて
2. utaeru, utaenai, utaemasu, utaete
   歌える、歌えない、歌えます、歌えて
3. hanaseru, hanasenai, hanasemasu, hanasete
   話せる、話せない、話せます、話せて
4. nomeru, nomenai, nomemasu, nomete
   飲める、飲めない、飲めます、飲めて
5. moteru, motenai, motemasu, motete
   持てる、持てない、持てます、持てて

Practice 15

1. konai, kimasu, kureba, koyō, kita
   来ない、来ます、来れば、来よう、来た
2. shinai, shimasu, sureba, shiyō, shita
   しない、します、すれば、しよう、した
3. shigoto shinai, shigoto shimasu, shigoto sureba, shigoto shiyō, shigoto shita
   仕事しない、仕事します、仕事すれば、仕事しよう、仕事した
4. shitsumon shinai, shitsumon shimasu, shitsumon sureba, shitsumon shiyō, shitsumon shita
   質問しない、質問します、質問すれば、質問しよう、質問した

Practice 16

1. de (wa) arimasen で（は）ありません
2. de(wa) nai deshō で（は）ないでしょう
3. de (wa) arimasen deshita で（は）ありませんでした
4. de (wa) nai darō で（は）ないだろう
5. de (wa) nakatta で（は）なかった
6. de (wa) nai で（は）ない

Practice 17

1. akimasu, akimasen, akimashita, akimasen deshita
   開きます、開きません、開きました、開きませんでした
2. tetsudaimasu, tetsudaimasen, tetsudaimashita, tetsudaimasen deshita
   手伝います、手伝いません、手伝いました、手伝いませんでした
3. kangaemasu, kangaemasen, kangaemashita, kangaemasen deshita
   考えます、考えません、考えました、考えませんでした
4. tsuzukemasu, tsuzukemasen, tsuzukemashita, tsuzukemasen deshita
   続けます、続けません、続けました、続けませんでした
5. kenbutsu shimasu, kenbutsu shimasen, kenbutsu shimashita, kenbutsu shimasen deshita
   見物します、見物しません、見物しました、見物しませんでした

Practice 18
1. nakanai, nakanakatta 泣かない、泣かなかった
2. yamenai, yamenakatta 辞めない、辞めなかった
3. kimenai, kimenakatta 決めない、決めなかった
4. konai, konakatta 来ない、来なかった
5. fukushū shinai, fukushū shinakatta 復習しない、復習しなかった

Practice 19
1. kotowaritai, kotowaritakatta 断りたい、断りたかった
2. iwaitai, iwaitakatta 祝いたい、祝いたかった
3. nokoshitai, nokoshitakatta 残したい、残したかった
4. sodatetai, sodatetakatta 育てたい、育てたかった
5. kitai shitai, kitai shitakatta 期待したい、期待したかった

Practice 20
1. oyogitagaru 泳ぎたがる　　2. shiritagaru 知りたがる　　3. mitagaru 見たがる
4. karitagaru 借りたがる　5. ryokō shitagaru 旅行したがる

Practice 21
1. makashite hoshii, makashite hoshikatta
   負かしてほしい、負かしてほしかった
2. ganbatte hoshii, ganbatte hoshikatta
   頑張ってほしい、頑張ってほしかった
3. atsumete hoshii, atsumete hoshikatta
   集めてほしい、集めてほしかった
4. akiramete hoshii, akiramete hoshikatta
   あきらめてほしい、あきらめてほしかった
5. shusseki shite hoshii, shusseki shite hoshikatta
   出席してほしい、出席してほしかった

Practice 22
1. maniau rashii 間に合うらしい
2. dekaketa rashii 出かけたらしい
3. okureru rashii 遅れるらしい
4. sanka shita rashii 参加したらしい

Practice 23
A.
1. kuru sō da 来るそうだ
2. aku sō da 開くそうだ
3. katta sō da 買ったそうだ
4. susumeta sō da 勧めたそうだ

B.
1. warai sō da 笑いそうだ
2. furi sō da 降りそうだ
3. yame sō da 辞めそうだ
4. naki sō da 泣きそうだ
5. hatten shi sō da 発展しそうだ

Practice 24

1. kakasemasu, kakaseta 書かせます、書かせた
2. hakobasemasu, hakobaseta 運ばせます、運ばせた
3. suwarasemasu, suwaraseta 座らせます、座らせた
4. hirowasemasu, hirowaseta 拾わせます、拾わせた
5. shimesasemasu, shimesaseta 示させます、示させた

Practice 25

1. atsumesasemasu, atsumesaseta 集めさせます、集めさせた
2. kisasemasu, kisaseta 着させます、着させた
3. shimesasemasu, shimesaseta 閉めさせます、閉めさせた
4. tomesasemasu, tomesaseta 止めさせます、止めさせた
5. orisasemasu, orisaseta 降りさせます、降りさせた

Practice 26

1. kosasemasu, kosaseta 来させます、来させた
2. sasemasu, saseta させます、させた
3. setsumei sasemasu, setsumei saseta 説明させます、説明させた

Practice 27

1. sasowaremasu, sasowareta 誘われます、誘われた
2. shikararemasu, shikarareta 叱られます、叱られた
3. shinaremasu, shinareta 死なれます、死なれた
4. tasukeraremasu, tasukerareta 助けられます、助けられた
5. chūkoku saremasu, chūkoku sareta 忠告されます、忠告された

Practice 28

1. mataserareru/matasareru 待たせられる・待たされる
2. nomaserareru/nomasareru 飲ませられる・飲まされる
3. odoraserareru/odorasareru 踊らせられる・踊らされる
4. sutesaserareru 捨てさせられる
5. kosaserareru 来させられる
6. hōkoku saserareru 報告させられる

ANSWERS TO PRACTICES (PART II, USAGE OF VERB FORMS)

Practice 1
1. okimasu 起きます 2. tsukimasu 着きます 3. kimashita 来ました, kimasen deshita 来ませんでした 4. mimashō 見ましょう 5. yakushimashō 訳しましょう
6. shōkai shimasen 紹介しません

Practice 2
A.
1. narabinasai 並びなさい   o-narabi kudasai お並びください
2. harainasai 払いなさい   o-harai kudasai お払いください
3. torinasai 取りなさい   o-tori kudasai お取りください
4. arainasai 洗いなさい   o-arai kudasai お洗いください
5. misenasai 見せなさい   o-mise kudasi お見せください

B.
1. o-azukari shimasu/itashimasu お預かりします・いたします
2. o-kotowari shimashita/itashimashita お断りしました・いたしました
3. o-shirabe shimasu/itashimasu お調べします・いたします

Practice 3
1. nori 乗り, ori 降り 2. hajime 始め, owari 終わり 3. kudari 下り, nobori 上り
4. shi し 5. naoshi 直し 6. de 出, kaeshi 返し 7. ai 会い, nomi 飲み

Practice 4
1. kiki 聞き, renshū shi 練習し 2. tsukai 使い, yakushi 訳し 3. ki 着 4. hataraki 働き 5. asobi 遊び, iki 行き 6. mi 見, sugoshi 過ごし

Practice 5
1. tsuzuki 続き 2. uri 売り 3. todoki 届き 4. nori 乗り, tōri 通り 5. ugoki 動き
6. dashi 出し 7. tsukuri 作り, narai 習い 8. hashiri 走り

Practice 6
1. hajimaru 始まる 2. agaru 上がる 3. kimeru 決める 4. yoru 寄る 5. nokoru 残る 6. korobu 転ぶ 7. hareru 晴れる 8. okosu 起こす

Practice 7
1. tanomu 頼む 2. mitsukaru 見付かる 3. odoroku 驚く 4. tsutawaru 伝わる 5. naku 鳴く, kiki 聞き 6. nyūin suru 入院する, shiri 知り 7. sōji suru 掃除する, tetsudai 手伝い

Practice 8

A.

1. hanasu koto ga dekiru/dekimasu 話すことが出来る・出来ます
2. yaku koto ga dekiru/dekimasu 焼くことが出来る・出来ます
3. kotaeru koto ga dekiru/dekimasu 答えることが出来る・出来ます
4. tomeru kato ga dekiru/dekimasu 止めることが出来る・出来ます
5. enzetsu suru koto ga dekiru/dekimasu 演説することが出来る・出来ます

B.

1. tsukuru koto ni suru/shimasu 作ることにする・します
2. sewa suru koto ga aru/arimasu 世話することがある・あります
3. au koto ni suru/shimasu 会うことにする・します
4. taiin suru koto ni naru darō/deshō 退院することになるだろう・でしょう
5. nemuru koto ga aru/arimasu 眠ることがある・あります
6. shutchō suru koto ni narimashita 出張することになりました

Practice 9

1. kiru 切る 2. anki suru 暗記する 3. narau 習う, oshieru 教える 4. oyogu 泳ぐ, noboru 登る 5. tayoru 頼る, yaru やる 6. yasumu 休む, hataraku 働く

Practice 10

1. taberu 食べる, arai 洗い 2. hairu 入る, undō shi 運動し 3. arawareru 現れる, machi 待ち 4. mitsukaru 見付かる, sagashi 探し 5. naru なる, shuppan suru 出版する 6. kireru 切れる, watari 渡り

Practice 11

1. tsukuru 作る, iri 要り 2. naraberu 並べる, kakari かかり 3. aru ある, benkyō shi 勉強し 4. yasumu 休む, sagari 下がり 5. kuru 来る, toke 溶け 6. susumu 進む, kikoe 聞こえ

Practice 12

1. suu 吸う, ake 開け 2. noru 乗る, isogi 急ぎ 3. iwau 祝う, shiri 知り 4. deru 出る, shirabe 調べ 5. okureru 遅れる, shirase 知らせ

Practice 13

1. naoru 治る, nomi 飲み 2. yaseru やせる, undō shi 運動し 3. musubu 結ぶ 4. kakinaosu 書き直す 5. machigaeru 間違える 6. kanjiru 感じる 7. oki 起き, neru 寝る 8. sasou 誘う

Practice 14

1. okureru 遅れる, nomi 飲み 2. chūi suru 注意する, futori 太り 3. otosu 落とす, hiroi 拾い 4. aru ある, komu 込む 5. kuru 来る, de 出 6. agaru 上がる, kau 買う

Practice 15

1. herasu 減らす   2. wasureru 忘れる   3. hairu 入る, iru いる   4. mise 見せ, yoru 寄る   5. hataraki 働き, kayou 通う

Practice 16

1. mieru 見える, utsuri 移り   2. iku 行く, iwai 祝い   3. iru 要る, kaki 書き   4. yomi 読み, ari あり   5. yaku 焼く, kau 買う

Practice 17

1. suteru 捨てる, ari あり   2. kasu 貸す, mōke もうけ   3. naraberu 並べる   4. hataraku 働く, asobi 遊び   5. suru する, nori 乗り   6. furu 降る, fuki 吹き

Practice 18

1. sasowanai 誘わない   2. atsumaranai 集まらない   3. inai いない   4. nakunaranai なくならない   5. intai shinai 引退しない   6. sumanai 住まない   7. konai 来ない   8. nai ない

Practice 19

A.

1. erabanai no/koto 選ばないの・こと   2. shirabenai no/koto 調べないの・こと   3. awanai no/koto 会わないの・こと   4. konai no/koto 来ないの・こと   5. oboenai no/koto 覚えないの・こと 6. junbi shinai no/koto 準備しないの・こと

B.

1. ikanai de kudasai 行かないでください
2. sutenai de kudasai 捨てないでください
3. wasurenai de kudasai 忘れないでください
4. matanai de kudasai 待たないでください
5. hitei shinai de kudasai 否定しないでください
6. machigaenai de kudasai 間違えないでください

C.

1. konai koto ga aru/arimasu 来ないことがある・あります
2. sōdan shinai koto ni shimashita 相談しないことにしました
3. okonawanai koto ni narimashita 行わないことになりました
4. hanasanai koto ni shiyō/shimashō 話さないことにしよう・しましょう
5. nenai koto ga aru/arimasu 寝ないことがある・あります
6. zōka shinai koto ni narimashita 増加しないことになりました

Practice 20

1. konai 来ない, sōji shi 掃除し   2. akenai 明けない, oki 起き   3. sagenai 下げない   4. owaru 終わる, hairanai 入らない   5. utawanai 歌わない, hiki 弾き   6. ryokō shinai 旅行しない, kau 買う

Practice 21

1. nai ない, kai 買い 2. senden shinai 宣伝しない, atsumari 集まり 3. naranai 鳴らない, hairi 入り 4. shusseki shinai 出席しない, kimaranai 決まらない 5. isoganai 急がない, aruki 歩き 6. tsukawanai 使わない, sute 捨て

Practice 22

1. okurenai 遅れない, oki 起き 2. korobanai 転ばない, kudari 下り 3. sawaganai 騒がない, shi し 4. okanai 置かない 5. odoranai 踊らない 6. asobanai 遊ばない 7. tsukaisuginai 使いすぎない 8. tōranai 通らない

Practice 23

A.

1. Kodomo-tachi wa sensei ni shikararemashita.
   子供達は先生に叱られました。

2. Ono-sensei wa gakusei ni pâtī ni shōtai saremashita.
   小野先生は学生にパーティーに招待されました。

3. Watashi wa ueitoresu ni sukâto o yogosaremashita.
   私はウエイトレスにスカートを汚されました。

4. Kida-san wa dorobō ni jitensha o nusumaremashita.
   木田さんは泥棒に自転車を盗まれました。

5. Yano-san wa okusan ni shinaremashita.
   矢野さんは奥さんに死なれました。

6. Watashi-tachi wa maiban kodomo ni nakareru/nakaremasu.
   私達は毎晩子供に泣かれる・泣かれます。

B.

1. yorare 寄られ 2. yomare 読まれ 3. kakare 書かれ 4. kansei deki 完成出来 5. sansei sare 賛成され

Practice 24

A.

1. ikaseru; ikaserareru/ikasareru
   行かせる；行かせられる・行かされる

2. kangaesaseru; kangaesaserareru
   考えさせる；考えさせられる

3. tetsudawaseru; tetsudawaserareru/tetsudawasareru
   手伝わせる；手伝わせられる・手伝わされる

4. shimesaseru; shimesaserareru
   閉めさせる；閉めさせられる

5. nomaseru; nomaserareru/nomasareru
   飲ませる；飲ませられる・飲まされる

6. shinpai saseru; shinpai saserareru
   心配させる；心配させられる

B.
1. asobase/asobashi 遊ばせ・遊ばし   2. yamesase/yamesashi やめさせ・やめさし
3. sōji sase/sōji sashi 掃除させ・掃除さし   4. migakaserare/migakasare 磨かせら
れ・磨かされ   5. nyūin saserare 入院させられ

Practice 25
1. ko 来, kakinaosa 書き直さ   2. noma 飲ま, sagara 下がら   3. okure 遅れ, nora
乗ら   4. okosa, 起こさ, mamora 守ら

Practice 26
A.
1. densha o norikaenakereba naranai/norikaenakute mo ii
   電車を乗りかえなければならない・乗りかえなくてもいい
2. kutsu o nuganakereba naranai/nuganakute mo ii
   くつを脱がなければならない・脱がなくてもいい
3. shiken o ukenakereba naranai/ukenakute mo ii
   試験を受けなければならない・受けなくてもいい
4. jisho o chūmon shinakereba naranai/chūmon shinakute mo ii
   辞書を注文しなければならない・注文しなくてもいい
5. ryōkin o harawanakereba naranai/harawanakute mo ii
   料金を払わなければならない・払わなくてもいい

B.
1. atara 当たら, saki 咲き   2. yasuma 休ま, hataraka 働か   3. fura 降ら, dekake 出
かけ   4. kaifuku shi 回復し, chūshi shi 中止し

Practice 27
1. nobore 登れ, mie 見え   2. nore 乗れ, tsuki 着き   3. migake 磨け, hikari 光り
4. kotaere 答えれ   5. yame やめ, tsuzukere 続けれ   6. ire いれ, ari あり

Practice 28
1. sutero/suteyo 捨てろ・捨てよ   2. watase 渡せ   3. mate 待て   4. shiji seyo/shiji
shiro 支持せよ・支持しろ   5. shimero/shimeyo 閉めろ・閉めよ

Practice 29
A.
1. kabe o shiroku nurō 壁を白く塗ろう
2. shiai o chūshi shiyō 試合を中止しよう
3. nimotsu o todokeyō 荷物を届けよう
4. Fuji-san ni noborō 富士山に登ろう

B.
1. deyō 出よう, hairi 入り   2. kaesō 返そう   3. oyogaseyō 泳がせよう   4. hōkoku shiyō 報告しよう   5. agare 上がれ, urō 売ろう

Practice 30
A.
1. kiite 聞いて   2. naratte 習って   3. wakatte 分かって   4. asonde 遊んで 5. kite 来て   6. naoshite 直して   7. junbi shite 準備して   8. orite 降りて

B.
1. aite 開いて, shimete 閉めて   2. isoide 急いで, kakinaoshite 書き直して   3. sōji shite 掃除して   4. irete 入れて, sutete 捨てて   5. mite 見て, yori 寄り   6. benkyō shite 勉強して, okirare 起きられ

Practice 31
1. nuide 脱いで, suwari 座り   2. yonde 読んで, mawashite 回して   3. kaeshi 返し, itte 行って   4. tabe 食べ, nete 寝て   5. kotae 答え, naite 泣いて

Practice 32
A.
1. enpitsu de kaite mo ii desu ka/kaite wa ikemasen
   鉛筆で書いてもいいですか・書いてはいけません
2. jugyō ni okurete mo ii desu ka/okurete wa ikemasen
   授業に遅れてもいいですか・遅れてはいけません
3. terebi o keshite mo ii desu ka/keshite wa ikemasen
   テレビを消してもいいですか・消してはいけません
4. shinbun o sutete mo ii desu ka/sutete wa ikemasen
   新聞を捨ててもいいですか・捨ててはいけません
5. kaigi o enki shite mo ii desu ka/enki shite wa ikemasen
   会議を延期してもいいですか・延期してはいけません

B.
1. yonde 呼んで   2. tsukatte 使って, tsukawa 使わ   3. fuite 吹いて   4. oyoide 泳いで   5. hajimatte 始まって, haitte 入って

Practice 33
1. hakonde agemashita 運んであげました
2. yakushite itadakimashita 訳していただきました
3. kashite kuremashita 貸してくれました
4. tomete morau 泊めてもらう
5. tetsudatte yarimashita 手伝ってやりました
6. naoshite kudasaimashita 直してくださいました
7. shirabete sashiagemashita 調べてさしあげました

Practice 34

1. kiite iru 聞いている   2. haite iru はいている   3. jikken shite iru 実験している
4. tomete aru 止めてある   5. hiite iru 弾いている   6. ryūgaku shite iru 留学している   7. yande iru やんでいる   8. aratte aru 洗ってある

Practice 35

A.
1. fukushū shite oku/okimasu 復習しておく・おきます
2. nomisugite shimau/shimaimasu 飲みすぎてしまう・しまいます
3. harete kimashita 晴れてきました
4. tsukatte mimashita 使ってみました
5. sodatte iku/ikimasu 育っていく・いきます
6. yonde shimaimashita 読んでしまいました
7. keshite okimashita 消しておきました

B.
1. wasurete 忘れて, shikararete 叱られて   2. asonde 遊んで, katazukete 片付けて
3. hantai shite 反対して, yatte やって   4. ganbatte 頑張って, agatte 上がって
5. tabe 食べ, futotte 太って

Practice 36

A.
1. shinda 死んだ   2. suwatta 座った   3. toketa 溶けた   4. tetsudatta 手伝った
5. taoshita 倒した   6. saita 咲いた   7. saketa 避けた   8. bōshi shita 防止した

B.
1. owat 終わっ, de 出   2. dashi 出し, it 行っ   3. okutta 送った, todoki 届き   4. taiin shite 退院して, nakunat 亡くなっ   5. ut 売っ, katta 買った   6. kotowatta 断った, ki 来

Practice 37

1. shimatte 閉まって, kaetta 帰った   2. owatte 終わって, yotta 寄った   3. sagat 下がっ, chūi sareta 注意された   4. hataraki 働き, sodateta 育てた

Practice 38

1. kiki 聞き, oboeta 覚えた   2. tabe 食べ, kaetta 帰った   3. isoida 急いだ, mani-awa 間に合わ   4. atta 会った, shokuji shita 食事した   5. nyūin shita 入院した, shiraseta 知らせた

Practice 39

1. kita 来た, kaette 帰って   2. tsukatta 使った, aratte 洗って   3. kireta 切れた, shinsei shi 申請し   4. tsuke つけ, okotta 起こった   5. yasunda 休んだ, atta あった

Practice 40

1. kikoku shita 帰国した, todoi 届い 2. haita はいた, haitte 入って 3. okure
遅れ, matasareta 待たされた 4. subet 滑っ, koronda 転んだ 5. sugita 過ぎた,
machigaeta 間違えた

Practice 41

1. totta とった, misete 見せて 2. atta 会った, shōkai sare 紹介され 3. mōshi-
konda 申し込んだ, sanka shi 参加し 4. tomatta 泊まった, atsumeta 集めた
5. komatta 困った, tasukete 助けて

Practice 42

A.

1. hakattara 計ったら 2. hiitara 引いたら 3. kayottara 通ったら 4. haretara 腫れ
たら 5. fukundara 含んだら 6. naretara 慣れたら 7. oretara 折れたら 8. shidō
shitara 指導したら

B.

1. at 会っ, watashite 渡して 2. tsukutta 作った, age 上げ 3. kawai 乾い, hakonde
運んで 4. ate 当て, tsukai 使い

Practice 43

1. fut 降っ, yan やん 2. nage 投げ, not 乗っ 3. sut 吸っ, suwa 吸わ 4. yomase
読ませ, kakase 書かせ

SENTENCE PATTERNS

1. Conjunctive Form

1.1 Vconj + masu ます "do/will do," "there is/will be", 48
1.2 Vconj + mashō ましょう "I will," "Let's ~", 49
1.3 Vconj + mashō ka/masen ka ましょうか・ませんか "Shall I ~" "Wouldn't
      you ~", 50
1.4 Vconj + nasai なさい "Do ~", 51
1.5 o + Vconj + kudasai お …. ください "Would you please do ~", 52
1.6 o + Vconj + shimasu/itashimasu お …. します・いたします "I'll do ~" "I'd
      like to do ~", 53
1.7 Vconj, Vconj + masu ます "do ~ and do ~", 54
1.8 Vconj used as a noun, 55
1.9 Vconj + ni に + motion verb "go/come/return/enter/leave to do something", 55
1.10 Vconj + nagara ながら "while doing ~", 57
1.11 Vconj + tai/tagaru たい・たがる "want to do ~", 58
1.12 Vconj + sō da そうだ "look like," "feel like", 60

3. Negative Form

BASIC JAPANESE VERBS

1. Regular I Verbs

agaru, 上がる (vi) go up, rise
aku, 開く (vi) open
aku, 空く (vi) become empty
amaru, 余る (vi) be left over, remain
arasou, 争う (vt) fight, compete
arau, 洗う (vt) wash
arawasu, 表す・現す (vt) show, express
arawasu, 著す (vt) write
aru, ある (vi) be, have
aruku, 歩く (vi) walk
asaru, あさる (vt) hunt for, scavenge
asobu, 遊ぶ (vi) play, enjoy oneself
ataru, 当たる (vi) hit, strike, shine upon
atatamaru, 暖まる (vi) get warm
atsukau, 扱う (vt) handle, deal
atsumaru, 集まる (vi) assemble, get together
au, 会う (vi) meet
au, 合う (vi) match, fit
ayamaru, 謝る (vt) apologize
ayamaru, 誤る (vt) make a mistake
azukaru, 預かる (vt) keep

butsukaru, ぶつかる (vi) hit, bump

chigau, 違う (vi) differ, be wrong
chigiru, ちぎる (vt) tear to pieces
chijimu, 縮む (vi) shrink
chikazuku, 近づく (vi) approach, get near

chirasu, 散らす (vt) scatter, disperse
chiru, 散る (vi) fall, scatter, disperse

daku, 抱く (vt) hold, hug
damasu, だます (vt) deceive, cheat
dasu, 出す (vt) put out, send, submit
donaru, どなる (vi) shout

erabu, 選ぶ (vt) choose, select, elect

fuku, 拭く (vt) wipe
fuku, 吹く (vi, vt) blow, play (wind instruments)
fukumu, 含む (vt) contain, include
fukuramu, 膨らむ (vi) swell, expand
fumu, 踏む (vt) step on
furu, 降る (vi) rain, snow
furu, 振る (vt) wave
fusagu, ふさぐ (vt) block up
futoru, 太る (vi) get fat
fuyasu, 増やす (vt) increase

ganbaru, 頑張る (vi) hold on

habuku, 省く (vt) omit
hagasu, はがす (vt) strip off, tear off
hagemasu, 励ます (vt) encourage
hagemu, 励む (vi) make efforts, strive
habuku, 省く (vt) omit
hagasu, はがす (vt) strip off, tear off

hagemasu, 励ます (vt) encourage

hagemu, 励む (vi) make efforts, strive

hairu, 入る (vi) enter

hajimaru, 始まる (vi) begin, start

hakaru, 計る (vt) measure, weigh

hakobu, 運ぶ (vt) carry, transport

haku, 履く (vt) wear (shoes)

haku, 吐く (vt) vomit

haku, 掃く (vt) sweep

hamidasu, はみ出す (vi) stick out

hanasu, 話す (vt) speak, talk

hanasu, 離す (vt) detach

hanasu, 放す (vt) set free, release

harau, 払う (vt) pay, brush off

haru, 張る (vt) paste, stick, stretch (a rope), spread (a net)

hashiru, 走る (vi) run

hataku, はたく (vt) beat, slap, dust

hataraku, 働く (vi) work

hayaru, はやる (vi) be popular, be in fashion, prevail

hayasu, 生やす (vt) grow (a mustache)

hazumu, 弾む (vi) spring, bound

hazusu, 外す (vt) take off, remove

hekomu, へこむ (vi) be dented

herasu, 減らす (vt) decrease

heru, 減る (vi) decrease

hikaru, 光る (vi) shine

hikizuru, 引きずる (vt) drag, trail

hikkomu, 引っ込む (vi) draw back

hikkosu, 引っ越す (vi) move to

hikkurikaesu, ひっくり返す (vt) turn over, upset

hiku, 引く (vt) pull, draw

hiku, 弾く (vt) play (string instruments)

hineru, ひねる (vt) twist, wrench

hipparu, 引っ張る (vt) pull, draw

hiraku, 開く (vi, vt) open, unfold

hirogaru, 広がる (vi) extend, spread

hirou, 拾う (vt) pick up, find (a purse)

hisomu, 潜む (vi) lurk

hiyakasu, 冷やかす (vt) tease

hiyasu, 冷やす (vt) cool, ice

hodoku, ほどく (vt) untie

hokoru, 誇る (vi, vt) be proud of

horu, 掘る (vt) dig

horu, 彫る (vt) engrave, sculpture

idomu, 挑む (vi, vt) challenge

ijiru, いじる (vt) fumble, tamper

ikigomu, 意気込む (vi) be eager

iku, 行く (vi) go

inoru, 祈る (vt) pray

iradatsu, いら立つ (vi) be irritated

irassharu, いらっしゃる (vi) be, go, come

iru, 要る (vi) need

isogu, 急ぐ (vi) hurry

itadaku, 頂く (vt) receive, eat, drink

itamu, 痛む (vi) feel a pain

itaru, 至る (vi) arrive, reach

itasu, 致す (vt) do

itawaru, いたわる (vt) console

itonamu, 営む (vt) perform, conduct (business)

itsuwaru, 偽る (vt) lie, feign

iu, 言う (vt) say, tell

iwau, 祝う (vt) congratulate, celebrate

jirasu, じらす (vt) irritate, tease

kaburu, かぶる (vt) wear (a hat)

kaeru, 帰る (vi) return

kaesu, 返す (vt) return, give back

kagamu, かがむ (vi) stoop

kajiru, かじる (vt) bite, gnaw

kakaru, かかる (vi) hang, cost, take time

kakimawasu, かき回す (vt) stir up

kaku, 書く (vt) write

kakusu, 隠す (vt) hide, conceal

kamu, かむ (vt) bite

kanashimu, 悲しむ (vt) feel sad

karamu, 絡む (vi) twine around

karu, 刈る (vt) cut, trim, mow
kasu, 貸す (vt) lend, rent
katamuku, 傾く (vi) slope, lean
katsu, 勝つ (vi) win
kau, 買う (vt) buy
kau, 飼う (vt) keep pets
kawakasu, 乾かす (vt) dry
kawaku, 乾く (vi) get dry
kawaku, 渇く (vi) get thirsty
kawaru, 変わる (vi) change
kawaru, 代わる (vi) replace
kayou, 通う (vi) commute
kazaru, 飾る (vt) decorate
kesu, 消す (vt) turn off, erase
kezuru, 削る (vt) sharpen
kiku, 聞く (vt) hear, listen, ask
kiku, 効く (vi) be effective
kimaru, 決まる (vi) be decided
kiru, 切る (vt) cut, switch off
kisou, 競う (vi, vt) compete
kizamu, 刻む (vt) chop
komaru, 困る (vi) be in trouble
komu, 込む (vi) be crowded
korobu, 転ぶ (vi) fall down
korogaru, 転がる (vi) roll
korogasu, 転がす (vt) roll
korosu, 殺す (vt) kill, murder
kōru, 凍る (vi) freeze
kosu, 超す (vi) cross, pass
kosuru, こする (vt) rub, scrub
kotowaru, 断る (vt) refuse, decline
kowasu, 壊す (vt) break, destroy
kubaru, 配る (vt) distribute, hand out
kudaku, 砕く (vt) smash, crush
kudaru, 下る (vi) go down
kudasaru, くださる (vt) give
kukuru, くくる (vt) tie, bind
kumoru, 曇る (vi) become cloudy
kumu, 組む (vt) pair, team up
kurikaesu, 繰り返す (vt) repeat
kurushimu, 苦しむ (vi) suffer, feel pain

kuruu, 狂う (vi) go mad, go wrong
kusaru, 腐る (vi) spoil
kusuguru, くすぐる (vt) tickle
kuyamu, 悔やむ (vt) regret

machigau, 間違う (vi, vt) make a mistake
magaru, 曲がる (vi) turn, bend, curve
mairu, 参る (vi) go, come
makasu, 負かす (vt) beat, defeat
maku, 巻く (vt) roll up
maku, まく (vt) sprinkle
mamoru, 守る (vt) defend, protect
maniau, 間に合う (vi) be in time, be
  enough, suffice
matsu, 待つ (vt) wait
mawaru, 回る (vi) turn, spin
mawasu, 回す (vt) turn, spin, pass round
mayou, 迷う (vi) get lost
mazaru, 混ざる (vi) blend, mix
medatsu, 目立つ (vi) be outstanding
mezasu, 目指す (vt) aim
midasu, 乱す (vt) disturb, corrupt
migaku, 磨く (vt) polish, brush
miharu, 見張る (vt) keep watch, stand
  guard
minoru, 実る (vi) bear fruit, ripen
miokuru, 見送る (vt) see off
mitasu, 満たす (vt) fill, satisfy (a need)
mitsukaru, 見付かる (vi) be found, be
  discovered
modoru, 戻る (vi) return
modosu, 戻す (vt) return, give back
mogaku, もがく (vi) struggle
moguru, 潜る (vi) dive
mōkaru, もうかる (vi) make a profit
momu, もむ (vt) massage
morasu, 漏らす (vt) let leak out
morau, もらう (vt) get, receive
mōshikomu, 申し込む (vt) apply, propose
motsu, 持つ (vt) have, hold, own
motteiku, 持って行く (vt) take (a thing)

moyasu, 燃やす (vt) burn
muku, 向く (vi) face, turn
muku, むく (vt) peel
musu, 蒸す (vt) steam
musubu, 結ぶ (vt) tie, contract

nagasu, 流す (vt) drain, float
naku, 泣く (vi) cry, weep
naku, 鳴く (vi) cry, sing
nakunaru, 亡くなる (vi) die, pass away
nakunaru, 無くなる (vi) be missing, run out
nakusu, 亡くす (vt) lose (a person)
nakusu, 無くす (vt) lose (a thing)
naoru, 治る (vi) get well, recover
naoru, 直る (vi) be corrected, be fixed, be repaired
naosu, 治す (vt) cure
naosu, 直す (vt) correct, fix, repair
narabu, 並ぶ (vi) stand in line
narasu, 慣らす (vt) tame
narasu, 鳴らす (vt) ring, sound
narau, 習う (vt) learn
naru, なる (vi) become
naru, 鳴る (vi) ring, sound
nasaru, なさる (vt) do
nayamu, 悩む (vi) be worried, suffer
nazoru, なぞる (vt) trace
nedaru, ねだる (vt) pester
negau, 願う (vt) desire, wish, hope
nejiru, ねじる (vt) twist, wrench
nemuru, 眠る (vi) sleep
nerau, ねらう (vt) aim
niau, 似合う (vi) suit, match well
niburu, 鈍る (vi) become dull
nigasu, 逃がす (vt) let escape
nigiru, 握る (vt) grasp, clasp
nigiwau, にぎわう (vi) prosper
nigoru, 濁る (vi) get muddy
nikumu, 憎む (vt) hate
niou, におう (vi) smell

niramu, にらむ (vt) stare, suspect
nobasu, 延ばす (vt) postpone
nobasu, 伸ばす (vt) stretch, extend
noboru, 上る (vi) go up
noboru, 登る (vi) climb
noboru, 昇る (vi) rise
nokoru, 残る (vi) remain
nokosu, 残す (vt) save, leave (a thing) behind
nomu, 飲む (vt) drink, take (medicine)
noru, 乗る (vi) ride, get on (a vehicle)
noru, 載る (vi) be printed, be reported
nozoku, 除く (vt) exclude
nozoku, のぞく (vt) peep
nozomu, 望む (vt) desire, wish, hope
nugu, 脱ぐ (vt) take off (clothes)
nuku, 抜く (vt) pull out, extract
nurasu, ぬらす (vt) wet, soak
nuru, 塗る (vt) paint
nusumu, 盗む (vt) steal
nuu, 縫う (vt) sew

ochitsuku, 落ち着く (vi) settle down
odokasu, 脅かす (vt) threaten
odoroku, 驚く (vi) be surprised, be shocked
odoru, 踊る (vi) dance
ogamu, 拝む (vt) worship
ogoru, おごる (vt) treat (a person) to
oikosu, 追い越す (vt) pass
okasu, 犯す (vt) commit (a crime)
okonau, 行う (vt) do, conduct, perform
okoru, 怒る (vi) get angry
okoru, 起こる (vi) occur
okosu, 起こす (vt) wake up, cause
oku, 置く (vt) put
okuru, 送る (vt) send, see off
omoidasu, 思い出す (vt) remember, recall
omou, 思う (vt) think
orosu, 下ろす (vt) lower, unload
oru, 折る (vt) bend, break, fold

osamaru, 治まる (vi) subside, quiet down
osou, 襲う (vt) attack, invade
osu, 押す (vt) push, press
otosu, 落とす (vt) drop, lose
ou, 追う (vt) run after, chase
ou, 負う (vt) bear on one's back
ōu, 覆う (vt) cover
owaru, 終わる (vi) end, finish
oyobosu, 及ぼす (vt) influence, affect
oyogu, 泳ぐ (vi) swim

sagaru, 下がる (vi) fall, drop, hang
sagasu, 探す (vt) look for, search
sakebu, 叫ぶ (vi) shout
saku, 咲く (vi) bloom
saku, 裂く (vt) tear, split
samasu, 冷ます (vt) cool
samasu, 覚ます (vt) awake
saru, 去る (vi) leave, go away
sasayaku, ささやく (vi) whisper
sasou, 誘う (vt) invite
sasu, 指す (vt) point to, indicate
sasu, 差す (vi, vt) shine upon, hold up
 (an umbrella)
sasu, 刺す (vt) stab, pierce
satoru, 悟る (vt) realize, understand
sawagu, 騒ぐ (vi) make a noise
sawaru, 触る (vi) touch
shaberu, しゃべる (vt) chat, talk
shibaru, 縛る (vt) tie, bind
shikaru, 叱る (vt) scold
shiku, 敷く (vt) lay, pave, spread (a mat)
shimaru, 閉まる (vi) be closed, be shut
shimaru, 締まる (vi) be tightened
shimau, しまう (vt) put away
shimesu, 示す (vt) show, point out
shinu, 死ぬ (vi) die
shiru, 知る (vt) know
shitagau, 従う (vi) follow, obey
shizumu, 沈む (vi) sink
sodatsu, 育つ (vi) grow

somaru, 染まる (vi) be dyed, be tinged
 with
somuku, 背く (vi) disobey
soru, そる (vt) shave
soru, 反る (vi) warp
suberu, 滑る (vi) slide, slip, skate
sugosu, 過ごす (vt) spend (one's time)
suku, 好く (vt) like
suku, すく (vi) become empty
sukuu, 救う (vt) rescue
sumu, 住む (vi) live, reside
sumu, 済む (vi) end
susumu, 進む (vi) advance
suu, 吸う (vt) inhale, suck, smoke
suwaru, 座る (vi) sit

tadasu, 正す (vt) correct
taku, 炊く (vt) boil
takuramu, たくらむ (vt) plot, scheme
takusu, 託す (vt) entrust
tamaru, たまる (vi) accumulate
tamesu, 試す (vt) try, test
tamotsu, 保つ (vt) keep, maintain
tanomu, 頼む (vt) ask, request
tanoshimu, 楽しむ (vt) enjoy
taosu, 倒す (vt) knock down, defeat
tarasu, 垂らす (vt) hang down, drip
tarumu, たるむ (vi) loosen
tasukaru, 助かる (vi) be saved, be rescued
tatakau, 戦う (vi) fight, struggle
tataku, たたく (vt) hit, strike, slap, knock
tatsu, 立つ (vi) stand, rise
tatsu, 建つ (vi) be built
tatsu, 経つ (vi) pass, elapse
tayoru, 頼る (vi) depend on, rely on
terasu, 照らす (vt) light up, illuminate
teru, 照る (vi) shine
tetsudau, 手伝う (vt) help, assist
tobasu, 飛ばす (vt) let fly, skip
tobu, 飛ぶ (vi) fly
tobu, 跳ぶ (vi) jump

todoku, 届く (vi) be delivered, arrive, reach

togaru, とがる (vi) become sharp

togu, 研ぐ (vt) sharpen, whet

tokasu, 溶かす (vt) melt, dissolve

toku, 解く (vt) untie, solve

toku, 溶く (vt) melt, dissolve

tomaru, 止まる (vi) stop, be parked

tomaru, 泊まる (vi) lodge, stay the night

toru, 取る (vt) get, take, catch

tōru, 通る (vi) pass

tōsu, 通す (vt) let (a person) pass

tsubusu, つぶす (vt) smash, scrap

tsugunau, 償う (vt) compensate

tsukamu, つかむ (vt) grasp, hold, grip

tsukau, 使う (vt) use, spend

tsukiau, 付き合う (vi) associate

tsuku, 付く (vi) stick, be installed

tsuku, 着く (vi) arrive

tsuku, つく (vi) be lighted

tsukurou, 繕う (vt) patch, repair

tsukuru, 作る (vt) make, produce

tsumamu, つまむ (vt) pick

tsumaru, 詰まる (vi) be blocked

tsumoru, 積もる (vi) be piled up

tsumu, 積む (vt) pile up

tsumu, 摘む (vt) pick, trim

tsunagaru, つながる (vi) be connected

tsunagu, つなぐ (vt) connect, link

tsureteiku, 連れて行く (vt) take (a person)

tsuru, 釣る (vt) fish

tsuru, つる (vt) hang down, suspend

tsutawaru, 伝わる (vi) be transmitted

tsutsumu, 包む (vt) wrap, envelop

tsuzuku, 続く (vi) continue, last

ubau, 奪う (vt) snatch, rob

ugokasu, 動かす (vt) move, run (a machine)

ugoku, 動く (vi) move, run

ukabu, 浮かぶ (vi) float

ukemotsu, 受け持つ (vt) take charge

uketoru, 受け取る (vt) get, receive

umu, 生む (vt) give birth

uragaesu, 裏返す (vt) overturn

uramu, 恨む (vt) resent

uranau, 占う (vt) tell fortunes

urayamu, うらやむ (vt) envy

uru, 売る (vt) sell

utagau, 疑う (vt) doubt, suspect

utau, 歌う (vt) sing

utsu, 打つ (vt) beat, hit, strike

utsuru, 移る (vi) move, transfer

utsuru, 映る (vi) be reflected

utsuru, 写る (vi) be copied, be in a picture

utsusu, 移す (vt) move, transfer

utsusu, 映す (vt) reflect

utsusu, 写す (vt) copy, take a picture

wakaru, 分かる (vi) understand, know

warau, 笑う (vi) laugh, smile

waru, 割る (vt) break, split, divide

wataru, 渡る (vi) cross

watasu, 渡す (vt) hand

yaburu, 破る (vt) tear, break

yaku, 焼く (vt) burn, bake, roast

yakusu, 訳す (vt) translate

yamu, やむ (vi) stop, cease

yaru, やる (vt) do, give

yasumu, 休む (vi) rest, be absent

yatou, 雇う (vt) employ, hire

yobu, 呼ぶ (vt) call, invite

yogosu, 汚す (vt) dirty

yomu, 読む (vt) read

yorokobu, 喜ぶ (vi) be glad, be delighted

yoru, 寄る (vi) drop in

you, 酔う (vi) get drunk

yugamu, ゆがむ (vi) warp

yurumu, 緩む (vi) loosen

yurusu, 許す (vt) forgive, permit

yusuru, 揺する (vt) shake, swing

yuzuru, 譲る (vt) concede, hand over

2. Regular II Verbs

abareru, 暴れる (vi) rage, storm
abiru, 浴びる (vt) take (a shower)
abiseru, 浴びせる (vt) pour on
afureru, あふれる (vi) overflow
ageru, 上げる (vt) raise, lift, give
akeru, 開ける (vt) open
akeru, 空ける (vt) empty
akeru, 明ける (vi) day breaks
akirameru, あきらめる (vt) give up
akiru, 飽きる (vi) be tired of
arawareru, 現れる (vi) appear
atatameru, 暖める (vt) heat, warm
ateru, 当てる (vt) hit, strike, guess
atsumeru, 集める (vt) assemble, collect
awaseru, 合わせる (vt) combine
awateru, 慌てる (vi) be in rush
azukeru, 預ける (vt) deposit, leave (a thing) in a person's care

butsukeru, ぶつける (vt) hit, throw

chijimeru, 縮める (vt) shorten, shrink

dekakeru, 出かける (vi) go out, depart
dekiru, 出来る (vi) can, be completed
deru, 出る (vi) leave, come out, attend

eru, 得る (vt) get, obtain

fueru, 増える (vi) increase
fukumeru, 含める (vt) include, contain
fureru, 触れる (vi) touch
fuzakeru, ふざける (vi) play pranks

haeru, 生える (vi) grow, sprout
haeru, 映える (vi) glow
hajimeru, 始める (vt) begin, start
hameru, はめる (vt) wear (a ring)
hanareru, 離れる (vi) be separated

haneru, 跳ねる (vi) leap, jump
hareru, 晴れる (vi) clear up
hareru, 腫れる (vi) swell
hazureru, 外れる (vi) come off, be detached
hieru, 冷える (vi) get cold, cool
hikiukeru, 引き受ける (vt) take charge
hirogeru, 広げる (vt) spread, extend
hoeru, ほえる (vi) bark, howl
homeru, 褒める (vt) praise

ijimeru, いじめる (vt) tease, bully
ikeru, 生ける (vt) arrange (flowers)
ikiru, 生きる (vi) live
ireru, 入れる (vt) put in, include
iru, いる (vi) be, stay

kaeru, 変える (vt) change
kaeru, 代える (vt) replace
kakaeru, 抱える (vt) hold
kakeru, 掛ける (vt) hang
kakureru, 隠れる (vi) hide
kangaeru, 考える (vt) think, consider
kanjiru, 感じる (vi, vt) feel
kareru, 枯れる (vi) wither
kariru, 借りる (vt) borrow, rent
kasaneru, 重ねる (vt) pile up
katazukeru, 片付ける (vt) put in order, tidy up
kazoeru, 数える (vt) count
kieru, 消える (vi) go out, disappear
kikoeru, 聞こえる (vi) be audible, can hear
kimeru, 決める (vt) decide, choose
kireru, 切れる (vi) cut off, expire, run out, be sharp
kiru, 着る (vt) wear, put on
koeru, 越える (vi) cross, pass
koeru, 肥える (vi) be fertile, get fat
kogeru, 焦げる (vi) burn, scorch
kotaeru, 答える (vi) answer, reply, respond

kowareru, 壊れる (vi) break, be out of order

kudakeru, 砕ける (vi) be smashed, be crushed

kumiawaseru, 組み合わせる (vt) combine

kumitateru, 組み立てる (vt) assemble

kuraberu, 比べる (vt) compare

kureru, くれる (vt) give

kureru, 暮れる (vi) get dark

kurushimeru, 苦しめる (vt) torment, torture

kutabireru, くたびれる (vi) be tired

kuwaeru, 加える (vt) add, increase

kuwaeru, くわえる (vt) hold in the mouth

kuzureru, 崩れる (vi) collapse

machigaeru, 間違える (vt) make a mistake

mageru, 曲げる (vt) bend, curve

makaseru, 任せる (vt) entrust

makeru, 負ける (vi) be defeated, lose (a game)

matomeru, まとめる (vt) put together, unify

mazeru, 混ぜる (vt) mix, blend

midareru, 乱れる (vi) go out of order, be corrupt

mieru, 見える (vi) be seen, can see

miru, 見る (vt) see, look, watch

miseru, 見せる (vt) show

mitomeru, 認める (vt) approve

mitsukeru, 見付ける (vt) find, discover

moeru, 燃える (vi) burn

mōkeru, もうける (vt) earn, make a profit

moreru, 漏れる (vi) leak

moteru, 持てる (vi) be popular with

motomeru, 求める (vt) demand, request

mukeru, 向ける (vt) turn (something) to

naderu, なでる (vt) smooth down

nagareru, 流れる (vi) stream, float

nageru, 投げる (vt) throw, pitch

naraberu, 並べる (vt) put (things) in order, display

nareru, 慣れる (vi) get used to

nejiru, ねじる (vt) twist, wrench

neru, 寝る (vi) go to bed, lie down

nigeru, 逃げる (vi) run away, escape

niru, 煮る (vt) boil

niru, 似る (vi) look like, resemble

nobiru, 延びる (vi) be postponed

nobiru, 伸びる (vi) extend, lengthen

norikaeru, 乗り換える (vi) change (trains)

noseru, 乗せる (vt) take (a person) on board

noseru, 載せる (vt) print, load

nureru, ぬれる (vi) get wet, be moist

obieru, おびえる (vi) be scared

oboeru, 覚える (vt) memorize, learn

ochiru, 落ちる (vi) fall

oikakeru, 追いかける (vt) run after, chase

okiru, 起きる (vi) wake up, get up, occur

okureru, 遅れる (vi) be late, be behind

oreru, 折れる (vi) break, bend

oriru, 降りる (vi) get off

oriru, 下りる (vi) go down

osaeru, 押さえる (vt) press down

osaeru, 抑える (vt) suppress

osameru, 治める (vt) govern, quiet

oshieru, 教える (vt) teach, tell

sabiru, さびる (vi) get rusty

sageru, 下げる (vt) lower, hang

sakaeru, 栄える (vi) prosper, flourish

sakeru, 裂ける (vi) tear, split

sakeru, 避ける (vt) avoid

sasaeru, 支える (vt) support, prop up

semeru, 攻める (vt) attack

semeru, 責める (vt) blame

shibireru, しびれる (vi) become numb

shiireru, 仕入れる (vt) stock

shimeru, 閉める (vt) shut, close

shimeru, 締める (vt) tie, fasten, tighten

shimiru, 染みる (vi) permeate, smart

shinjiru, 信じる (vt) believe, trust

shiraberu, 調べる (vt) check, investigate

shiraseru, 知らせる (vt) inform, tell

shizumeru, 沈める (vt) sink

shizumeru, 静める (vt) quiet, suppress

sodateru, 育てる (vt) bring up, raise

soeru, 添える (vt) attach

someru, 染める (vt) dye, color

somukeru, 背ける (vt) turn (one's face) away

sonaeru, 供える (vt) offer (to a god)

sonaeru, 備える (vt) prepare, be furnished with

sugiru, 過ぎる (vi) pass, exceed

sugureru, 優れる (vi) be excellent

surikireru, 擦り切れる (vi) be worn out

susumeru, 進める (vt) advance

susumeru, 勧める (vt) recommend

suteru, 捨てる (vt) throw away, abandon

taberu, 食べる (vt) eat

taeru, 耐える (vi) endure

takameru, 高める (vt) raise, lift

takuwaeru, 蓄える (vt) save, store, stock

tameru, ためる (vt) accumulate

taoreru, 倒れる (vi) fall down, collapse

tariru, 足りる (vi) be enough, suffice

tashikameru, 確かめる (vt) confirm

tasukeru, 助ける (vt) help, save, rescue

tateru, 立てる (vt) stand, erect

tateru, 建てる (vt) build

tazuneru, 尋ねる (vt) ask

tazuneru, 訪ねる (vt) visit

todokeru, 届ける (vt) deliver, report

tojiru, 閉じる (vi, vt) shut, close

tokeru, 溶ける (vi) melt, dissolve

tokeru, 解ける (vi) be solved, become untied

tomeru, 止める (vt) stop, turn off, park

tomeru, 泊める (vt) give lodging

tomeru, 留める (vt) fasten, detain

toraeru, 捕らえる (vt) catch, capture

toreru, 取れる (vi) come off, be caught

toriireru, 取り入れる (vt) adopt

torikaeru, 取り替える (vt) exchange, renew

totonoeru, 整える (vt) adjust, put in order

tsubureru, つぶれる (vi) be smashed, go bankrupt

tsūjiru, 通じる (vi) be laid, be understood

tsukamaeru, 捕まえる (vt) catch, arrest

tsukareru, 疲れる (vi) be tired

tsukeru, 付ける (vt) attach, install

tsukeru, つける (vt) light, switch on

tsutaeru, 伝える (vt) report, tell, transmit

tsutomeru, 勤める (vi) work for, be employed

tsutomeru, 努める (vi) make efforts

tsuzukeru, 続ける (vt) continue, proceed

ueru, 植える (vt) plant

ukaberu, 浮かべる (vt) float, set afloat

ukeireru, 受け入れる (vt) accept, assent to (a proposal)

ukeru, 受ける (vt) get, receive

uketsukeru, 受け付ける (vt) accept (applications)

umareru, 生まれる (vi) be born

ureru, 売れる (vi) sell

urikireru, 売り切れる (vi) be sold out

uttaeru, 訴える (vt) appeal, complain

wakareru, 分かれる (vi) be divided

wakareru, 別れる (vi) part from, separate from

wakeru, 分ける (vt) divide, separate, share

wareru, 割れる (vi) break, split

wasureru, 忘れる (vt) forget, leave (a thing) behind

yabureru, 破れる (vi) tear
yabureru, 敗れる (vi) be defeated, lose (a game)
yakeru, 焼ける (vi) be burnt, be baked, be roasted
yameru, やめる (vt) quit, stop doing
yameru, 辞める (vt) resign
yaseru, やせる (vi) lose weight, become thin
yogoreru, 汚れる (vi) get dirty
yoseru, 寄せる (vt) bring (a thing) near
yuderu, ゆでる (vt) boil
yureru, 揺れる (vi) quake, shake, swing
yurumeru, 緩める (vt) loosen

zureru, ずれる (vi) slip, slide

3. Irregular and *Suru* Verbs

•Irregular Verbs
kuru, 来る (vi) come
mottekuru, 持って来る (vt) bring (a thing)

tsuretekuru, 連れて来る (vt) bring (a person)

suru, する (vt) do, play

•Noun + *Suru* Verbs
adobaisu suru, アドバイスする (vi) advise
aisatsu suru, あいさつする (vi) greet
akushu suru, 握手する (vi) shake hands
akuyō suru, 悪用する (vt) misuse, abuse
anaunsu suru, アナウンスする (vt) announce
anki suru, 暗記する (vt) learn by heart, memorize

annai suru, 案内する (vt) guide
anshin suru, 安心する (vi) feel at ease
antei suru, 安定する (vi) become stable
apīru suru, アピールする (vi) appeal
atakku suru, アタックする (vt) attack

bakuhatsu suru, 爆発する (vi) explode
bengo suru, 弁護する (vt) defend
benkyō suru, 勉強する (vt) study
bōgai suru, 妨害する (vt) interrupt, obstruct
bōshi suru, 防止する (vt) prevent
boshū suru, 募集する (vt) recruit
bunseki suru, 分析する (vt) analyze

charenji suru, チャレンジする (vi) challenge
chekku suru, チェックする (vt) check
chenji suru, チェンジする (vi, vt) change
chikoku suru, 遅刻する (vi) be late (for school)
chinretsu suru, 陳列する (vt) display
chokin suru, 貯金する (vi) deposit, save money
chōsa suru, 調査する (vt) investigate
chūi suru, 注意する (vi) pay attention, warn
chūkoku suru, 忠告する (vi) advise
chūmon suru, 注文する (vt) order (goods)
chūshi suru, 中止する (vt) cancel

daihyō suru, 代表する (vt) represent
dakyō suru, 妥協する (vi) compromise
dansu suru, ダンスする (vi) dance
debyū suru, デビューする (vi) make one's debut
denwa suru, 電話する (vi) phone, ring
dēto suru, デートする (vi) date
disupurē suru, ディスプレーする (vt) display

dōi suru, 同意する (vi) agree

dokuritsu suru, 独立する (vi) become independent

doryoku suru, 努力する (vi) make efforts

eigyō suru, 営業する (vi) do business

enjo suru, 援助する (vt) aid, assist

enjoi suru, エンジョイする (vt) enjoy

enki suru, 延期する (vt) postpone

enzetsu suru, 演説する (vi) make a speech

esukēpu suru, エスケープする (vi) escape

fukushū suru, 復習する (vt) review

fukyū suru, 普及する (vi, vt) spread, be popular

fusoku suru, 不足する (vi) be short of

futan suru, 負担する (vt) bear (expenses)

gaishoku suru, 外食する (vi) eat out

gaishutsu suru, 外出する (vi) go out

gaman suru, 我慢する (vt) be patient

genshō suru, 減少する (vi, vt) decrease

giron suru, 議論する (vi) argue, debate

gokai suru, 誤解する (vt) misunderstand

gōkaku suru, 合格する (vi) pass (an exam)

gōkei suru, 合計する (vt) total

haishi suru, 廃止する (vt) abolish

haitatsu suru, 配達する (vt) deliver

hakai suru, 破壊する (vi, vt) destroy

hakkō suru, 発行する (vt) publish

hakushu suru, 拍手する (vi) clap

handan suru, 判断する (vt) judge

hannō suru, 反応する (vi) react, respond

hansha suru, 反射する (vi, vt) reflect

hantai suru, 反対する (vi) oppose

happyō suru, 発表する (vt) announce

hasan suru, 破産する (vi) go bankrupt

hassō suru, 発送する (vt) send out

hatsugen suru, 発言する (vi) speak

hatsumei suru, 発明する (vt) invent

hatten suru, 発展する (vi) develop

heiten suru, 閉店する (vi) close a shop

henji suru, 返事する (vi) answer, reply

henka suru, 変化する (vi) change

henkō suru, 変更する (vi, vt) change

henpin suru, 返品する (vi) return goods

herupu suru, ヘルプする (vt) help

hihan suru, 批判する (vt) criticize

hihyō suru, 批評する (vt) criticize

hitei suru, 否定する (vt) deny

hōkoku suru, 報告する (vt) report

hōmon suru, 訪問する (vt) visit

hon'yaku suru, 翻訳する (vt) translate

hoshō suru, 保証する (vt) guarantee

hōsō suru, 放送する (vt) broadcast

hozon suru, 保存する (vt) preserve

ichi suru, 位置する (vi) be located

idō suru, 移動する (vi, vt) move

ihan suru, 違反する (vi) violate

iji suru, 維持する (vt) maintain

insatsu suru, 印刷する (vt) print

intabyū suru, インタビューする (vi) interview

intai suru, 引退する (vi) retire

irai suru, 依頼する (vt) request

ishoku suru, 移植する (vt) transplant

iten suru, 移転する (vi, vt) move to

jama suru, 邪魔する (vt) interrupt

jikken suru, 実験する (vt) experiment

jiman suru, 自慢する (vt) be proud of

jiritsu suru, 自立する (vi) become independent

jisatsu suru, 自殺する (vi) commit suicide

jishoku suru, 辞職する (vi, vt) resign

jitsugen suru, 実現する (vi, vt) come true, turn into reality

234

jōho suru, 譲歩する (vi) concede, compromise

jukutatsu suru, 熟達する (vi) master

junbi suru, 準備する (vt) prepare

kabâ suru, カバーする (vt) cover

kâbu suru, カーブする (vi) curve

kaichiku suru, 改築する (vt) rebuild

kaifuku suru, 回復する (vi, vt) get well, recover

kaigi suru, 会議する (vi) hold a conference

kaihatsu suru, 開発する (vt) develop, exploit

kaikaku suru, 改革する (vt) reform

kaiketsu suru, 解決する (vt) solve

kaisai suru, 開催する (vt) hold/open (an exhibition)

kaisan suru, 解散する (vi, vt) break up, dissolve

kaitei suru, 改訂する (vt) revise

kaiten suru, 開店する (vi) open a shop

kaiten suru, 回転する (vi) rotate, turn

kaitō suru, 回答する (vi) answer, reply

kaiwa suru, 会話する (vi) talk

kaiyaku suru, 解約する (vt) cancel a contract

kaizen suru, 改善する (vt) improve

kakō suru, 加工する (vt) process

kakudai suru, 拡大する (vi, vt) enlarge

kakunin suru, 確認する (vt) confirm

kangei suru, 歓迎する (vt) welcome

kankō suru, 観光する (vt) see the sights

kanri suru, 管理する (vt) manage

kansatsu suru, 観察する (vt) observe

kansei suru, 完成する (vi, vt) complete

kanshin suru, 感心する (vi) admire

katei suru, 仮定する (vi, vt) suppose

katsudō suru, 活動する (vi) be active

katto suru, カットする (vt) cut

keiei suru, 経営する (vt) run (a company)

keika suru, 経過する (vi) pass, elapse

keikaku suru, 計画する (vt) plan

keiken suru, 経験する (vt) experience

keisan suru, 計算する (vt) calculate

keiyaku suru, 契約する (vt) contract

kekkon suru, 結婚する (vi) marry

kenbutsu suru, 見物する (vt) see the sights

kenka suru, けんかする (vi) quarrel, fight

kenkyū suru, 研究する (vt) research

kensetsu suru, 建設する (vt) build, construct

kesseki suru, 欠席する (vi) be absent

kettei suru, 決定する (vi, vt) decide

kikoku suru, 帰国する (vi) return to one's country

kin'en suru, 禁煙する (vi) quit smoking

kinen suru, 記念する (vt) commemorate

kiroku suru, 記録する (vt) record

kisu suru, キスする (vi) kiss

kitai suru, 期待する (vt) expect, hope

kōchi suru, コーチする (vt) coach

kōgeki suru, 攻撃する (vt) attack

kōgi suru, 講義する (vt) lecture

kōji suru, 工事する (vt) construct

kōkan suru, 交換する (vt) exchange

kōkoku suru, 広告する (vt) advertise

kontorōru suru, コントロールする (vt) control

kōryo suru, 考慮する (vt) consider

koshō suru, 故障する (vi) break down, be out of order

kōshō suru, 交渉する (vi) negotiate

kyanpu suru, キャンプする (vi) camp

kyanseru suru, キャンセルする (vt) cancel

kyatchi suru, キャッチする (vt) catch

kyohi suru, 拒否する (vt) refuse

kyōiku suru, 教育する (vt) educate

kyoka suru, 許可する (vt) permit

kyōryoku suru, 協力する (vi) cooperate

kyōsei suru, 強請する (vt) force

kyōsō suru, 競争する (vi) compete

kyūjo suru, 救助する (vt) rescue

kyūkei suru, 休憩する (vi) rest

kyūshū suru, 吸収する (vt) absorb

manzoku suru, 満足する (vi) be satisfied

massâji suru, マッサージする (vt) massage

masutâ suru, マスターする (vt) master

matchi suru, マッチする (vi) match

mensetsu suru, 面接する (vi) interview

mikkusu suru, ミックスする (vt) mix

mujun suru, 矛盾する (vi) contradict

mushi suru, 無視する (vt) ignore

nattoku suru, 納得する (vi) consent, agree

ninmei suru, 任命する (vt) appoint

ninshin suru, 妊娠する (vi) get pregnant

nokku suru, ノックする (vt) knock

nyūgaku suru, 入学する (vi) enter a school

nyūin suru, 入院する (vi) be hospitalized

ōbâ suru, オーバーする (vi, vt) exceed

ōbo suru, 応募する (vi) apply

ōdâ suru, オーダーする (vt) order

ōdan suru, 横断する (vt) cross

ōen suru, 応援する (vt) aid, cheer

ōfuku suru, 往復する (vi) go and return, make a round trip

omitto suru, オミットする (vt) omit

ōpun suru, オープンする (vt) open

ōryō suru, 横領する (vt) usurp

ōyō suru, 応用する (vi) put into practice

pasu suru, パスする (vi) pass

pikkuappu suru, ピックアップする (vt) pick up

purinto suru, プリントする (vt) print

puropōzu suru, プロポーズする (vi) propose

rakudai suru, 落第する (vi) fail (an exam)

renraku suru, 連絡する (vi, vt) contact

renshū suru, 練習する (vt) practice

rikai suru, 理解する (vt) understand

rikon suru, 離婚する (vi) divorce

ritaia suru, リタイアする (vi) retire

riyō suru, 利用する (vt) use

rokuon suru, 録音する (vt) record (on tape)

ryokō suru, 旅行する (vi) travel, take a trip

ryōri suru, 料理する (vt) cook

ryūgaku suru, 留学する (vi) study abroad

ryūkō suru, 流行する (vi) be in fashion, be popular

saiban suru, 裁判する (vt) try (a case)

sain suru, サインする (vi) sign

saiyō suru, 採用する (vt) adopt, employ

sanka suru, 参加する (vi) participate, join

sanpo suru, 散歩する (vi) take a walk

sansei suru, 賛成する (vi) agree

seichō suru, 成長する (vi) grow

seikatsu suru, 生活する (vi) live, make a living

seikō suru, 成功する (vi) succeed

seiri suru, 整理する (vt) put in order

seisan suru, 生産する (vt) produce

senden suru, 宣伝する (vt) advertise

senkyo suru, 選挙する (vt) elect, vote

sensō suru, 戦争する (vi) make war

sentaku suru, 洗濯する (vt) wash (clothes)

setsumei suru, 説明する (vt) explain

setsuyaku suru, 節約する (vt) save

settoku suru, 説得する (vt) persuade

sewa suru, 世話する (vt) take care of

shibō suru, 死亡する (vi) die

shidō suru, 指導する (vt) lead, coach

shigoto suru, 仕事する (vi) work

shihai suru, 支配する (vt) control

shiji suru, 指示する (vt) instruct

shiji suru, 支持する (vt) support

shiken suru, 試験する (vt) examine, test

shinpai suru, 心配する (vi, vt) be worried

shinpo suru, 進歩する (vi) progress

shinsei suru, 申請する (vt) apply

shin'yō suru, 信用する (vt) trust

shippai suru, 失敗する (vi) fail

shitsumon suru, 質問する (vi, vt) ask a question

shiyō suru, 使用する (vt) use

shōhi suru, 消費する (vt) consume

shōkai suru, 紹介する (vt) introduce

shokuji suru, 食事する (vi) dine

shomei suru, 署名する (vi) sign

shōmei suru, 証明する (vt) prove

shōshin suru, 昇進する (vi) be promoted

shōtai suru, 招待する (vt) invite

shōtotsu suru, 衝突する (vi) collide

shoyū suru, 所有する (vt) have, own

shozoku suru, 所属する (vi) belong

shuchō suru, 主張する (vt) assert, insist

shukkō suru, 出航する (vi) sail off

shukushō suru, 縮小する (vi, vt) reduce

shuppan suru, 出版する (vt) publish

shuppatsu suru, 出発する (vi) depart, leave

shūri suru, 修理する (vt) repair, fix

shusseki suru, 出席する (vi) attend

shutchō suru, 出張する (vi) go on a business trip

sōdan suru, 相談する (vt) consult

sōji suru, 掃除する (vt) clean, sweep

sōkin suru, 送金する (vi) remit money

sonkei suru, 尊敬する (vt) respect

sōsa suru, 捜査する (vt) investigate

soshiki suru, 組織する (vt) organize

sotsugyō suru, 卒業する (vi) graduate

suisen suru, 推薦する (vt) recommend

suraido suru, スライドする (vi, vt) slide

surippu suru, スリップする (vi) slip

sutāto suru, スタートする (vi) start

sutoppu suru, ストップする (vi, vt) stop

taiho suru, 逮捕する (vt) arrest

taiin suru, 退院する (vi) get out of a hospital

tantō suru, 担当する (vt) take charge

tatchi suru, タッチする (vi) touch

teian suru, 提案する (vt) propose

teikyō suru, 提供する (vt) offer

teishutsu suru, 提出する (vt) submit

tenkin suru, 転勤する (vi) be transferred (to another office)

tesuto suru, テストする (vt) test

tetsuya suru, 徹夜する (vi) stay up all night

tōchaku suru, 到着する (vi) arrive

tōhyō suru, 投票する (vi) vote

tōitsu suru, 統一する (vt) unify

tōroku suru, 登録する (vt) register

tōsan suru, 倒産する (vi) go bankrupt

tōsen suru, 当選する (vi) be elected

tōshi suru, 投資する (vi) invest

tsuika suru, 追加する (vt) add

tsuikyū suru, 追求する (vt) pursue

tsuiraku suru, 墜落する (vi) fall, crash

tsūka suru, 通過する (vi) pass

tsūkin suru, 通勤する (vi) commute (to work)

tsūshin suru, 通信する (vi) correspond, communicate

undō suru, 運動する (vi) exercise

unsō suru, 運送する (vt) transport

unten suru, 運転する (vt) drive (a car), operate (a machine)

yakusoku suru, 約束する (vt) promise

yōkyū suru, 要求する (vt) demand

yoshū suru, 予習する (vt) prepare one's lessons

yosō suru, 予想する (vt) expect, forecast

yoyaku suru, 予約する (vt) reserve

yūkai suru, 誘拐する (vt) kidnap

yunyū suru, 輸入する (vt) import

yūshō suru, 優勝する (vi) win a championship

yushutsu suru, 輸出する (vt) export

yūsō suru, 郵送する (vt) mail

zangyō suru, 残業する (vi) work overtime

zōka suru, 増加する (vi, vt) increase

ENGLISH-JAPANESE VERB LIST

Note: numbers indicate conjugation: 1 = regular I, 2 = regular II, 3 = irregular.

abandon, suteru 捨てる (vt, 2)

abolish, haishi suru 廃止する (vt, 3)

absent (be absent), yasumu 休む (vi, 1), kesseki suru 欠席する (vi, 3)

absorb, kyūshū suru 吸収する (vt, 3)

abuse, akuyō suru 悪用する (vt, 3)

accept, ukeireru 受け入れる (vt, 2); accept applications, uketsukeru 受け付ける (vt, 2)

accumulate, tamaru たまる (vi, 1), tameru ためる (vt, 2)

active (be active), katsudō suru 活動する (vi, 3)

add, kuwaeru 加える (vt, 2), tsuika suru 追加する (vt, 3)

adjust, totonoeru 整える (vt, 2)

admire, kanshin suru 感心する (vi, 3)

adopt, toriireru 取り入れる (vt, 2), saiyō suru 採用する (vt, 3)

advance, susumu 進む (vi, 1), susumeru 進める (vt, 2)

advertise, senden suru 宣伝する (vt, 3), kōkoku suru 広告する (vt, 3)

advise, chūkoku suru 忠告する (vi, 3), adobaisu suru アドバイスする (vi, 3)

affect, oyobosu 及ぼす (vt, 1)

agree, sansei suru 賛成する (vi, 3), nattoku suru 納得する (vi, 3), dōi suru 同意する (vi, 3)

aid, enjo suru 援助する (vt, 3), ōen suru 応援する (vt, 3)

aim, nerau ねらう (vt, 1), mezasu 目指す (vt, 1)

analyze, bunseki suru 分析する (vt, 3)

angry (get angry), okoru 怒る (vi, 1)

announce, happyō suru 発表する (vt, 3), anaunsu suru アナウンスする (vt, 3)

answer, kotaeru 答える (vi, 2), henji suru 返事する (vi, 3), kaitō suru 回答する (vi, 3)

apologize, ayamaru 謝る (vt, 1)

appeal, uttaeru 訴える (vt, 2), apīru suru アピールする (vi, 3)

appear, arawareru 現れる (vi, 2)

apply, mōshikomu 申し込む (vt, 1), ōbo suru 応募する (vi, 3), shinsei suru 申請する (vt, 3)

appoint, ninmei suru 任命する (vt, 3)

approach, chikazuku 近づく (vi, 1)

approve, mitomeru 認める (vt, 2)

argue, giron suru 議論する (vi, 3)

arrange (flowers), ikeru 生ける (vt, 2)

arrest, tsukamaeru 捕まえる (vt, 2), taiho suru 逮捕する (vt, 3)

arrive, tsuku 着く (vi, 1), tōchaku suru 到着する (vi, 3), todoku 届く (vi, 1), itaru 至る (vi, 1)

ask, kiku 聞く (vt, 1), tazuneru 尋ねる (vt, 2), tanomu 頼む (vt, 1); ask a question, shitsumon suru 質問する (vi, vt, 3)

assemble, atsumaru 集まる (vi, 1), atsumeru 集める (vt, 2), kumitateru 組み立てる (vt, 2)

assent (to a proposal), ukeireru 受け入れる (vt, 2)

assert, shuchō suru 主張する (vt, 3)

assist, tetsudau 手伝う (vt, 1), enjo suru 援助する (vt, 3)

associate, tsukiau 付き合う (vi, 1)

attach, tsukeru 付ける (vt, 2), soeru 添える (vt, 2)

attack, osou 襲う (vt, 1), semeru 攻める (vt, 2), kōgeki suru 攻撃する (vt, 3), atakku suru アタックする (vt, 3)

attend, deru 出る (vi, 2), shusseki suru 出席する (vi, 3)

attention (pay attention), chūi suru 注意する (vi, 3)

audible (be audible), kikoeru 聞こえる (vi, 2)

avoid, sakeru 避ける (vt, 2)

awake, samasu 覚ます (vt, 1)

bake, yaku 焼く (vt, 1); be baked, yakeru 焼ける (vi, 2)

bankrupt (go bankrupt), tsubureru つぶれる (vi, 2), tōsan suru 倒産する (vi, 3), hasan suru 破産する (vi, 3)

bark, hoeru ほえる (vi, 2)

be, aru ある (vi, 1), iru いる (vi, 2), irassharu いらっしゃる (vi, 1)

bear (fruit), minoru 実る (vi, 1); bear on one's back, ou 負う (vt, 1); bear expenses, futan suru 負担する (vt, 3)

beat, utsu 打つ (vt, 1), hataku はたく (vt, 1), makasu 負かす (vt, 1)

become, naru なる (vi, 1)

bed (go to bed), neru 寝る (vi, 2)

begin, hajimaru 始まる (vi, 1), hajimeru 始める (vt, 2)

behind (be behind), okureru 遅れる (vi, 2)

believe, shinjiru 信じる (vt, 2)

belong, shozoku suru 所属する (vi, 3)

bend, magaru 曲がる (vi, 1), mageru 曲げる (vt, 2), oreru 折れる (vi, 2), oru 折る (vt, 1)

bind, shibaru 縛る (vt, 1), kukuru くくる (vt, 1)

birth (give birth), umu 生む (vt, 1)

bite, kamu かむ (vt, 1), kajiru かじる (vt, 1)

blame, semeru 責める (vt, 2)

blend, mazaru 混ざる (vi, 1), mazeru 混ぜる (vt, 2)

block, fusagu ふさぐ (vt, 1); be blocked, tsumaru 詰まる (vi, 1)

bloom, saku 咲く (vi, 1)

blow, fuku 吹く (vi, 1)

board (take people on board), noseru 乗せる (vt, 2)

boil, niru 煮る (vt, 2), taku 炊く (vt, 1), yuderu ゆでる (vt, 2)

born (be born), umareru 生まれる (vi, 2)

borrow, kariru 借りる (vt, 2)

bound, hazumu 弾む (vi, 1)

break, kowasu 壊す (vt, 1), kowareru 壊れる (vi, 2), waru 割る (vt, 1), wareru 割れる (vi, 2), oru 折る (vt, 1), oreru 折れる (vi, 2), yaburu 破る (vt, 1); break up, kaisan suru 解散する (vi, 3); break down, koshō suru 故障する (vi, 3); day breaks, akeru 明ける (vi, 2)

bring (a thing), mottekuru 持って来る (vt, 3); bring a person, tsuretekuru

連れて来る(vt, 3); bring up, sodateru 育てる (vt, 2)

broadcast, hosō suru 放送する (vt, 3)

brush, migaku 磨く (vt, 1); brush off, harau 払う (vt, 1)

build, tateru 建てる(vt, 2), kensetsu suru 建設する(vt, 3); be built, tatsu 建つ (vi, 1)

bully, ijimeru いじめる (vt, 2)

bump, butsukaru ぶつかる (vi, 1)

burn, yaku 焼く (vt, 1), kogeru 焦げる (vi, 2); be burnt, yakeru 焼ける (vi, 2)

business (do business), eigyō suru 営業 する (vi, 3)

buy, kau 買う (vt, 1)

calculate, keisan suru 計算する (vt, 3)

call, yobu 呼ぶ (vt, 1)

camp, kyanpu suru キャンプする (vi, 3)

can, dekiru 出来る (vi, 2)

cancel, chūshi suru 中止する (vt, 3), kyanseru suru キャンセルする (vt, 3)

capture, toraeru 捕らえる (vt, 2)

carry, hakobu 運ぶ (vt, 1); carry out, jikkō suru 実行する (vt, 3)

catch, toru 取る (vt, 1), tsukamaeru 捕 まえる (vt, 2), toraeru 捕らえる (vt, 2), kyatchi suru キャッチする (vt, 3); be caught, toreru 取れる (vi, 2)

cause, okosu 起こす (vt, 1)

cease, yamu やむ (vi, 1)

celebrate, iwau 祝う (vt, 1)

challenge, idomu 挑む (vi, vt, 1), charenji suru チャレンジする (vi, 3)

change, kawaru 変わる (vi, 1), kaeru 変える (vt, 2), henkō suru 変更する (vi, vt, 3), chenji suru チェンジする (vi, vt, 3); change trains, norikaeru 乗り換える (vi, 2)

charge (take charge), ukemotsu 受け 持つ (vt, 1), hikiukeru 引き受ける

(vt, 2), tantō suru 担当する (vt, 3)

chase, ou 追う (vt, 1), oikakeru 追いか ける (vt, 2)

chat, shaberu しゃべる (vt, 1)

cheat, damasu だます (vt, 1)

check, shiraberu 調べる (vt, 2), chekku suru チェックする (vt, 3)

cheer, ōen suru 応援する (vt, 3)

choose, erabu 選ぶ (vt, 1), kimeru 決 める (vt, 2)

chop, kizamu 刻む (vt, 1)

clap, hakushu suru 拍手する (vi, 3)

clasp, nigiru 握る (vt, 1)

clean, sōji suru 掃除する (vt, 3)

clear (up), hareru 晴れる (vi, 2)

climb, noboru 登る (vi, 1)

close, shimeru 閉める (vt, 2), tojiru 閉 じる (vi, vt, 2); be closed, shimaru 閉 まる (vi, 1); close a shop, heiten suru 閉店する (vi, 3)

cloudy (become cloudy), kumoru 曇る (vi, 1)

coach, shidō suru 指導する (vt, 3), kōchi suru コーチする (vt, 3)

collapse, taoreru 倒れる (vi, 2), kuzureru 崩れる (vi, 2)

collect, atsumeru 集める (vt, 2), kaishū suru 回収する (vt, 3)

collide, shōtotsu suru 衝突する (vi, 3)

color, someru 染める (vt, 2)

combine, awaseru 合わせる (vt, 2), kumiawaseru 組み合わせる (vt, 2)

come, kuru 来る (vi, 3), mairu 参る (vi, Reg. 1), irassharu いらっしゃる (vi, 1); come off, toreru 取れる (vi, 2), hazureru 外れる (vi, 2); come out, deru 出る (vi, 2); come true, jitsugen suru 実現する (vi, 3)

commemorate, kinen suru 記念する (vt, 3)

commit (a crime), okasu 犯す (vt, 1);

commit suicide, jisatsu suru 自殺する (vi)

communicate, tsūshin suru 通信する (vi, 3)

commute, kayou 通う (vi, 1); commute to work, tsūkin suru 通勤する (vi, 3)

compare, kuraberu 比べる (vt, 2)

compensate, tsugunau 償う (vt, 1)

compete, arasou 争う (vt, 1), kisou 競う (vi, vt, 1), kyōsō suru 競争する (vi, 3)

complain, uttaeru 訴える (vt, 2)

complete (be completed), dekiru 出来る (vi, 2), kansei suru 完成する (vi, vt, 3)

compromise, dakyō suru 妥協する (vi, 3), jōho suru 譲歩する (vi, 3)

conceal, kakusu 隠す (vt, 1)

concede, yuzuru 譲る (vt, 1), jōho suru 譲歩する (vi, 3)

conceive (get pregnant), ninshin suru 妊娠する (vi)

conduct, okonau 行う (vt, 1); conduct business, itonamu 営む (vt, 1)

conference (hold a conference), kaigi suru 会議する (vi, 3)

confirm, tashikameru 確かめる (vt, 2), kakunin suru 確認する (vt, 3)

congratulate, iwau 祝う (vt, 1)

connect, tsunagu つなぐ (vt, 1); be connected, tsunagaru つながる (vi, 1)

consent, nattoku suru 納得する (vi, 3)

consider, kangaeru 考える (vt, 2), kōryo suru 考慮する (vt, 3)

console, itawaru いたわる (vt, 1)

construct, kōji suru 工事する (vt, 3), kensetsu suru 建設する (vt, 3)

consult, sōdan suru 相談する (vt, 3)

consume, shōhi suru 消費する (vt, 3)

contact, renraku suru 連絡する (vi, vt, 3)

contain, fukumu 含む (vt, 1), fukumeru 含める (vt, 2)

continue, tsuzuku 続く (vi, 1), tsuzukeru 続ける (vt, 2)

contract, musubu 結ぶ (vt, 1), keiyaku suru 契約する (vt, 3), cancel a contract, kaiyaku suru 解約する (vt, 3)

contradict, mujun suru 矛盾する (vi, 3)

control, shihai suru 支配する (vt, 3), kontorōru suru コントロールする (vt, 3)

cook, ryōri suru 料理する (vt, 3)

cool, hiyasu 冷やす (vt, 1), samasu 冷ます (vt, 1); get cold, hieru 冷える (vi, 2)

cooperate, kyōryoku suru 協力する (vi, 3)

copy, utsusu 写す (vt, 1); be copied, utsuru 写る (vi, 1)

correct, naosu 直す (vt, 1), tadasu 正す (vt, 1); be corrected, naoru 直る (vi, 2)

correspond (communicate), tsūshin suru 通信する (vi, 3)

corrupt, midasu 乱す (vt, 1); be corrupt, midareru 乱れる (vi, 2)

cost, kakaru かかる (vi, 1)

count, kazoeru 数える (vt, 2)

cover, ōu 覆う (vt, 1), kabā suru カバーする (vt, 3)

crash, kudaku 砕く (vt, 1), tsuiraku suru 墜落する (vi, 3)

criticize, hihan suru 批判する (vt, 3), hihyō suru 批評する (vt, 3)

cross, wataru 渡る (vi, 1), ōdan suru 横断する (vt, 3), kosu 越す (vi, 1), koeru 越える (vi, 2)

crowd (be crowded), komu 込む (vi, 1)

crush, kudaku 砕く (vt, 1); be crushed, kudakeru 砕ける (vi, 2)

cry, naku 泣く・鳴く (vi, 1)

cure, naosu 治す (vt, 1)

curve, magaru 曲がる (vi, 1), kābu suru カーブする (vi, 3), mageru 曲げる (vt, 2)

cut, kiru 切る (vt, 1), katto suru カット

する (vt, 3); cut off, kireru 切れる (vi, 2)

dance, odoru 踊る (vi, 1), dansu suru ダンスする (vi, 3)

date, dēto suru デートする (vi, 3)

deal, atsukau 扱う (vt, 1)

debate, giron suru 議論する (vi, 3)

debut (make one's debut), debyū suru デビューする (vi, 3)

deceive, damasu だます (vt, 1)

decide, kimeru 決める (vt, 2), kettei suru 決定する (vi, vt, 3); be decided, kimaru 決まる (vi, 1)

decline, kotowaru 断る (vt, 1)

decorate, kazaru 飾る (vt, 1)

decrease, heru 減る (vi, 1), herasu 減らす (vt, 1), genshō suru 減少する (vi, vt, 3)

defeat, taosu 倒す (vt, 1), makasu 負かす (vt, 1); be defeated, makeru 負ける (vi, 2), yabureru 敗れる (vi, 2)

defend, mamoru 守る (vt, 1), bengo suru 弁護する (vt, 3)

delight (be delighted), yorokobu 喜ぶ (vi, 1)

deliver, todokeru 届ける (vt, 2), haitatsu suru 配達する (vt, 3); be delivered, todoku 届く (vi, 1)

demand, motomeru 求める (vt, 2), yōkyū suru 要求する (vt, 3)

dent (be dented), hekomu へこむ (vi, 1)

deny, hitei suru 否定する (vt, 3)

depart, dekakeru 出かける (vi, 2), shuppatsu suru 出発する (vi, 3)

depend (on), tayoru 頼る (vi, 1)

deposit, azukeru 預ける (vt, 2), chokin suru 貯金する (vi, 3)

desire, negau 願う (vt, 1), nozomu 望む (vt, 1)

destroy, kowasu 壊す (vt, 1), hakai suru 破壊する (vi, vt, 3)

detach, hanasu 離す (vt, 1); be detached, hazureru 外れる (vi, 2)

detain, tomeru 留める (vt, 2)

develop, hatten suru 発展する (vi, 3), kaihatsu suru 開発する (vt, 3)

die, shinu 死ぬ (vi, 1), nakunaru 亡くなる (vi, 1), shibō suru 死亡する (vi, 3)

differ, chigau 違う (vi, 1)

dig, horu 掘る (vt, 1)

dine, shokuji suru 食事する (vi, 3)

dirty, yogosu 汚す (vt, 1); get dirty, yogoreru 汚れる (vi, 2)

disappear, kieru 消える (vi, 2)

discover, mitsukeru 見付ける (vt, 2); be discovered, mitsukaru 見付かる (vi, 1)

disobey, somuku 背く (vi, 1)

disperse, chiru 散る (vi, 1), chirasu 散らす (vt, 1)

display, naraberu 並べる (vt, 2), chinretsu suru 陳列する (vt, 3), disupurē suru ディスプレーする (vt, 3)

dissolve, tokeru 溶ける (vi, 2), toku 溶く (vt, 1), tokasu 溶かす (vt, 1), kaisan suru 解散する (vi, vt, 3)

distribute, kubaru 配る (vt, 1)

disturb, midasu 乱す (vt, 1)

dive, moguru 潜る (vi, 1)

divide, waru 割る (vt, 1), wakeru 分ける (vt, 2); be divided, wakareru 分かれる (vi, 2)

divorce, rikon suru 離婚する (vi, 3)

do, suru する (vt, 3), okonau 行う (vt, 1), yaru やる (vt, 1), itasu 致す (vt, 1)

doubt, utagau 疑う (vt, 1)

drag, hikizuru 引きずる (vt, 1)

drain, nagasu 流す (vt, 1)

draw, hiku 引く (vt, 1), hipparu 引っ張る (vt, 1); draw back, hikkomu 引っ込む (vi, 1)

drink, 飲む (vt, 1), itadaku 頂く (vt, 1); get drunk, you 酔う (vi, 1)

drip, tarasu 垂らす (vt, 1)

drive (a car), unten suru 運転する (vt, 3)

drop, otosu 落とす (vt, 1), sagaru 下がる (vi, 1); drop in, yoru 寄る (vi, 1)

dry, kawakasu 乾かす (vt, 1); get dry, kawaku 乾く (vi, 1)

dull (become dull), niburu 鈍る (vi, 1)

dust, hataku はたく (vt, 1)

dye, someru 染める (vt, 2); be dyed, somaru 染まる (vi, 1)

eager (be eager), ikigomu 意気込む (vi, 1)

earn, mōkeru もうける (vt, 2)

eat, taberu 食べる (vt, 2), itadaku 頂く (vt, 1); eat out, gaishoku suru 外食する (vi, 3)

educate, kyōiku suru 教育する (vt, 3)

effective (be effective), kiku 効く (vi, 1)

effort (make efforts), tsutomeru 努める (vi, 2), doryoku suru 努力する (vi, 3), hagemu 励む (vi, 1)

elapse, tatsu 経つ (vi, 1), keika suru 経過する (vi, 3)

elect, erabu 選ぶ (vt, 1), senkyo suru 選挙する (vt, 3); be elected, tōsen suru 当選する (vi, 3)

employ, yatou 雇う (vt, 1), saiyō suru 採用する (vt, 3); be employed, tsutomeru 勤める (vi, 2)

empty, akeru 空ける (vt, 2); become empty, aku 空く (vi, 1), suku すく (vi, 1)

encourage, hagemasu 励ます (vt, 1)

end, owaru 終わる (vi, 1), sumu 済む (vi, 1)

endure, taeru 耐える (vi, 2)

engrave, horu 彫る (vt, 1)

enjoy, tanoshimu 楽しむ (vt, 1), enjoi suru エンジョイする (vt, 3); enjoy oneself, asobu 遊ぶ (vi, 1)

enlarge, kakudai suru 拡大する (vi, vt, 3)

enter, hairu 入る (vi, 1); enter a school, nyūgaku suru 入学する (vi, 3)

entrust, takusu 託す (vt, 1), makaseru 任せる (vt, 2)

envelop, tsutsumu 包む (vt, 1)

envy, urayamu うらやむ (vt, 1)

erase, kesu 消す (vt, 1)

erect, tateru 立てる (vt, 2)

escape, nigeru 逃げる (vi, 2), esukēpu suru エスケープする (vi, 3); let escape, nigasu 逃がす (vt, 1)

examine, shiken suru 試験する (vt, 3)

exceed, sugiru 過ぎる (vi, 2), ōbā suru オーバーする (vi, vt, 3)

excel (be excellent), sugureru 優れる (vi, 2)

exchange, torikaeru 取り替える (vt, 2), kōkan suru 交換する (vt, 3)

exclude, nozoku 除く (vt, 1)

exercise, undō suru 運動する (vi, 3)

expand, fukuramu 膨らむ (vi, 1)

expect, kitai suru 期待する (vt, 3), yosō suru 予想する (vt, 3)

experience, keiken suru 経験する (vt, 3)

experiment, jikken suru 実験する (vt, 3)

expire, kireru 切れる (vi, 2)

explain, setsumei suru 説明する (vt, 3)

explode, bakuhatsu suru 爆発する (vi, 3)

exploit, kaihatsu suru 開発する (vt, 3)

export, yushutsu suru 輸出する (vt, 3)

express, arawasu 表す・現す (vt, 1)

extend, nobasu 伸ばす (vt, 1), nobiru 伸びる (vi, 2), hirogeru 広げる (vt, 2), hirogaru 広がる (vi, 1)

extract, nuku 抜く (vt, 1)

face, muku 向く (vi, 1)

fail, shippai suru 失敗する (vi, 3); fail an exam, rakudai suru 落第する (vi, 3) fall, ochiru 落ちる (vi, 2), sagaru 下がる (vi, 1), chiru 散る (vi, 1), tsuiraku suru 墜落する (vi, 3); fall down, korobu 転ぶ (vi, 1), taoreru 倒れる (vi, 2)

fashion (be in fashion), hayaru はやる (vi, 1), ryūkō suru 流行する (vi, 3)

fasten, shimeru 締める (vt, 2), tomeru 留める (vt, 2)

fatten (get fat), futoru 太る (vi, 1), koeru 肥える (vi, 2)

feel, kanjiru 感じる (vi, vt, 2); feel at ease, anshin suru 安心する (vi, 3)

feign, itsuwaru 偽る (vt, 1)

fertile (be fertile), koeru 肥える (vi, 2)

fight, arasou 争う (vt, 1), tatakau 戦う (vi, 1), kenka suru けんかする (vi, 3)

fill, mitasu 満たす (vt, 1)

find, mitsukeru 見付ける (vt, 2); be found, mitsukaru 見付かる (vi, 1); find a purse, hirou 拾う (vt, 1)

finish, owaru 終わる (vi, 1)

fish, tsuru 釣る (vt, 1)

fit, au 合う (vi, 1)

fix, naosu 直す (vt, 1), shūri suru 修理する (vt, 3); be fixed, naoru 直る (vi, 1)

float, ukabu 浮かぶ (vi, 1), uku 浮く (vi, 1), ukaberu 浮かべる (vt, 2), nagasu 流す (vt, 1), nagareru 流れる (vi, 2)

flourish, sakaeru 栄える (vi, 2)

fly, tobu 飛ぶ (vi, 1); let fly, tobasu 飛ばす (vt, 1)

fold, oru 折る (vt, 1)

follow, shitagau 従う (vi, 1)

force, kyōsei suru 強請する (vt, 3)

forecast, yosō suru 予想する (vt, 3)

forget, wasureru 忘れる (vt, 2)

forgive, yurusu 許す (vt, 1)

freeze, kōru 凍る (vi, 1)

fumble, ijiru いじる (vt, 1)

furnish (be furnished with), sonaeru 備える (vt, 2)

get, eru 得る (vt, 2), morau もらう (vt, 1), toru 取る (vt, 1), ukeru 受ける (vt, 2), uketoru 受け取る (vt, 1); get on a vehicle, noru 乗る (vi, 1); get off, oriru 降りる (vi, 2); get together, atsumaru 集まる (vi, 1); get up, okiru 起きる (vi, 2); get used to, nareru 慣れる (vi, 2)

give, ageru 上げる (vt, 2), yaru やる (vt, 1), kureru くれる (vt, 2), kudasaru 下さる (vt, 1); give back, kaesu 返す (vt, 1), modosu 戻す (vt, 1); give up, akirameru あきらめる (vt, 2)

glad (be glad), yorokobu 喜ぶ (vi, 1)

glow, haeru 映える (vi, 2)

gnaw, kajiru かじる (vt, 1)

go, iku 行く (vi, 1), irassharu いらっしゃる (vi, 1), mairu 参る (vi, 1); go out, dekakeru 出かける (vi, 2), gaishutsu suru 外出する (vi, 3), kieru 消える (vi, 2); go up, agaru 上がる (vi, 1), noboru 上る (vi, 1); go down, kudaru 下る (vi, 1), oriru 下りる (vi, 2); go away, saru 去る (vi, 1); go and return, ōfuku suru 往復する (vi, 3)

govern, osameru 治める (vt, 2)

graduate, sotsugyō suru 卒業する (vi, 3)

grasp, nigiru 握る (vt, 1), tsukamu つかむ (vt, 1)

greet, aisatsu suru あいさつする (vi, 3)

grip, tsukamu つかむ (vt, 1)

grow, sodatsu 育つ (vi, 1), seichō suru 成長する (vi, 3), haeru 生える (vi, 2); grow a mustache, hayasu 生やす (vt, 1); grow dark, kureru 暮れる (vi, 2)

guarantee, hoshō suru 保証する (vt, 3)

guard (stand guard), miharu 見張る (vt, 1)

guess, ateru 当てる (vt, 2)

guide, annai suru 案内する (vt, 3)

hand (over), watasu 渡す (vt, 1); hand out, kubaru 配る (vt, 1)

handle, atsukau 扱う (vt, 1)

hang, kakaru かかる (vi, 1), kakeru かける (vt, 2), sagaru 下がる (vi, 1), sageru 下げる (vt, 2); hang down, tarasu 垂らす (vt, 1), tsuru つる (vt, 1)

hate, nikumu 憎む (vt, 1)

have, motsu 持つ (vt, 1), aru ある (vi, 1), shoyū suru 所有する (vt, 3)

hear, kiku 聞く (vt, 1); can hear, kikoeru 聞こえる (vi, 2)

heat, atatameru 暖める (vt, 2)

help, tetsudau 手伝う (vt, 1), tasukeru 助ける (vt, 2), herupu suru ヘルプする (vt, 3)

hide, kakusu 隠す (vt, 1), kakureru 隠れる (vi, 2)

hire, yatou 雇う (vt, 1)

hit, utsu 打つ (vt, 1), tataku たたく (vt, 1), ataru 当たる (vi, 1), ateru 当てる (vt, 2), butsukaru ぶつかる (vi, 1), butsukeru ぶつける (vt, 2)

hold, motsu 持つ (vt, 1), tsukamu つかむ (vt, 1), kakaeru 抱える (vt, 2), daku 抱く (vt, 1); hold on, ganbaru 頑張る (vi, 1); hold an exhibition, kaisai suru 開催する (vt, 3); hold in the mouth, kuwaeru くわえる (vt, 2); hold up (an umbrella), sasu 差す (vt, 1)

hope, negau 願う (vt, 1), nozomu 望む (vt, 1), kitai suru 期待する (vt, 3)

hospitalize (be hospitalized), nyūin suru 入院する (vi, 3)

howl, hoeru ほえる (vi, 2)

hunt (for), asaru あさる (vt, 1)

hug, daku 抱く (vt, 1)

hurry, isogu 急ぐ (vi, 1)

ice, hiyasu 冷やす (vt, 1)

ignore, mushi suru 無視する (vt, 3)

illuminate, terasu 照らす (vt, 1)

import, yunyū suru 輸入する (vt, 3)

improve, kaizen suru 改善する (vt, 3)

include, fukumu 含む (vt, 1), fukumeru 含める (vt, 2), ireru 入れる (vt, 2)

increase, fuyasu 増やす (vt, 1), fueru 増える (vi, 2), zōka suru 増加する (vi, vt, 3)

independent (become independent), dokuritsu suru 独立する (vi, 3), jiritsu suru 自立する (vi, 3)

indicate, sasu 指す (vt, 1)

influence, oyobosu 及ぼす (vt, 1)

inform, shiraseru 知らせる (vt, 2), tsūchi suru 通知する (vt, 3)

inhale, suu 吸う (vt, 1)

insist, shuchō suru 主張する (vt, 3)

install, tsukeru 付ける (vt, 2); be installed, tsuku 付く (vi, 1)

instruct, shiji suru 指示する (vt, 3)

interrupt, jama suru 邪魔する (vt, 3), bōgai suru 妨害する (vt, 3)

interview, mensetsu suru 面接する (vi, 3), intabyū suru インタビューする (vi, 3)

introduce, shōkai suru 紹介する (vt, 3)

invade, osou 襲う (vt, 1)

invent, hatsumei suru 発明する (vt, 3)

invest, tōshi suru 投資する (vi, 3)

investigate, shiraberu 調べる (vt, 2), chōsa suru 調査する (vt, 3), sōsa suru 捜査する (vt, 3)

invite, sasou 誘う (vt, 1), yobu 呼ぶ (vt, 1), shōtai suru 招待する (vt, 3)

irritate, jirasu じらす (vt, 1); be irritated, iradatsu いら立つ (vi, 1)

join, sanka suru 参加する (vi, 3)

judge, handan suru 判断する (vt, 3)

jump, tobu 跳ぶ (vi, 1), haneru 跳ねる (vi, 2)

keep, tamotsu 保つ (vt, 1), azukaru 預かる (vt, 1); keep pets, kau 飼う (vt, 1)

kidnap, yūkai suru 誘拐する (vt, 3)

kill, korosu 殺す (vt, 1)

kiss, kisu suru キスする (vi, 3)

knock, tataku たたく (vt, 1), nokku suru ノックする (vt, 3); kock down, taosu 倒す (vt, 1)

know, shiru 知る (vt, Reg. 1), wakaru 分かる (vi, 1)

last, tsuzuku 続く (vi, 1)

late (be late), okureru 遅れる (vi, 2); be late for school, chikoku suru 遅刻する (vi, 3)

laugh, warau 笑う (vi, 1)

lay, shiku 敷く (vt, 1); be laid, tsūjiru 通じる (vi, 2)

lead, shidō suru 指導する (vt, 3)

leak moreru 漏れる (vi, 2); let leak, morasu 漏らす (vt, 1)

lean katamuku 傾く (vi, 1)

leap, haneru 跳ねる (vi, 2)

learn, narau 習う (vt, 1), oboeru 覚える (vt, 2); learn by heart, anki suru 暗記する (vt, 3)

leave, deru 出る (vi, 2), saru 去る (vi, 1), shuppatsu suru 出発する (vi, 3); leave a thing behind, nokosu 残す (vt, 1), wasureru 忘れる (vt, 2); leave a thing in a person's care, azukeru 預ける (vt, 2); leave hospital, taiin suru 退院する (vi, 3)

lecture, kōgi suru 講義する (vt, 3)

left (be left over), amaru 余る (vi, 1)

lend, kasu 貸す (vt, 1)

lie, itsuwaru 偽る (vt, 1); lie down, neru 寝る (vi, 2)

lift, ageru 上げる (vt, 2), takameru 高める (vt, 2)

light, tsukeru つける (vt, 2); be lighted, tsuku つく (vi, 1); light up, terasu 照らす (vt, 1)

like, suku 好く (vt, 1)

link, tsunagu つなぐ (vt, 1)

listen, kiku 聞く (vt, 1)

live, sumu 住む (vi, 1), ikiru 生きる (vi, 2), seikatsu suru 生活する (vi, 3); make a living, seikatsu suru 生活する (vi, 3)

load, noseru 載せる (vt, 2)

locate (be located), ichi suru 位置する (vi, 3)

lodge, tomaru 泊まる (vi, 1); give lodging, tomeru 泊める (vt, 2)

look, miru 見る (vt, 2); look for, sagasu 探す (vt, 1); look like, niru 似る (vi, 2)

loosen, tarumu たるむ (vi, 1), yurumu 緩む (vi, 1), yurumeru 緩める (vt, 2)

lose, otosu 落とす (vt, 1); lose a thing, nakusu 無くす (vt, 1); lose a person, nakusu 亡くす (vt, 1); loose a game, makeru 負ける (vi, 2), yabureru 敗れる (vi, 2); lose weight, yaseru やせる (vi, 2); get lost, mayou 迷う (vi, 1)

lower, sageru 下げる (vt, 2), orosu 下ろす (vt, 1)

lurk, hisomu 潜む (vi, 1)

mad (go mad), kuruu 狂う (vi, 1)

mail, yūsō suru 郵送する (vt, 3)

maintain, tamotsu 保つ (vt, 1), iji suru 維持する (vt, 3)

make, tsukuru 作る (vt, 1)

manage, kanri suru 管理する (vt, 3)

marry, kekkon suru 結婚する (vi, 3)

massage, momu もむ (vt, 1), massâji suru マッサージする (vt, 3)

master, jukutatsu suru 熟達する (vi, 3), masutâ suru マスターする (vt, 3)

match, au 合う (vi, 1); match well, niau 似合う (vi, 1), matchi suru マッチする (vi, 3) measure, hakaru 計る (vt, 1)

meet, au 会う (vi, 1)

melt, tokeru 溶ける (vi, 2), tokasu 溶かす (vt, 1), toku 溶く (vt, 1)

memorize, oboeru 覚える (vt, 2), anki suru 暗記する (vt, 3)

miss (be missing), nakunaru 無くなる (vi, 1)

mistake (make a mistake), machigau 間違う (vi, vt, 1), machigaeru 間違える (vt, 2), ayamaru 誤る (vt, 1)

misunderstand, gokai suru 誤解する (vt, 3)

misuse, akuyō suru 悪用する (vt, 3)

mix, mazaru 混ざる (vi, 1), mazeru 混ぜる (vt, 2), mikkusu suru ミックスする (vt, 3)

moist (be moist), nureru ぬれる (vi, 2)

move, ugokasu 動かす (vt, 1), ugoku 動く (vi, 1), utsusu 移す (vt, 1), utsuru 移る (vi, 1), idō suru 移動する (vi, vt, 3); move to, hikkosu 引っ越す (vi, 1), iten suru 移転する (vi, vt, 3)

mow, karu 刈る (vt, 1)

muddy (get muddy), nigoru 濁る (vi, 1)

murder, korosu 殺す (vt, 1)

near, chikazuku 近づく (vi, 1); bring a thing near, yoseru 寄せる (vt, 2)

need, iru 要る (vi, 1)

negotiate, kōshō suru 交渉する (vi, 3)

noise (make a noise), sawagu 騒ぐ (vi, 1)

numb (become numb), shibireru しびれる (vi, 2)

obey, shitagau 従う (vi, 1)

observe, kansatsu suru 観察する (vt, 3)

obstruct, bōgai suru 妨害する (vt, 3)

obtain, eru 得る (vt, 2)

occur, okoru 起こる (vi, 1), okiru 起きる (vi, 2)

offer, teikyō suru 提供する (vt, 3); offer to a god, sonaeru 供える (vt, 2)

omit, habuku 省く (vt, 1), omitto suru オミットする (vt, 3)

open, aku 開く (vi, 1), akeru 開ける (vt, 2), hiraku 開く (vi, vt, 1); open an exhibition, kaisai suru 開催する (vt, 3); open a shop, kaiten suru 開店する (vi, 3), ōpun suru オープンする (vt, 3)

operate (a machine), unten suru 運転する (vt, 3)

oppose, hantai suru 反対する (vi, 3)

order (put in order), totonoeru 整える (vt, 2), seiri suru 整理する (vt, 3), katazukeru 片付ける (vt, 2); order goods, chūmon suru 注文する (vt, 3), ōdâ suru オーダーする (vt, 3); go out of order, midareru 乱れる (vi, 2); be out of order, kowareru 壊れる (vi, 2), koshō suru 故障する (vi, 3)

organize, soshiki suru 組織する (vt, 3)

outstanding (be outstanding), midatsu 目立つ (vi, 1)

overflow, afureru あふれる (vi, 2)

overturn, uragaesu 裏返す (vt, 1)

own, motsu 持つ (vt, 1), shoyū suru 所有する (vt, 3)

pain (feel a pain), itamu 痛む (vi, 1), kurushimu 苦しむ (vi, 1)

paint, nuru 塗る (vt, 1)

pair, kumu 組む (vt, 1)

park, tomeru 止める (vt, 2); be parked, tomaru 止まる (vi, 1)

part (from), wakareru 別れる (vi, 2)

participate, sanka suru 参加する (vi, 3)

pass, tōru 通る (vi, 1), sugiru 過ぎる (vi, 2), tsūka suru 通過する (vi, 3), tatsu 経つ (vi, 1), keika suru 経過する (vi, 3), kosu 越す (vi, 1), koeru 越える (vi, 2), oikosu 追い越す (vt, 1);

let a person pass, tōsu 通す (vt, 1); pass around, mawasu 回す (vt, 1); pass away, nakunaru 亡くなる (vi, 1); pass an exam, gōkaku suru 合格する (vi, 3), pasu suru パスする (vi, 3)

paste (a poster), haru 張る (vt, 1)

patch, tsukurou 繕う (vt, 1)

patient (be patient), gaman suru 我慢する (vt, 3)

pave, shiku 敷く (vt, 1)

pay, harau 払う (vt, 1)

peel, muku むく (vt, 1)

peep, nozoku のぞく (vt, 1)

perform, okonau 行う (vt, 1), itonamu 営む (vt, 1)

permeate, shimiru 染みる (vi, 2)

permit, yurusu 許す (vt, 1), kyoka suru 許可する (vt, 3)

persuade, settoku suru 説得する (vt, 3)

pester, nedaru ねだる (vt, 1)

phone, denwa suru 電話する (vi, 3)

pick, tsumu 摘む (vt, 1), tsumamu つまむ (vt, 1); pick up, hirou 拾う (vt, 1), pikkuappu suru ピックアップする (vt, 3)

picture (take a picture), utsusu 写す (vt, 1); be in a picture, utsuru 写る (vi, 1)

pierce, sasu 刺す (vt, 1)

pile (up), tsumu 積む (vt, 1), kasaneru 重ねる (vt, 2); be piled up, tsumoru 積もる (vi, 1)

pitch, nageru 投げる (vt, 2)

plan, keikaku suru 計画する (vt, 3)

plant, ueru 植える (vt, 2)

play, asobu 遊ぶ (vi, 1), play string instruments, hiku 弾く (vt, 1); play wind instruments, fuku 吹く (vt, 1); play pranks, fuzakeru ふざける (vi, 2)

plot, takuramu たくらむ (vt, 1)

point (out), shimesu 示す (vt, 1); point to, sasu 指す (vt, 1)

polish, migaku 磨く (vt, 1)

popular (be popular), hayaru はやる (vi, 1), ryūkō suru 流行する (vi, 3), fukyū suru 普及する (vi, vt, 3); be popular with, moteru 持てる (vi, 2)

postpone, nobasu 延ばす (vt, 1), enki suru 延期する (vt, 3); be postponed, nobiru 延びる (vi, 2)

pour (on), abiseru 浴びせる (vt, 2)

practice, renshū suru 練習する (vt, 3); put into practice, ōyō suru 応用する (vi, 3)

praise, homeru 褒める (vt, 2)

pray, inoru 祈る (vt, 1)

prepare, sonaeru 備える (vt, 2), junbi suru 準備する (vt, 3); prepare one's lessons, yoshū suru 予習する (vt, 3)

preserve, hozon suru 保存する (vt, 3)

press, osu 押す (vt, 1); press down, osaeru 押さえる (vt, 2)

prevail, hayaru はやる (vi, 1)

prevent, bōshi suru 防止する (vt, 3), yobō suru 予防する (vt, 3)

print, insatsu suru 印刷する (vt, 3), purinto suru プリントする (vt, 3), noseru 載せる (vt, 2); be printed, noru 載る (vi, 1)

proceed, tsuzukeru 続ける (vt, 2)

process, kakō suru 加工する (vt, 3)

produce, tsukuru 作る (vt, 1), seisan suru 生産する (vt, 3)

profit (make a profit), mōkeru もうける (vt, 2), mōkaru もうかる (vi, 1)

progress, shinpo suru 進歩する (vi, 3)

promise, yakusoku suru 約束する (vt, 3)

promote (be promoted), shōshin suru 昇進する (vi, 3)

prop (up), sasaeru 支える (vt, 2)

propose, mōshikomu 申し込む (vt, 1), teian suru 提案する (vt, 3), puropōzu suru プロポーズする (vi, 3)

prosper, nigiwau にぎわう (vi, 1), sakaeru 栄える (vi, 2)

protect, mamoru 守る (vt, 1)

proud (be proud of), hokoru 誇る (vi, vt, 1), jiman suru 自慢する (vt, 3)

prove, shōmei suru 証明する (vt, 3)

publish, hakkō suru 発行する (vt, 3), shuppan suru 出版する (vt, 3)

pull, hiku 引く (vt, 1), hipparu 引っ張る (vt, 1); pull out, nuku 抜く (vt, 1)

pursue, tsuikyū suru 追求する (vt, 3)

push, osu 押す (vt, 1)

put, oku 置く (vt, 1); put things in order, naraberu 並べる (vt, 2); put away, shimau しまう (vt, 1); put in, ireru 入れる (vt, 2); put on, kiru 着る (vt, 2); put out, dasu 出す (vt, 1); put together, matomeru まとめる (vt, 2)

quake, yureru 揺れる (vi, 2)

quarrel, kenka suru けんかする (vi, 3)

quiet, shizumeru 静める (vt, 2), osameru 治める (vt, 2); quiet down, osamaru 治まる (vi, 1)

quit, yameru やめる (vt, 2); quit smoking, kin'en suru 禁煙する (vi, 3)

rage, abareru 暴れる (vi, 2)

rain, ame ga furu 雨が降る (vi, 1)

raise, ageru 上げる (vt, 2), takameru 高める (vt, 2), sodateru 育てる (vt, 2)

reach, todoku 届く (vi, 1), itaru 至る (vi, 1)

react, hannō suru 反応する (vi, 3)

read, yomu 読む (vt, 1)

realize, satoru 悟る (vt, 1); turn into reality, jitsugen suru 実現する (vi, vt, 3)

rebuild, kaichiku suru 改築する (vt, 3)

recall, omoidasu 思い出す (vt, 1)

receive, morau もらう (vt, 1), itadaku 頂く (vt, 1), ukeru 受ける (vt, 2), uke-toru 受け取る (vt, 1)

recommend, susumeru 勧める (vt, 2), suisen suru 推薦する (vt, 3)

record, kiroku suru 記録する (vt, 3); record on tape, rokuon suru 録音する (vt, 3)

recover, naoru 治る (vi, 1), kaifuku suru 回復する (vi, vt, 3)

recruit, boshū suru 募集する (vt, 3)

reduce, shukushō suru 縮小する (vi, vt, 3)

reflect, utsusu 映す (vt, 1), hansha suru 反射する (vi, vt, 3); be reflected, utsuru 映る (vi, 1)

reform, kaikaku suru 改革する (vt, 3)

refuse, kotowaru 断る (vt, 1), kyohi suru 拒否する (vt, 3)

register, tōroku suru 登録する (vt, 3)

regret, kuyamu 悔やむ (vt, 1)

release, hanasu 放す (vt, 1)

rely (on), tayoru 頼る (vi, 1)

remain, nokoru 残る (vi, 1), be left over, amaru 余る (vi, 1)

remember, omoidasu 思い出す (vt, 1)

remit (money), sōkin suru 送金する (vi, 3)

remove, hazusu 外す (vt, 1)

renew, torikaeru 取り替える (vt, 2)

rent, kariru 借りる (vt, 2), kasu 貸す (vt, 1)

repair, naosu 直す (vt, 1), tsukurou 繕う (vt, 1), shūri suru 修理する (vt, 3); be repaired, naoru 直る (vi, 1)

repeat, kurikaesu 繰り返す (vt, 1)

replace, kaeru 代える (vt, 2), kawaru 代わる (vi, 1)

reply, kotaeru 答える (vi, 2), henji suru 返事する (vi, 3), kaitō suru 回答する (vi, 3)

report, tsutaeru 伝える (vt, 2), hōkoku suru 報告する (vt, 3), todokeru 届ける

(vt, 2); be reported, noru 載る (vi, 1)

represent, daihyō suru 代表する (vt, 3)

request, tanomu 頼む (vt, 1), motomeru 求める (vt, 2), irai suru 依頼する (vt, 3)

rescue, sukuu 救う (vt, 1), tasukeru 助ける (vt, 2), kyūjo suru 救助する (vt, 3); be rescued, tasukaru 助かる (vi, 1)

research, kenkyū suru 研究する (vt, 3)

resemble, niru 似る (vi, 2)

resent, uramu 恨む (vt, 1)

reserve, yoyaku suru 予約する (vt, 3)

reside, sumu 住む (vi, 1)

resign, yameru 辞める (vt, 2), jishoku suru 辞職する (vi, vt, 3)

respect, sonkei suru 尊敬する (vt, 3)

respond, kotaeru 答える (vi, 2), hannō suru 反応する (vi, 3)

rest, yasumu 休む (vi, 1), kyūkei suru 休憩する (vi, 3)

retire, intai suru 引退する (vi, 3), ritaia suru リタイアする (vi, 3)

return, kaeru 帰る (vi, 1), modoru 戻る (vi, 1); return something, kaesu 返す (vt, 1), modosu 戻す (vt, 1); return to one's country, kikoku suru 帰国する (vi, 3); return goods, henpin suru 返品する (vi, 3)

review, fukushū suru 復習する (vt, 3)

revise, kaitei suru 改訂する (vt, 3)

ride, noru 乗る (vi, 1)

ring, naru 鳴る (vi, 1), narasu 鳴らす (vt, 1), denwa suru 電話する (vi, 3)

ripen, minoru 実る (vi, 1)

rise, agaru 上がる (vi, 1), noboru 昇る (vi, 1), tatsu 立つ (vi, 1)

roast, yaku 焼く (vt, 1); be roasted, yakeru 焼ける (vi, 2)

rob, ubau 奪う (vt, 1)

roll, korogaru 転がる (vi, 1), korogasu 転がす (vt, 1); roll up, maku 巻く (vt, 1)

rotate, kaiten suru 回転する (vi, 3)

rub, kosuru こする (vt, 1)

run, hashiru 走る (vi, 1), ugoku 動く (vi, 1); run a machine, ugokasu 動かす (vt, 1); run away, nigeru 逃げる (vi, 2); run out, kireru 切れる (vi, 2), nakunaru 無くなる (vi, 1); run after, ou 追う (vt, 1), oikakeru 追いかける (vt, 2); run a company, keiei suru 経営する (vt, 3)

rush (be in rush), awateru 慌てる (vi, 2)

rust, sabiru さびる (vi, 2)

sad (feel sad), kanashimu 悲しむ (vt, 1)

sail (off), shukkō suru 出航する (vi, 3)

satisfy (a need), mitasu 満たす (vt, 1); be satisfied, manzoku suru 満足する (vi, 3)

save, tasukeru 助ける (vt, 2), nokosu 残す (vt, 1), takuwaeru 蓄える (vt, 2), setsuyaku suru 節約する (vt, 3); save money, chokin suru 貯金する (vi, 3); be saved, tasukaru 助かる (vi, 1)

say, iu 言う (vt, 1)

scare (be scared), obieru おびえる (vi, 2)

scatter, chirasu 散らす (vt, 1), chiru 散る (vi, 1)

scavenge, asaru あさる (vt, 1)

scheme, takuramu たくらむ (vt, 1)

scold, shikaru 叱る (vt, 1)

scorch, kogeru 焦げる (vi, 2)

scrap, tsubusu つぶす (vt, 1)

scrub, kosuru こする (vt, 1)

sculpture, horu 彫る (vt, 1)

search, sagasu 探す (vt, 1)

see, miru 見る (vt, 2); see off, okuru 送る (vt, 1), miokuru 見送る (vt, 1); be seen/ can see, mieru 見える (vi, 2)

select, erabu 選ぶ (vt, 1)

sell, uru 売る (vt, 1), ureru 売れる (vi, 2); be sold out, urikireru 売り切れる (vi, 2) send, okuru 送る (vt, 1), dasu 出す (vt, 1); send out, hassō suru 発送する (vt, 3)

separate, wakeru 分ける (vt, 2); separate from, wakareru 別れる (vi, 2); be separated, hanareru 離れる (vi, 2)

set (free), hanasu 放す (vt, 1); set afloat, ukaberu 浮かべる (vt, 2)

settle (down), ochitsuku 落ち着く (vi, 1)

sew, nuu 縫う (vt, 1)

shake, yusuru 揺する (vt, 1), yureru 揺れる (vi, 2); shake hands, akushu suru 握手する (vi, 3)

share, wakeru 分ける (vt, 2)

sharp (be sharp), kireru 切れる (vi, 2); become sharp, togaru とがる (vi, 1)

sharpen, kezuru 削る (vt, 1), togu 研ぐ (vt, 1)

shave, soru そる (vt, 1)

shine, hikaru 光る (vi, 1), teru 照る (vi, 1); shine upon, ataru 当たる (vi, 1), sasu 差す (vi, 1)

shock (be shocked), odoroku 驚く (vi, 1)

short (be short of), fusoku suru 不足する (vi, 3)

shorten, chijimeru 縮める (vt, 2)

shout, sakebu 叫ぶ (vi, 1), donaru どなる (vi, 1)

show, miseru 見せる (vt, 2), shimesu 示す (vt, 1), arawasu 表す・現す (vt, 1)

shower (take a shower), abiru 浴びる (vt, 2)

shrink, chijimu 縮む (vi, 1), chijimeru 縮める (vt, 2)

shut, shimeru 閉める (vt, 2), tojiru 閉じる (vi, vt, 2); be shut, shimaru 閉まる (vi, 1)

sight-see, kenbutsu suru 見物する (vt, 3), kankō suru 観光する (vt, 3)

sign, shomei suru 署名する (vi, 3), sain suru サインする (vi, 3)

sing, utau 歌う (vt, 1), naku 鳴く (vi, 1)

sink, shizumu 沈む (vi, 1), shizumeru 沈める (vt, 2)

sit, suwaru 座る (vi, 1)

skate, suberu 滑る (vi, 1)

skip, tobasu 飛ばす (vt, 1)

slap, hataku はたく (vt, 1), tataku たたく (vt, 1)

sleep, nemuru 眠る (vi, 1)

slide, suberu 滑る (vi, 1), suraido suru スライドする (vi, vt, 3), zureru ずれる (vi, 2)

slip, suberu 滑る (vi, 1), surippu suru スリップする (vi, 3), zureru ずれる (vi, 2)

slope, katamuku 傾く (vi, 1)

smart, shimiru 染みる (vi, 2)

smash, kudaku 砕く (vt, 1), tsubusu つぶす (vt, 1); be smashed, kudakeru 砕ける (vi, 2), tsubureru つぶれる (vi, 2)

smile, warau 笑う (vi, 1)

smoke, suu 吸う (vt, 1)

smooth (down), naderu (vt, 2)

snatch, ubau 奪う (vt, 1)

snow, yuki ga furu 雪が降る (vi, 1)

soak, nurasu ぬらす (vt, 1)

solve, toku 解く (vt, 1), kaiketsu suru 解決する (vt, 3); be solved, tokeru 解ける (vi, 2)

sound, naru 鳴る (vi, 1), narasu 鳴らす (vt, 1)

speak, hanasu 話す (vt, 1), hatsugen suru 発言する (vi, 3); make a speech, enzetsu suru 演説する (vi, 3)

spend, tsukau 使う (vt, 1); spend one's time, sugosu 過ごす (vt, 1)

spin, mowasu 回す (vt, 1), mawaru 回る (vi, 1)

split, saku 裂く (vt, 1), sakeru 裂ける (vi, 2), waru 割る (vt, 1), wareru 割れる (vi, 2)

spoil, kusaru 腐る (vi, 1)

spread, hirogeru 広げる (vt, 2), hirogaru 広がる (vi, 1), fukyū suru 普及する (vi, vt, 3); spread a mat, shiku 敷く (vt, 1); spread a net, haru 張る (vt, 1)

spring, hazumu 弾む (vi, 1)

sprinkle, maku まく (vt, 1)

sprout, haeru 生える (vi, 2)

stab, sasu 刺す (vt, 1)

stable (become stable), antei suru 安定する (vi, 3)

stand, tatsu 立つ (vi, 1), tateru 立てる (vt, 2); stand in a line, narabu 並ぶ (vi, 1)

stare, niramu にらむ (vt, 1)

start, hajimaru 始まる (vi, 1), sutāto suru スタートする (vi, 3), hajimeru 始める (vt, 2)

stay, iru いる (vi, 2); stay the night, tomaru 泊まる (vi, 1); stay up all night, tetsuya suru 徹夜する (vi, 3)

steal, nusumu 盗む (vt, 1)

steam, musu 蒸す (vt, 1)

step (on), fumu 踏む (vt, 1)

stick, tsuku 付く (vi, 1), haru 張る (vt, 1); stick out, hamidasu はみ出す (vi, 1)

stir, kakimawasu かき回す (vt, 1)

stock, takuwaeru 蓄える (vt, 2), shi-ireru 仕入れる (vt, 2)

stoop, kagamu かがむ (vi, 1)

stop, tomaru 止まる (vi, 1), sutoppu suru ストップする (vi, 3), tomeru 止める (vt, 2), yamu やむ (vi, 1); stop doing, yameru やめる (vt, 2)

store, takuwaeru 蓄える (vt, 2)

storm, abareru 暴れる (vi, 2)

stream, nagareru 流れる (vi, 2)

stretch, nobasu 伸ばす (vt, 1); stretch a rope, haru 張る (vt, 1)

strike, utsu 打つ (vt, 1), tataku たたく (vt, 1), ateru 当てる (vt, 2), ataru 当たる (vi, 1)

strip (off), hagasu はがす (vt, 1)

strive, hagemu 励む (vi, 1)

struggle, tatakau 戦う (vi, 1), mogaku もがく (vi, 1)

study, benkyō suru 勉強する (vt, 3); study abroad, ryūgaku suru 留学する (vi, 3)

submit, dasu 出す (vt, 1), teishutsu suru 提出する (vt, 3)

subside, osamaru 治まる (vi, 1)

succeed, seikō suru 成功する (vi, 3)

suck, suu 吸う (vt, 1)

suffer, kurushimu 苦しむ (vi, 1), nayamu 悩む (vi, 1)

suffice, tariru 足りる (vi, 2); maniau 間に合う (vi)

suit, niau 似合う (vi, 1)

support, sasaeru 支える (vt, 2), shiji suru 支持する (vt, 3)

suppose, katei suru 仮定する (vi, vt, 3)

suppress, shizumeru 静める (vt, 2)

surprise (be surprised), odoroku 驚く (vi, 1)

suspect, utagau 疑う (vt, 1), niramu にらむ (vt, 1)

suspend, tsuru つる (vt, 1)

sweep, haku 掃く (vt, 1), sōji suru 掃除する (vt, 3)

swell, hareru 腫れる (vi, 2), fukuramu 膨らむ (vi, 1)

swim, oyogu 泳ぐ (vi, 1)

swing, yureru 揺れる (vi, 2), yusuru 揺する (vt, 1)

switch (on), tsukeru つける (vt, 2); switch off, kiru 切る (vt, 1)

take, toru 取る (vt, 1); take a thing, motteiku 持って行く (vt, 1); take a person, tsureteiku 連れて行く (vt, 1); take medicine, nomu 飲む (vt, 1); take off, hazusu 外す (vt, 1); take off clothes, nugu 脱ぐ (vt, 1); take time, kakaru かかる (vi, 1); take care of, sewa suru 世話する (vt, 3)

talk, hanasu 話す (vt, 1), shaberu しゃべる (vt, 1), kaiwa suru 会話する (vi, 3)

tame, narasu 慣らす (vt, 1)

tamper, ijiru いじる (vt, 1)

teach, oshieru 教える (vt, 2)

team (up), kumu 組む (vt, 1)

tear, saku 裂く (vt, 1), sakeru 裂ける (vi, 2), yaburu 破る (vt, 1), yabureru 破れる (vi, 2); tear to pieces, chigiru ちぎる (vt, 1); tear off, hagasu はがす (vt, 1)

tease, ijimeru いじめる (vt, 2), jirasu じらす (vt, 1), hiyakasu 冷やかす (vt, 1)

tell, iu 言う (vt, 1), oshieru 教える (vt, 2), shiraseru 知らせる (vt, 2), tsutaeru 伝える (vt, 2); tell fortunes, uranau 占う (vt)

test, tamesu 試す (vt, 1), shiken suru 試験する (vt, 3), tesuto suru テストする (vt, 3)

thin (become thin), yaseru やせる (vi, 2)

think, kangaeru 考える (vt, 2), omou 思う (vt, 1)

thirsty (get thirsty), kawaku 渇く (vi, 1)

threaten, odokasu 脅かす (vt, 1)

throw, nageru 投げる (vt, 2), butsukeru ぶつける (vt, 2); throw away, suteru 捨てる (vt, 2)

tickle, kusuguru くすぐる (vt, 1)

tidy (up), katazukeru 片付ける (vt, 2)

tie, musubu 結ぶ (vt, 1), shimeru 締める (vt, 2), shibaru 縛る (vt, 1), kukuru くくる (vt, 1)

tighten, shimeru 締める (vt, 2); be tighten, shimaru 締まる (vi, 1)

time (be in time), maniau 間に合う (vi, 1)

tinge (be tinged with), somaru 染まる (vi, 1)

tire (be tired), tsukareru 疲れる (vi, 2), kutabireru くたびれる (vi, 2); be tired of, akiru 飽きる (vi, 2)

torment, kurushimeru 苦しめる (vt, 2)

torture, kurushimeru 苦しめる (vt, 2)

touch, fureru 触れる (vi, 2), sawaru 触る (vi, 1), tatchi suru タッチする (vi, 3)

trace, nazoru なぞる (vt, 1)

trail, hikizuru 引きずる (vt, 1)

transfer, utsusu 移す (vt, 1), utsuru 移る (vi, 1); be transferred to another office, tenkin suru 転勤する (vi, 3)

translate, yakusu 訳す (vt, 1), hon'yaku suru 翻訳する (vt, 3)

transmit, tsutaeru 伝える (vt, 2); be transmitted, tsutawaru 伝わる (vi, 1)

transplant, ishoku suru 移植する (vt, 3)

transport, hakobu 運ぶ (vt, 1), unsō suru 運送する (vt, 3)

travel, ryokō suru 旅行する (vi, 3)

treat (a person to), ogoru おごる (vt, 1)

trim, karu 刈る (vt, 1), tsumu 摘む (vt, 1)

trip (take a trip), ryokō suru 旅行する (vi, 3); go on a business trip, shutchō suru 出張する (vi, 3); make a round trip, ōfuku suru 往復する (vi, 3)

trouble (be in trouble), komaru 困る (vi, 1)

trust, shinjiru 信じる (vt, 2), shin'yō suru 信用する (vt, 3)

try, tamesu 試す (vt, 1); try a case, saiban suru 裁判する (vt, 3)

turn, mawasu 回す (vt, 1), mawaru 回る (vi, 1), kaiten suru 回転する (vi, 3), magaru 曲がる (vi, 1), muku 向く (vi, 1); turn something to, mukeru 向ける (vt, 2); turn one's face away, somukeru 背ける (vt, 2); turn off, kesu 消す (vt, 1), tomeru 止める (vt, 2); turn over, hikkurikaesu ひっくり返す (vt, 1) twine (around), karamu 絡む (vi, 1)

twist, hineru ひねる (vt, Reg. 1), nejiru ねじる (vt, 2)

understand, wakaru 分かる (vi, 1), rikai suru 理解する (vt, 3), satoru 悟る (vt, 1); be understood, tsūjiru 通じる (vi, 2)

unfold, hiraku 開く (vi, vt, 1)

unify, matomeru まとめる (vt, 2), tōitsu suru 統一する (vt, 3)

unload, orosu 下ろす (vt, 1)

untie, hodoku ほどく (vt, 1), toku 解く (vt, 1); become untied, tokeru 解ける (vi, 2)

upset, hikkurikaesu ひっくり返す (vt, 1)

use, tsukau 使う (vt, 1), shiyō suru 使用する (vt, 3), riyō suru 利用する (vt, 3)

usurp, ōyō suru 横領する (vt, 3)

violate, ihan suru 違反する (vi, 3)

visit, tazuneru 訪ねる (vt, 2), hōmon suru 訪問する (vi, 3)

vomit, haku 吐く (vt, 1)

vote, tōhyō suru 投票する (vi, 3), senkyo suru 選挙する (vt, 3)

wait, matsu 待つ (vt, 1)

wake (up), okiru 起きる (vi, 2), okosu 起こす (vt, 1)

walk, aruku 歩く (vi, 1); take a walk, sanpo suru 散歩する (vi, 3)

war (make war), sensō suru 戦争する (vi, 3)

warm, atatameru 暖める (vt, 2); get warm, atatamaru 暖まる (vi, 1)

warn, chūi suru 注意する (vi, 3)

warp, soru 反る (vi, 1), yugamu ゆがむ (vi, 1)

wash, arau 洗う (vt, 1); wash clothes, sentaku suru 洗濯する (vt, 3)

watch, miru 見る (vt, 2); keep watch, miharu 見張る (vt, 1)

wave, furu 振る (vt, 1)

wear, kiru 着る (vt, 2); wear shoes, haku 履く (vt, 1); wear a hat, kaburu かぶる (vt, 1); wear a ring, hameru はめる (vt, 2); be worn out, surikireru 擦り切れる (vi, 2)

weep, naku 泣く (vi, 1)

weigh, hakaru 計る (vt, 1)

welcome, kangei suru 歓迎する (vt, 3)

well (get well), naoru 治る (vi, 1), kaifuku suru 回復する (vi, vt, 3)

wet, nurasu ぬらす (vt, 1); get wet, nureru ぬれる (vi, 2)

whet, togu 研ぐ (vt, 1)

whisper, sasayaku ささやく (vi, 1)

win, katsu 勝つ (vi, 1); win a championship, yūshō suru 優勝する (vi, 3)

wipe, fuku 拭く (vt, 1)

wish, negau 願う (vt, 1), nozomu 望む (vt, 1)

wither, kareru 枯れる (vi, 2)

work, hataraku 働く (vi, 1), shigoto suru 仕事する (vi, 3); work for, tsutomeru 勤める (vi, 2); work overtime, zangyō suru 残業する (vi, 3)

worry (be worried), nayamu 悩む (vi, 1), shinpai suru 心配する (vi, vt, 3)

worship, ogamu 拝む (vt, 1)

wrap, tsutsumu 包む (vt, 1)

wrench, hineru ひねる (vt, Reg. 1), nejiru ねじる (vt, Reg. 1)

write, kaku 書く (vt, 1), arawasu 著す (vt, 1)

wrong (be wrong), chigau 違う (vi, 1); go wrong, kuruu 狂う (vi, 1)

日本語動詞ハンドブック
THE HANDBOOK OF JAPANESE VERBS

2001 年 4 月　第 1 刷発行
2003 年 5 月　第 4 刷発行

著　者　　神谷妙子

発行者　　畑野文夫

発行所　　講談社インターナショナル株式会社
　　　　　〒112–8652　東京都文京区音羽 1–17–14
　　　　　電話　03–3944–6493（編集部）
　　　　　　　　03–3944–6492（営業部・業務部）
　　　　　ホームページ　www.kodansha-intl.co.jp

印刷所　　大日本印刷株式会社

製本所　　大日本印刷株式会社

落丁本・乱丁本は購入書店名を明記のうえ、小社業務部宛にお送りください。送料
小社負担にてお取替えします。なお、この本についてのお問い合わせは、編集部
宛にお願いいたします。本書の無断複写（コピー）、転載は著作権法の例外を除き、
禁じられています。

定価はカバーに表示してあります。

© 神谷妙子 2001
Printed in Japan
ISBN 4–7700–2683–8

JAPANESE SYLLABARY CHART

(for Regular I Verb Conjugation)

	1	2	3	4
BASE	Ka か行	Ga が行	Sa さ行	Ta た行
1st A	ka か	ga が	sa さ	ta た
2nd I	ki き	gi ぎ	shi し	chi ち
3rd U	ku く	gu ぐ	su す	tsu つ
4th E	ke け	ge げ	se せ	te て
5th O	ko こ	go ご	so そ	to と

*In modern Japanese, *w* disappears before all vowels except *a*.
**を is used as a particle to mark the object of a sentence.